Incidence
of Travel

Incidence *of* Travel

RECENT JOURNEYS IN ANCIENT SOUTH AMERICA

Jerry D. Moore

UNIVERSITY PRESS OF COLORADO

Boulder

© 2017 by University Press of Colorado

Published by University Press of Colorado
5589 Arapahoe Avenue, Suite 206C
Boulder, Colorado 80303

 The University Press of Colorado is a proud member of
the Association of American University Presses.

The University Press of Colorado is a cooperative publishing enterprise supported, in part, by Adams State University, Colorado State University, Fort Lewis College, Metropolitan State University of Denver, Regis University, University of Colorado, University of Northern Colorado, Utah State University, and Western State Colorado University.

∞ This paper meets the requirements of the ANSI/NISO Z39.48-1992 (Permanence of Paper).

ISBN: 978-1-60732-599-4 (pbk)
ISBN: 978-1-60732-600-7 (ebook)
DOI: 10.5876/9781607326007

Library of Congress Cataloging-in-Publication Data

Names: Moore, Jerry D., author.
Title: Incidence of travel : recent journeys in ancient South America / Jerry D. Moore.
Description: Boulder : University Press of Colorado, 2017. | Includes bibliographical
    references.
Identifiers: LCCN 2016053403| ISBN 9781607325994 (pbk.) | ISBN 9781607326007 (ebook)
Subjects: LCSH: South America—Antiquities. | Moore, Jerry D.—Travel—South America. |
    South America—Description and travel.
Classification: LCC F2229 .M65 2017 | DDC 980/.01—dc23
LC record available at https://lccn.loc.gov/2016053403

Front cover illustrations, clockwise from top left: Machu Picchu; Cueva de las Manos; eruption of Tungurahua; trekkers near Quebrada Cusco; the author at Ciudad Perdida. Back cover illustration: Laguna Quilatoa. Tungurahua photo from public domain; all other photos by the author.

Contents

Incidence *of* Travel

CHAPTER ONE

Incidence of Travel

In the present state of the world, it is almost presumptuous to put forth a book of travels.

> JOHN L. STEPHENS, *Incidents of Travel in Egypt,
> Arabia Petræa and the Holy Land* (1838)

MAY 2015

LEAVING CUSCO, THE ROAD TO THE FIESTA of the Lord of the Snows actually continues across South America to São Paulo, Brazil, but after five hours we got off the bus at Mahuayani. Usually, Mahuayani is a small settlement that straggles along the two-lane blacktop, but in late May and early June impromptu food stalls and shops sprout up at the trailhead leading to the chapel of the Lord of the Snows, or El Señor de Qoyllur Rit'i. The Fiesta de Qoyllur Rit'i has deep and tangled origins. The fiesta may have pre-Columbian roots and is certainly embedded in indigenous Andean belief and practice.[1] The fiesta is a movable feast, calibrated by the reappearance of the Pleiades in the southern Andean night. The Pleiades mark the important beginning of an agricultural cycle, and the brightness of the constellation in mid-June is used to predict the abundance of future rains.[2] Some anthropologists have suggested that Qoyllur Rit'i began as pilgrims from the eastern tropical lowlands climbed west into the high Andes.[3] The ritual guardians who police the fiesta are the *ukukus*, young men in shaggy, black wool chaps who represent the spectacled bear (*Tremarctos ornatus*) that live in the cloud forests in the eastern montaña and allegedly sneak into the Andes to have sex with Quechua women. Today, Qoyllur Rit'i attracts *campesinos* from Quechua and Aymara villages but also large numbers of mestizos from Cusco and other Peruvian cities and towns, some New Age adherents attracted by the spectacle and sacredness, other foreign tourists, and—of course—me.

I am here because I am an archaeologist. I am interested in the ways humans mark their presence on the landscape, a broad field of inquiry into cultural landscapes and the archaeology of place, exploring "the ways in which people impart meaning—both symbolically and through action—to their cultural and physical surroundings at multiple scales and . . . the material forms these meaning may take."[4] I conduct archaeological fieldwork in South America, principally on the northern coast of Peru, but I also travel across South America to visit other sites, museums, places, and ceremonies to learn about the ways humans inscribe their presence on the earth. And that is why I am here.

I was guided to the fiesta by Angel Callañaupa Alvarez, an extremely accomplished man from Chinchero, Peru: climber, expedition guide, an activist working on problems of food security in high Andean villages, and an artist with several book credits. (Angel's early artwork was used in the seldom-seen 1971 film *The Last Movie*, directed by Dennis Hopper.) We were joined by Arnold, a quiet young man in his mid-twenties who studied archaeology and museum studies at the Universidad San Abad del Cusco. In Mahuayani, Angel led us to a tarp-covered kitchen run by friends from Chinchero, where we sat at rough plank tables and ate bowls of mutton and noodle soup. Great commotions swirled around us. This was the beginning of the four-day festival, and while

some of the kitchens and stalls were already in business, other folks were still stringing blue plastic tarps, arranging cooking hearths, and unloading goods to sell to the pilgrims. The pilgrims hike 9 km to over 4,300 m above sea level to the chapel of Qoyllur Rit'i that sits below three glaciers at the base of Mount Qulqipunku, the "Silver Gate," an *apu*, or mountain deity, who watches over the health and well-being of people.

Angel arranged for a packhorse to carry our gear and another horse for him to ride, and he went on to set up camp. Arnold and I began to hike, lightly burdened with water, camera, and rain gear. The sun was out, and it was about 50°F as we hiked. The first pitch of the trail was extremely steep. We began at 3,880 m and climbed higher. I was constantly out of breath. The trail leveled to a more gentle but constant grade, following a stream that flowed from distant glaciers. The hillsides flanking the trail were very steep. White llamas grazed on the slopes.

We passed clusters of vendors' shops at various points along the trail, generally at broad, flat spots or at specific kilometer posts. On the lower reaches of the trail the vendors sold food and drink, but as we climbed, more and more of the shops offered ritual items. Candles and images of Christ were for sale, but most of the items were miniature objects of desire. A principal reason for journeying to Qoyllur Rit'i is to demonstrate one's faith to the Lord of the Snow Star and to ask for help in attaining one's dreams. There were small automobiles and pickup trucks for those who desired transportation and miniature bundles of money (both Peruvian *soles* and US dollars) for those who wished for wealth. A variety of types of miniature real estate was offered—houses, apartment buildings, and entire hardware stores—none larger than a pack of cigarettes. If you wanted to be well-educated or improve your professional standing, you could buy miniature diplomas and certificates that would ensure you would become *un maestro* or *un doctor*. These miniatures could be purchased along the trail and carried to the shrine high above.

It took almost three hours to climb to the broad basin that held the Santuario del Señor de Qoyllur Rit'i. The basin ran northeast-southwest, edged by steep slopes, and a stream curved through it. The slopes were pocked by small rectangular terraces, camping spots associated with specific families and passed down by generations of devotees. The santuario and plaza were on the south side of the stream. A market area with more kitchens and shops bordered the stream. North of the stream, dance troupes staked out camping spots in the flat and muddy area, pitching small tents and building large cooking fires.

We found Angel in his traditional camping spot across from the san-tuario on the north side of the basin overlooking the muddy flat. Angel had set up his tent, and he and Arnold set up a small tent for me as the sun went over the ridge and temperatures dropped quickly. I unpacked my sleeping bag and pad and put on warmer clothes. This was the eve-ning of the first of four days, and the basin already held tens of thou-sands of the faithful. I was the only gringo I had seen so far.

Incidence (physics): The falling of a line or anything moving in a line upon a surface.

OXFORD ENGLISH DICTIONARY

This book is about journeys and what I have learned in the course of travel about the archaeology of South America, particularly by looking at the creation of ancient cultural landscapes. My journeys are lines of movement—sometimes planned, often diverted by unforeseen events—that intersect with the lives and acts of other humans, past and present. Journeys are intersections, and I refer to the intersection between my travels and the material traces of other lives as "the incidence of travel." Of course, my title also plays on the titles of nineteenth-century archaeo-logical narratives, such as John Stephens's 1838 *Incidents of Travel in Egypt, Arabia Petræa and the Holy Land*; his 1841 *Incidents of Travel in Central America, Chiapas and Yucatán*, illustrated by Frederick Catherwood; and Ephraim George Squier's 1871 *Peru: Incidents and Explorations in the Land of the Inca*—books that were wildly popular and widely reviewed in their day.[5] A more recent connection is with the American artist Robert Smithson's 1969 project, *Incidents of Mirror-Travel in the Yucatan*, a work that preceded his best-known earthwork, *Spiral Jetty*, the coiled embankment he built on the edge of the Great Salt Lake in Utah.[6] These texts and objects recurrently intersect at the creation of and inquiry into cultural landscapes, past and present. My encounters with such cultural landscapes are described in the narratives in this book.

The following chapters intentionally braid narratives that occurred at different moments but were knotted together at a particular place. Obviously, my encounter with an archaeological site implies such an intersection, but other historical narratives and events wrap around such spaces: historical expeditions, creative and artistic reactions to places, or strands of previous archaeological investigations that produced insights into the meanings imbued in particular places. Thus, my own journeys become enmeshed with others' travels, and these are described throughout this book. These various travels by others had different motives—conquests, inquiry, explorations, settlement, diversion, devotion, escape, among others—and the tales of those journeys are interwoven with the fabrics of my own narratives.

Today, archaeological writings rarely incorporate narrative. Most archaeologists (myself included) are more comfortable writing in other genres with more stable expectations: scientific articles, excavation reports, or monographs. The very rigidity of the format of a scientific article—Introduction, Problem, Data, Methods, Results, and Discussion—is extraordinarily comforting; as a writer, one knows what comes next. Journeys are less predictable, their intersections difficult to foresee.

Journeys are barely visible in most archaeological writings—limited to an acknowledgment to a foundation for travel funds or a brief mention of the challenges involved in "implementing a research strategy"— but the travel and transit are usually absent, implicit, or placed in the background. In such writings, the tale is often lost.

Yet tales of journeys are central to archaeology—and to literature in general. Nicholas Delbanco argues,

> Travel writing is, I think, coeval with writing itself. We move and remember the place that we left; from a distance we send letters home . . . An account of journeys taken or a report at journey's end, a message from the provinces or a dispatch from the capital: each must be written down . . . One way to read the Book of Genesis is to consider that expulsion as a journey out of Eden; the long travail of Moses is a

hunt for promised land. So too is the Aeneid a travelogue that starts in Troy and ends hard years later in Rome. "The Wanderer" and "The Seafarer" are descriptions of waterlogged distance traversed; Captain Cook and Magellan and Lewis and Clark get parsed now for their prose. Although we're not certain how widely he traveled, Avon's Bard set many of his plays abroad; it sometimes seems as though all texts we hold to be enduring ones evoke a world of wonders that at first seem passing strange.[7]

In *Reclaiming Travel*, Ilan Stavans and Joshua Ellison argue that "travel writing is related to memoir; the life story is circumscribed by a journey . . . Travel writing is a form of thinking aloud, with the journey as the narrative frame. The elision of travel and thought—of travel as a metaphor for thoughts—has a long history. Our English word 'theory' comes from the Greek *theorin*, which refers specifically to a journey beyond the city to witness an unfamiliar religious rite."[8] More broadly, *θεωρία*, according to the *Oxford English Dictionary*, references "a looking at, viewing contemplation, speculation, theory, also a sight, a spectacle."[9] Travel is therefore "an enduring human enterprise. Travel is embedded in the origins of species, in our journey from African plains to every other corner of the inhabited world. It is central to our mythology and our earliest efforts to comprehend the human condition and make sense of the world around us."[10]

⸬

Many people climb to the shrine of Qoyllur Rit'i and return in a single exhausting day, carrying images of their loved ones to the shrine and returning with jugs of sanctified spring water. Qoyllur Rit'i encompasses many meanings, some of which have changed over the years. From the late 1970s until the early twenty-first century, one of the key passages in the ceremony occurred when a select platoon of ukukus climbed to the glaciers overlooking the basin, cut out huge blocks of ice, and carried the frozen relics down the mountain on their backs. Once in the basin, the blocks were chopped into smaller chunks and parceled

out to pilgrims from different communities who would, in turn, carry the ice chunks back to their villages where the ice was used in rituals to sustain the flow of water in their own springs, streams, and farmlands. Also, large loads of sacred ice were transported in trucks to Cusco, where the ice was displayed in the main plaza. Yet around 2009 the effects of global warming became obvious as glaciers withered in the Andes and in other high-elevation tropical zones around the world. The ukukus decided to end the ritual of collecting ice and now only allow small plastic bottles and jugs to be filled—a gallon at most—which are carried home to cure ill kinfolk after the water has been blessed in the Santuario del Señor de Qoyllur Rit'i.

The santuario is the principal religious structure, but it is not the only sacred space. The santuario is a long, narrow building with a bell tower on its north wall and a modest altar inside. The ukukus attempt to control the crush of faithful moving toward the altar to view the image of the Lord, offer a candle, and receive a sprig of white gladiola. The sheer density of the worshipers is potentially dangerous. Several years ago, the vast quantities of flaming candles—some small tapers, others thick wax cylinders as long as your leg—posed a fire hazard, and one child was asphyxiated in the smoke. As we shoved toward the altar in the santuario, the crowd became anxious and people began to shout in alarm. The first acrid smell of panic mixed with the reverence of the worshippers. I glanced at the altar from a distance and slid out a side door. I was no longer among the faithful.

Just as the earliest human stories are tales of journey—the discovery of a waterhole or the encounter with an enemy—similarly, the earliest archaeological writings were entwined with narratives of travel: accounts of discoveries, mishaps of travel, and encounters with modern people living in ancient places. Consider the opening paragraphs of *Monumenta Britannica* by the British archaeologist John Aubrey (1626–97), describing his first encounter with the Neolithic dolmens of Avebury:

TO THE READER

I was inclined by my genius,[11] from my childhood to the love of antiquities: and my fate dropped me in a country most suitable for such enquiries.

Salisbury Plain, and Stonehenge I had known from eight years old: but, I never saw the country about Marlborough, till Christmas 1648 ... Charles Seymour and Sir William Button, met with their packs of hounds at the Grey Wethers ... The chase led us (at length) through the village of Avebury, into the closes there; where I was wonderfully surprised at the sight of those vast stones: of which I had never heard before: as also at the mighty bank and graff [ditch] about it: I observed in the enclosures some segments of rude circles, made with these stones; whence I concluded, they had been in the old time complete.[12]

Here, in this early archaeological observation, we see some of the basic elements in archaeological narratives: journey, encounter, surprise, observation, and inference.

Nearly a century before Aubrey's journey to Avebury, John Leland (1503–52)—the English poet, bookman, and antiquarian—traveled across England to consult monastic libraries, journeys that led him to note the presence of other antiquities. Bearing the authorization of King's Antiquary, Leland crisscrossed England and Wales, as he noted in the opening lines of *The Laboryouse Journey and Serche of John Leylande for Englandes Antiquitees* addressed to Henry VIII:

Amonge all the nacions, in whome I have wandered, for the knowledge
  of thynges
(moste benygne soueraygne)
I haue founde nene so negligent and vntoward,
as I haue found England in the due serch of theyr auncyent
hystores, to the syngulare fame and bewtye therof.[13]

Unfortunately, Leland died of madness before completing his magnum opus, which was only published in the late nineteenth century. Yet the themes of arduous travel, the entrancing beauty of things, and the modern world's shameful neglect of the past—all of these echo with my experience as an archaeologist six centuries later.

Narrative—and especially tales of travel—dominated archaeological writings well into the late nineteenth century, became less prominent in the mid-twentieth century, and thereafter rendered nearly invisible—except when archaeologists share their experiences over beers. And yet, as Rosemary Joyce has written, "Archaeology is a storytelling discipline from its inception in the field or lab."[14]

The dominant genres of archaeological writing—the report and the essay—often overlook the journeys that led to archaeological insights, not only the physical journeys but the intellectual transits, the passages through modern cultures, and the movement from ignorance to insight. Since these early texts, narrative has been gradually eliminated from archaeological writings, especially from technical reports in which the author's voice—and, often, presence—is erased from the text.

The act of writing is integral to archaeology. Joyce adds: "Writing pervades archaeology, from the creation of field notes and other records of research observations to the creation of informal and formal presentations. Archaeology is continually being scripted and rescripted from previous fragments, both in these writing practices and in its other embodied activities."[15]

The following narratives of encounter have several specific goals, while I intentionally avoid other matters. First, they present my own journeys in South America to archaeological sites and landscapes with a particular emphasis on place-making in the past and present. I am primarily interested in cultural landscapes and the creation of place in the archaeological record, and this is true whether I have written on the creation of ancient architecture, the development of cultural landscapes, the construction of sacred space, the prehistory of home, or the social adaptations by hunters and gatherers in the deserts of northern Baja California.[16] My own journeys to these "sites"—a term intriguingly stripped of valence—were also inquiries into how they were transformed into "places" by the people who once lived there, but they also became "places" to me through the act of journeying. I do not claim to fully understand the original meanings of these places for their inhabitants: I would never be so bold, as I am acutely aware of my ignorance. Yet by seeing these places with my own eyes, I have gained a deeper appreciation of, a greater empathy about, these landscapes and the people who created them.

Second, the narratives of my journeys interweave with historical accounts, archaeological reports, and other sources of information that create an intellectual landscape of contexts and relevancies. In many cases, I planned a specific journey because I was intrigued by a particular site or ceremony; in other cases, I blundered upon places whose significance I only later understood. In every case, the information and insights of others—whether explorers, archaeologists, artists, ethnographers, soldiers, or writers—deepened my experience of travels in South America.

Third, I have tried to write this book in a way that will engage a general reader. For this reason, I intentionally emphasize the narrative line, avoid unnecessary jargon, and direct the reader to scholarly references modestly consigned to endnotes. I believe archaeologists must write for a broader and sophisticated reading audience. A few archaeologists do.[17] For example, the prolific Brian Fagan has written scores of books on archaeology and related topics, such as climate change, food, and pets. The classical archaeologist Ian Morris has written four books exploring the broad sweep of human history to understand patterns of conflict and cohesion among modern societies. The biblical archaeologist Eric H. Cline wrote an outstanding book about the complex factors leading to the collapse of the eastern Mediterranean and Egypt during the Bronze Age. In the United Kingdom, the archaeologist, farmer, and novelist Francis Pryor has written numerous books about British archaeology and landscape, as well as being a principal in the *Time Team* television series. These archaeologists write for academic and popular audiences, and I apologize in advance for overlooking others of whom I am not aware. But note: the Society for American Archaeology has over 7,000 members, and it is estimated that 11,000 archaeologists work in the United States alone. When the most widely read and reviewed books about New World archaeology were the excellent *1491: New Revelations of the Americas before Columbus* (2005) and *1493: Uncovering the New World Columbus Created* (2011) by science journalist Charles Mann or journalist Marilyn Johnson's *Lives in Ruins* (2015), there should be room for an archaeologist to actually write about what we archaeologists actually do: uncover and retrieve forgotten elements of the past and incorporate them into the consultable record of the human experience.

Finally, the following chapters are not narratives of self-discovery. With the extraordinary popularity of Elizabeth Gilbert's *Eat, Pray, Love: One Woman's Search for Everything across Italy, India, and Indonesia*, an expectation has emerged that travel narrative necessarily involves personal self-discovery or, as an editor who wished to remain anonymous explained to me, "the emotional journey . . . along the way." Frankly, I do not travel to discover myself; I don't think I am interesting. My vision is outward and I travel, as John Leland did, "for the knowledge of thynges."

The sun went over the ridge and the temperature dropped. I was in my sleeping bag by 6:30 p.m., exhausted. The midwinter night was cold and long at Qoyllur Rit'i. I slept fully dressed with thermal long-johns, pants, long-sleeved T-shirt, flannel shirt, parka, gloves, stocking cap, and my stocking feet shoved into the pockets of a down vest in the bottom of my sleeping bag. I shook in the cold. I propped up my upper body to help me breathe. I was in the sleeping bag for nearly twelve hours, and I dozed for less than six hours of shivering, air-gasping sleep.

The fiesta continued throughout the night. Many pilgrims departed from Mahuayani after nightfall—climbing the trail in the darkness, bearing raised pennants on upright poles, and following dancers and musicians in transitory pools of sound and light. All night, other groups danced and paraded in the plaza on the east side of the santuario. The bands played bass and snare drums, clarinets and trumpets, and often saxophones. In the plaza, the dancers had choreographed routines, their phrasings signaled by a choreographer's blasts on a police whistle. The music reverberated through loudspeakers the size of refrigerators. Fireworks and mortar shots blasted throughout the night, echoing across the basin. The sounds of the fiesta ebbed slightly at around 3 a.m. but never silenced.

I crawled out of my tent around 6 a.m. The sky was thinly silvered. My tent was needled with hoarfrost, as was the flat basin below. I stumbled about on the uneven terrain in frozen boots. Around 20,000 to 30,000 pilgrims had arrived overnight and camped in the basin, their small tents covered in sheets of cobalt blue plastic. Sometime during the night, a Quechua couple had rigged a makeshift tent right below my terrace. Their "tent" was simply a 2-m-wide flat sheet of plastic anchored with stones and no higher than the undercarriage of a Volkswagen. They had arrived in last night's darkness, made camp, and now lay in front of me softly snoring in a thick mantle of heavy woolen blankets. I almost tumbled down onto them when I squirmed out of my tent.

The dance troupes stirred, arranging capes and masks, tightening drum-skins. As the sun rose over the glaciered ridges, the dance troupes prepared their first songs of the day, which they played to the sun—facing east to the Inti rather than toward the santuario. Gestures like these made me wonder whether Catholicism was a thin veneer over indigenous practice or whether—more probably—such questions were meaningless and misguided. Rather than remnants of past traditions or impositions of Catholicism, it is probably more reasonable to think of these gestures as ongoing and evolving attempts by people trying to understand and represent their place in the world.

And this is certainly true of the area above the santuario that consists of *las piedritas* and el Banco del Señor. The zone is called *las piedritas* (the little rocks) because the vendors of dreams stack small chunks of shale into lot boundaries, create small skyscrapers and buildings, or mark the areas where they sell other miniatures. The notion is that if you buy a miniature, your wish will be granted. Most of the vendors are women, members of a sellers' association all wearing identical day-glow orange vests. Ritual miniatures are used in various ceremonies in the southern Andes, such as in the Alasitas Fiesta in Bolivia, in which

small objects of desire—small stacks of dollar bills, miniature auto-mobiles, or tiny jumbo jets—are used to ask for wealth, vehicles, or a journey to Miami from Ekeko, the god of abundance, prosperity, and fecundity.[18] This practice may have originated in prehistory, with min-iature projectile points found in hunting-and-gathering sites dating to 5,000 to 4,400 years ago.[19] Over the last decades, versions of Ekeko have become more widespread in Argentina and Chile, although I didn't see any images of Ekeko himself at Qoyllur Rit'i; the miniatures were seen throughout the las piedritas area.

According to Angel, these miniatures are relatively recent at Qoyllur Rit'i. In past decades, small stones were the sole tokens; and they represented only llamas, alpacas, and sheep. Instead, I heard a young man offer, like a circus midway huckster, "Parcels! Parcels! I am selling lots in New York City worth $100,000, but you can have one for only a single *sol*"—about thirty cents.

Once you have bought your miniature or certificate of ownership, you go to the Banco del Señor.

Just downslope from las piedritas, the Banco del Señor is a building about 12 m long, with a plaza and altar to the Virgin on the east side and three bank teller windows—Caja 1, Caja 2, Caja 3—on the long north wall. The banco is a recent construction, according to Angel, built to enclose and contain a large boulder, a *wak'a*.[20] In the Andes, the Quechua term *wak'a* (also spelled "huaca" or "guaca") is broadly applied to sacred places and things, objects of veneration that are often natural landforms with special significance. This particular wak'a was a large boulder venerated by young girls and single women, who gave offerings of thread and candles and asked the wak'a for aid in finding a husband, for good health, or in other requests. Recently, the wak'a was expropriated by enclosing the stone within the walls of the banco, physically incorporating the boulder into the altar for the Virgin Mary, who is adored and honored by pilgrims in the small plaza on the east side of the building. But on the north side of the building, the ukukus control the crowds lined up before the bank tellers' windows. Having purchased your miniature deed to a $100,000 lot in New York for one sol, you can go to the Banco del Señor, be attended at one of the tellers' windows, and make an additional payment of a few soles to the Virgin to help ensure that the deal comes true.

Other dreams are sought in the las piedritas zone. Next to a large boulder, a man wearing a cheap version of a priest's stole and holding a plastic Coke bottle of "holy water" shouted, "Okay! Who wants to get married?" A raucous clutch of teenagers shoved one boy to the front, laughing—"Here! He does! He has a girlfriend!"—but the boy scrambled back into the crowd. Across the crowd, an embarrassed girl looked at the ground. The "priest" bantered in a rapid and slang-filled mix of Spanish and Quechua that I couldn't really follow, but the crowd roared with laughter. The priest stepped toward the crowd, spraying the onlookers with surprising streams of holy water. Convulsions of laughter. "Okay! Okay! Who wants to be married?" the priest demanded. More laughter and confusion. Finally, a middle-aged couple stepped forward. Based on their street clothes, they were not campesinos but from Cusco or another town. The couple stood in front of the priest. An assistant appeared with a selection of copper wedding rings of different sizes slotted into a wooden box lined with cheap velveteen. The couple and the ring assistant fumbled a bit, finding rings the correct size. The priest shouted, "And now—who will be the godfather and godmother?" Another middle-aged couple came forward and stood on each side of the betrothed. "*Bueno*," the priest began and launched into another sermon for the next five minutes, a monologue that convulsed the onlookers. Whenever hilarity flagged, the priest squirted holy water. The mass concluded with a hand wave of benediction. The couple kissed, signed a "marriage certificate," and paid the priest. The copper rings were twisted from fingers and replaced in their slots in the velveteen-lined box. The newlyweds headed downhill to validate their wedding at the Banco del Señor.

Angel observed that a spatial and moral axis runs through the Fiesta of Qoyllur Rit'i, from the Santuario upslope to the Banco del Señor and las piedritas. Downslope, the Santuario del Señor, the secondary chapel flickering with masses of candles, and plazas filled with dancers and musicians comprise a solemn, sacred, collective, and reverent zone, policed by ukukus armed with llama whips. Uphill, the banco and las piedritas are ironic areas, focused on everyday wishes, individual and irreverent. Along this gradient, there are different gestures and enactments of faith, marked by different material traces—what I, as an archaeologist, think of as diverse artifacts, features, and sites.

Each year when the Pleiades reappear in the southern Andes, this high cirque is reanimated by human actions and beliefs, anchoring a broad variety of gestures, dreams, and desires. In turn, these human hopes and actions are enacted in this specific place on this particular and resonant segment of terrain, and in that process landscape is imbued with meaning.

∏

The following chapters explore different aspects of place-making in ancient South America, regions and times past that I encountered in my journeys between 1981 and 2015. **Chapter 2** discusses a common class of archaeological monument—human-made earthen mounds—and considers how these apparently simple masses may have complex constructions and subtle associations, insights I gained during excavations in far northern Peru. **Chapter 3** describes a ritual procession I joined in southern Ecuador, walking through a landscape that was imbued with the sacred and made sacred through human actions. **Chapter 4** is an account of a journey I made to Patagonia to see a remarkable example of prehistoric rock art, a beautiful human creation in a featureless, wind-scoured landscape. This is followed by an essay (**chapter 5**) about how people have marked their presence by inscribing lines on the land, including such famous examples as the Nasca lines but also literally hundreds of other examples of geoglyphs across South America, ancient and modern, including in the Atacama Desert where I journeyed to see the longest poem in the world. **Chapter 6** is based on my trek in the mountains of northern Colombia—two-and-a-half days on foot, two-and-a-half days on mule—to visit a remote site associated with the Kaaga people and their ancestors, a culture of surpassing sophistication and complexity whose priests are entrusted with defending the Earth. Moving south to Ecuador (**chapter 7**), I describe a beautiful region periodically destroyed by fierce volcanic eruptions, cataclysmic events that obliterated ancient societies and became encoded in myth and legend. This region of Ecuador is also the principal location for the following chapter (**chapter 8**), which explores the different ways Western scientists and Andean astronomers approached the measurement of the cosmos. **Chapter 9** describes a journey on "the beautiful road," the Qhapaq Ñan, the roadway the Incas created to unify their empire—that inadvertently became the avenue of conquest for the expedition led by Francisco Pizarro and the chaos and destruction that occurred in its aftermath. The last chapter serves as an epilogue, exploring the ways archaeologists and others see the past as more stable and coherent than it was seen by the people who made place across the length of South America.

A final note: throughout this book, sections within chapters are separated by a trapezoidal symbol, as below. This is based on a common map symbol used in South America, which stands for a *tampu/tambo*, a way station along the Inca road. By extension, its presence in the following pages marks a waypoint on the reader's journey through this text.

▥

At Qoyllur Rit'i the morning dawned cold and clear, but by 9 a.m. it looked like rain. Fog rose up the valley, and the eastern sky weighed with water. I asked Angel if we needed to buy plastic sheets from the vendors who wandered among the pilgrims, selling meters of tarp from long blue rolls. Angel thought it wasn't necessary as the rain would freeze and quickly slide from our backpacking tents. The rain came at around 10:30 a.m., and we crawled back into the tents. As Angel predicted, the rain immediately froze on the tent's rip-stop nylon, but the walls slumped under the rime. Inside the tent, I batted the walls so the ice slid off the fly. After an hour or so, the rain paused and we got out and surveyed the situation. The broad flat below us was a muddy bog. Other pilgrims were climbing out to check their tents, call for more blue plastic, and try to get dry. In the plaza by the Santuario del Señor, the bands and dancers never halted.

Angel looked east at the clouds above the glaciers and predicted "viene el nevado," and the first snowflakes fell as we climbed back into

the tents. Over the next half hour, two to three inches of snow fell. The tent walls pressed to my face and seemed to make breathing that much harder. The snow stopped and we climbed out of our tents once again. Angel and I discussed the situation. Since it had snowed at noon, he was fairly certain it would snow again during the night, and he didn't know if the tents would bear the weight. The prospect of a long winter night sleeping in snowdrifts did not appeal to us. We decided to break camp and head down.

We left around 2 p.m. and passed large crowds of pilgrims and tourists heading up to Qoyllur Rit'i. The pilgrimage troupes danced up the mountain. The tourists ranged from large parties of a dozen people to single, ill-equipped travelers. One large group of gringo tourists with a trekking group, some on horseback, was accompanied by *arrieros* who drove pack mules that carried luggage, gear, and bundles of firewood. As I passed them going downhill, they looked at me quizzically, as if to ask why I was leaving when the major events were just beginning. Angel looked back at the clouds and remarked at how dark and foreboding they appeared. Despite this, the mountain path was thronged with travelers on their way to the Santuario del Señor de Qoyllur Rit'i, drawn by faith or curiosity to this specific valley in the southern Andes transformed by ancient practices and modern rituals into a complex and deeply human place.

NOTES

1. There are differences in scholarly opinion about when the Fiesta de Qoyllur Rit'i originated. Randall argued that it was originally an Inca fiesta; see Robert Randall, "Qoyllur Rit'i: An Inca Fiesta of the Pleiades: Reflections on Time and Space in the Andean World," *Bulletin de l'Institut Français d'études andines* 11, no. 1–2 (1982): 37–81; Robert Randall, "The Mythstory of Kuri Qoyllur: Sex, Seqes, and Sacrifice in Inka Agricultural Festivals," *Journal of Latin American Lore* 16, no. 1 (1990): 3–45. In contrast, Salas Carreño notes that the earliest historical account mentioning the pilgrimage dates to the 1780s and the current fiesta became more developed in the 1930s; see Guillermo Salas Carreño, "Acerca de la antigua importancia de las comparsas de *wayri ch'unchu* y su contemporánea marginalidad en la peregrinación de Quyllurit'i," *Antropologica* 28 (2010): 67–91; Guillermo Salas Carreño, "The Glacier, the Rock, the Image: Emotional Experience and Semiotic Diversity at the Quyllurit'i Pilgrimage (Cuzco, Peru)," *Signs and Society* 2.S1 (2014): S188–S214. For historical images of the fiesta, see pictures by the great Cusqueño photographer Martin Chambi (1891–1973), who photographed the fiesta in 1931 and 1935; see *Martín Chambi: Photographs, 1920–1950* (Washington, DC: Smithsonian Institution Press, 1993), 105–6.

2. Benjamin Orlove, John Chiang, and Mark Cane, "Forecasting Andean Rainfall and Crop Yield from the Influence of El Niño on Pleiades Visibility," *Nature* 403 (January 6, 2000): 68–71.

3. Randall, *Bulletin de l'Institut Français*, 54.

4. Maria Nieves Zedeño and Brenda J. Bowser, "The Archaeology of Meaningful Places," in *The Archaeology of Meaningful Places*, edited by Brenda J. Bowser and Maria Nieves Zedeño, 1–14 (Salt Lake City: University of Utah Press, 2009), 5.

5. For example, see excerpts from Edgar Allen Poe's reviews of Stephens's book, as discussed by Roscoe Hill, "John Lloyd Stephens and His American Book," *The Americas: A Quarterly Review of Inter-American Cultural History* 6, no. 2 (1949): 197–207.

6. See *Robert Smithson: The Collected Writings*, edited by Jack Flam (Berkeley: University of California Press, 1996).

7. Nicholas Delbanco, "Review: Anywhere out of This World: On Why All Writing Is Travel Writing," *Harper's Magazine* 309, no. 1852 (September 2004): 91–92.

8. Ilan Stavans and Joshua Ellison, *Reclaiming Travel* (Durham, NC: Duke University Press, 2015), 29.

9. Ibid., 29.

10. Ibid., 99.

11. Here, Aubrey uses "genius" in its classical Roman sense: "the tutelary god or attendant spirit allotted to every person at his birth," *Oxford English Dictionary*.

12. John Aubrey, *Monumenta Britannica*, annotated by Rodney Legg, 2 vols. (Sherborne, Dorset, UK: Dorset Publishing Company, 1980 [1665–93]), part I: 17–18, accessed March 11, 2016, https://archive.org/details/laboryousejourn00balegoog.

13. See also Matthew Johnson, "Commentary: Archaeology as Travel and Tourism," *International Journal of Historical Archaeology* 15 (2011): 298–303.

14. Rosemary Joyce with Robert Preucel, Jeanne Lopiparo, Carolyn Guyer, and Michael Joyce, *The Languages of Archaeology: Dialogue, Narrative, and Writing* (Oxford: Blackwell, 2008), 17.

15. Ibid., 7.

16. For example, *Cultural Landscapes in the Prehispanic Andes: Archaeologies of Place* (Gainesville: University Press of Florida, 2006); *The Prehistory of Home* (Berkeley: University of California Press, 2012).

17. The archaeologist Brian Fagan has spent most of his career writing for a non-archaeological reader, having written more than forty-six books and numerous articles about archaeology and related topics; for a full list and other information, see http://www.brianfagan.com. Ian Morris's books for a general audience include *Why the West Rules—For Now: The Patterns of History, and What They Reveal about the Future* (New York: Farrar, Straus, and Giroux, 2010); *The Measure of Civilisation: How Social Development Decides the Fate of Nations* (Princeton: Princeton University Press, 2013); *War! What Is It Good For? Conflict and the Progress of Civilization from Primates to Robots* (New York: Farrar, Straus, and Giroux, 2014); *Foragers, Farmers, and Fossil Fuels: How Human Values Evolve* (Princeton: Princeton University Press, 2015). Among his many books, Eric H. Cline's 2014 *1177 BC: The Year Civilization Collapsed* (Princeton: Princeton University Press, 2014) was widely reviewed. In the United Kingdom, Francis Pryor has written numerous books about British archaeology and landscape; see https://pryorfrancis.wordpress.com. A recent effort to extend archaeologists' reach to a broader readership was initiated by Brown University's Joukousky Institute for Archaeology and the Ancient World with a competition titled "Archaeology for the People: The Joukowsky Institute Competition for Accessible Archaeological Writing"; nearly 150 articles were submitted, and a selection of the ten best articles is forthcoming.

18. Michèle Cros and Daniel Dory, "Apprivoiser le marché: Éléments d'interprétation des alacitas en Bolivie," *Journal des anthropologues: Association française des anthropologues* 98–99 (2004): 171–201; Jim Weil, "From Ekeko to Scrooge McDuck: Commodity Fetishism and Ideological Change in a Bolivian Fiesta," *Ideologies and Literature* 4, no. 1 (1989): 7–29; Jim Weil, "The Articulated Peasant: Household Economies in the Andes," *American Anthropologist* 105, no. 2 (2003): 444–45.

19. Mark Aldenderfer, "Continuity and Change in Ceremonial Structures at Late Preceramic Asana, Southern Peru," *Latin American Antiquity* 2 (1991): 227–58.

20. For a recent discussion, see the volume edited by Tamara Bray, *The Archaeology of Wak'as: Explorations of the Sacred in the Pre-Columbian Andes* (Boulder: University Press of Colorado, 2015).

CHAPTER TWO

Making Mounds

I know of no such thing existing as an Indian monument: unless
indeed it be the Barrows, of which many are to be found all over
this country. These are of different sizes, some of them constructed of earth, and some of loose stones. That they were repos-
itories of the dead, has been obvious to all: but on what particular
occasion constructed, was [a] matter of doubt.

THOMAS JEFFERSON, *Notes on the State of Virginia*

EVEN DURING THE AUSTRAL WINTER IN FAR NORTHERN PERU, Tumbes
is hot. In 2007 we excavated a site called Santa Rosa, located about 15 km
inland from the Pacific Ocean on the south bank of the Tumbes River.
The terraces that flank the river have stands of dry tropical forest with
kapok and acacia trees and a tangle of thorn-covered vines. The site of
Santa Rosa was easy to overlook, although local residents knew it as a
mound and *wak'a*. It was also an extremely confusing and profoundly
illuminating site. The site was behind a row of modest houses made
from wattle and daub and roofed with corrugated aluminum that bakes

in the intense, tropical sun. The area behind the houses held chicken coops and pigpens, and behind them was an area where folks threw trash. It was a lurid modern midden—dirty diapers, paper scraps, dog-gnawed bones, used syringes, bloodied rags—a foot-thick layer of foul garbage. This unappealing stratum covered the site of Santa Rosa. But amid the trash and stench, you could see the signs of earlier occupants. In a few patches of bare earth, brief lines of cobblestones hinted at the presence of ancient walls. The surface was not level; it was highest at the southern end, somewhat higher along the west, north, and east sides, and lower in the center. It looked as if a rectangular enclosure made from adobe walls had slumped down, the sun-dried bricks melting over centuries of rainy seasons.

In 1996 we had found two small but exciting artifacts at Santa Rosa. On the northwest corner we found the shell of a thorny oyster, *Spondylus princeps*. *Spondylus* was highly revered across the ancient Andes, given as offerings to ensure the flow of water and good crop harvests, made into tiny beads, and carved into figurines used in funerals and other ceremonies.[1] *Spondylus* was widely traded and deeply esteemed throughout the Andes. Finding a *Spondylus* fragment at Santa Rosa was potentially very important. The other artifact was a small potsherd, black as charcoal and burnished smooth except for the upraised figure of a pelican. Because of my previous experience at other sites, I recognized this sherd at a glance: it was a fragment of a Chimú mold-made pot. The Chimú forged a pre-Inca state on the Peruvian coast. According to Colonial accounts, the Chimú had extended their empire northward to Tumbes in the late 1400s; this small sherd seemed confirmation of that notion. There were few other ancient artifacts on the surface, all but overwhelmed by the foul debris of modern times.

Based on the Chimú blackware sherd, we proposed that Santa Rosa was a late prehispanic site, possibly dating to the centuries when the Chimú Empire spread north. I thought we had found a rectangular adobe compound, about 30 m long and 20 m wide. My Peruvian colleagues, Wilson Puell and Bernardino Olaya, and I wrote a brief article in Spanish summarizing our survey results. I began the process of trying to get grant money to excavate at Santa Rosa and three other sites in Tumbes. In 2007 I returned to Tumbes to excavate at Santa Rosa.

On an early evening in mid-March, Bernardino, the local director of the Institute of Culture, and I went to Santa Rosa to meet with the community to discuss the excavations we hoped to begin in a few days. It was the end of the rainy season, but showers still welled up in the late afternoons. At dusk, black crickets crawled from the cornfields toward any source of light. The crickets oozed under the doors and flowed through gaps in windowsills. Thick, crunchy mats of the insects pooled below streetlights.

We met with the villagers on the concrete bleachers of an outdoor basketball court. We were welcomed by the *teniente gobernador*, a man serving as the local official for a two- or three-year term. He announced to the community that we were here to explain our project. I was introduced by the local director of the Institute of Culture, who vouched for my seriousness, said I was a long-standing friend of the people of Tumbes, and mentioned that our project would provide jobs for local men and women for the next two months. Then I spoke, saying that my hope was to discover more about the prehistory of Tumbes and share that knowledge with the people of Tumbes and all Peruvians who did not know that Tumbes had such a rich history and culture. We were going to excavate in the mound behind their houses, the huaca, and learn about the ancient lives of their ancestors. And we would hire between twelve and twenty people for various lengths of time over the next eight to ten weeks. There was a quiet murmur of assent. I asked, "Do you have any questions?" There was a long silence punctuated by metallic chirpings.

Finally, one man cleared his throat and said, "Is it true that if you dig into the wak'a, the people will sicken and children will die?"

Frankly, I was so surprised by this question that all I could do was stammer "well . . . no." Fortunately, Bernardino came to the rescue. "It is a common belief," he said, "that digging into the huacas disturbs the spirits of the ancestors, and many people believe this around the world. But this does not happen. You can ask your neighbors and friends at other places where we have excavated, and they have not sickened nor have their children died because we dug there. Do not just believe us. Ask your neighbors and friends, and you will learn that no ill will occur because of our excavations. Instead, we will learn about the past of your community and you will gain in pride by knowing about the history of this place."

There was a general nodding of heads, and the teniente gobernador said, "Then you are welcome to do this project here, and I will help you find the people you need as workers." Two women carried a case of beer bottles from a nearby store. There was a single glass. The teniente gobernador poured me a glass of beer. I drank, then carefully flicked the last foam to earth as an offering to Pachamama, Mother Earth, before passing the glass on so we could all drink together.

We began work the next day. We hired a half-dozen workmen who raked the garbage from the site. We burned great piles of toxic trash. When the fires burned down, we strung a barbed-wire fence around the excavation area to keep out goats and cattle. We laid out a line of 2 m × 2 m excavation pits, eight contiguous units forming a 2 m × 16 m trench that would slice through the center of the rectangular adobe compound. As I wrote in my field notes, the trench would "provide a stratigraphic cross-section of the compound including walls and plaza area"; since "the central portion is lower, excavations there should give us a better idea of pre-compound strata."

My plan was logical, straightforward, and wrong.

<hr />

Every archaeological project is a journey along multiple routes and different dimensions. My 2007 journey to Santa Rosa began three months earlier at Los Angeles International waiting by the gate for a 1 a.m. flight to Lima. The crowd was cranky, babies cried, and a Chinese grandmother harangued a bunch of kids in Mandarin. Once onboard, things settled down. The connection in Panama was only forty minutes but I made it, as did the equipment and luggage. In my carry-on knapsack I had my laptop and a total station—a laser-based transit used

for mapping—while the tripod and reflective prism were in checked luggage, along with books, trowels, work boots, and clothes for six months. In Lima, I sped through customs without a hitch and on to the Miraflores neighborhood of Lima, where I stayed in a small hostel a few blocks from the sea.

That journey had other antecedents. The 2007 trip was based on planning I had begun in 2001. The project was funded by a grant from the

National Science Foundation, a grant I had applied and been rejected for four times before receiving the award. The Tumbes research built on even earlier researches in Peru. I first went to Peru in 1981 as a graduate student working on an excavation at the Chimú site of Manchan, located in the Casma Valley about 350 km north of Lima. The project was directed by Carol Mackey and Ulana Klymyshyn, who supervised my dissertation research. The Chimú had founded the largest prehispanic state on the North Coast of Peru, ruling a long strip of territory between AD 900 and 1470. Manchan was the largest provincial center in the southern frontier of the Chimú Empire, and my research examined how this imperial presence affected the daily lives of ordinary people. I pursued these lines of research over the next nine years, returning to Peru for fieldwork totaling two more years, writing my dissertation, publishing articles, and presenting conference papers—all the things a young and aspiring archaeologist must do.

But then the terror in Peru became too intense. After starting its guerrilla war in 1980, the Maoist revolutionary force Sendero Luminoso (or "Shining Path") was active in most of the central and highland departments of Peru over the next decade. In 1990 I was in Lima pursuing a research project that involved working in the National Library and other archives, but rather than some tranquil, bookish interlude, this was when Peru's conflict with Sendero Luminoso was most intense. The revolutionary forces bombed electrical transmission towers, sending Lima into dark anarchy. The war was very close and terrifying. At the same time, hyperinflation peaked at 9,700 percent. The currency, the Peruvian *sol,* devalued as rapidly. People paid bus fares with bread rolls because buns held their value longer than the currency. Cell phones were not yet common, so Peru still relied on public pay phones, but instead of using coins—whose value evaporated hourly—one bought metal phone tokens called *rines* at newspaper kiosks. As inflation rocketed upward, a moment would arrive when the value of the rines as phone tokens was less than their value as scrap metal. All the rines disappeared, bought up by an unknown scrap metal cartel.

People on fixed salaries—teachers, nurses, and anyone on a government salary—saw their incomes decimated and called for *huelgas parciales*, or "partial strikes," that lasted from midnight until noon. During these daily twelve-hour strikes, chaos reigned. The major bus lines went on strike, so the *combis*—owner-operated vans that trolled the streets for passengers—were packed with as many as twenty people crammed into a vehicle with seats for eight. At the National Library, the doors opened hours after the posted 9 a.m. time, sometimes not until 11 a.m., when the staff straggled in. Given their devalued salaries—some were earning less than $100 a month—the major reason many library staff showed up was to receive a daily free lunch.

I completed my archival research and returned to Antigua Guatemala, where my wife and I were living. I swore that I would never return to Peru, deciding that I could enjoy doing archaeology in another Latin American country less blighted by chaos, but I followed events in Peru from a distance. Things only got worse. In April 1992 the Peruvian president, Alberto Fujimori, suspended the constitution, dismissed Congress, and began replacing judges—a coup against his own government dubbed *un autogolpe*. In July 1992 Sendero Luminoso detonated a massive car bomb that ripped through Miraflores (less than two blocks from the tranquil pension where I usually stayed)—killing 18 people, injuring 140 civilians, destroying apartment complexes, and shattering windows within a 15-block radius. Other, coordinated bombs exploded across Lima. Fujimori's government responded savagely, the army executing innocent people swept up in the violence. In September 1992 Sendero Luminoso's leader, Abimael Guzmán, and other guerrilla leaders were captured in Lima. The army continued to press the guerrillas. Fujimori's government began to invest in rural communities. Communal kitchens were established. Roads were repaired. Inflation slowed. A few years later foreign archaeologists—many of whom had shifted to other nations for their fieldwork—began to return to Peru. And in 1996, so did I.

In June 1996 I met my former student and longtime friend Patrick Kehoe in Lima. We picked up a rental car the next day and headed north on the Pan-American Highway to Tumbes, a 1,200-km journey we spread over five days, stopping to visit archaeological sites en route. We stayed the first night in Casma, where we visited the massive mound site of Sechin Alto.

For decades, the archaeology of mounds has been considered a relatively straightforward matter, with excavations targeted on the features and artifacts on top of or within the mound rather than focusing on the construction of the mound itself. In *Notes on the State of Virginia*, Thomas Jefferson described his excavation of a burial mound near the Rivanna River, a dig credited with being the first archaeological excavation in North America.

Jefferson provided some details about the mound, noting it was "spheroidical" in shape, 40 ft in diameter and originally 12 ft high, although reduced to 7½ ft by plowing, and that it contained stones and clay transported to this location. Nonetheless, Jefferson's attention was focused on the 1,000 human burials it contained, as the mound "has derived both origin and growth from the accustomary collection of bones, and deposition of them together."[2]

In the centuries since Jefferson's exploration, it has been more common for archaeologists to focus on the contents of mounds or to consider them as platforms for constructions rather than to consider how the mounds were constructed. Prehistoric anthropogenic mounds are found on every continent except Antarctica. Whether made from earth, stone, or shells, the basic process of making a mound seems unproblematic. The archaeologists Sarah C. Sherwood and Tristram R. Kidder—who specialize in the prehistory of the southeastern United States—write, "Traditionally, archaeologists have assumed mounds were erected by a simple process of accumulating sediments or soil material into a pile and shaping it to whatever architectural form was desired."[3] Yet these apparently unproblematic human creations are neither as obvious nor as straightforward as they might seem.

Consider two very different mounds. In the Casma Valley on the North Coast of Peru, the site of Sechin Alto extends over 1.4 km, a line of plazas and sunken circular courts that culminates in a massive mound built from blocks of granite and hand-modeled conical adobes. The mound is a dun-brown hulk looming above the surrounding corn-fields. This mound stood 35 m tall, and its base was the size of two-and-a half-football fields (300 m × 250 m). When it was built between 1800 and 1400 BC, the mound at Sechin Alto was the largest construction in the Americas. About 2 million m³ of material went into the mound. The project probably required more workers than actually lived at Sechin Alto, demanding labor from throughout the Casma Valley and beyond. The water and mud for the adobes were carried from a river a kilometer away. The stone was quarried and dragged 1.4 km to the site, some of the blocks weighing more than 4 tons. It is estimated that the initial construction phase between 1800 and 1600 BC would have required more than 66,000 person-years to complete.[4]

The scale of the construction is impressive; the implications of the project are tantalizing. What type of society built this enormous pile? Was it a powerful centralized authority that scoured the countryside for laborers, commanded workers, and coordinated the different aspects of the monument's design and completion? Or rather, was a monument like Sechin Alto the cumulative product of smaller, less hierarchical social groups motivated by religious devotion to place stone

upon stone? And what was this massive mound for? Was it a passive monument admired from afar, or was it the stage for sacred or royal ceremonies performed by priests or rulers and watched by crowds of commoners from below? If we could answer these questions for Sechin Alto, what about other mounds built elsewhere by prehispanic peoples in South America? Many questions remain unanswered, the evidence buried deep in this massive, ancient mound.

Contrast Sechin Alto with another massive mound construction, the twentieth-century work *Effigy Tumuli*, an example of earth art built by the artist Michael Heizer (b. 1944). The son of the archaeologist Robert Heizer (1915–79), who conducted major excavations at the monumental Olmec site of La Venta on the Gulf Coast of Mexico as well as extensive and diverse research in western North America, Michael Heizer's monumental constructions frequently draw on Native American mound-building traditions. In the early 1980s, Heizer built a series of massive mounds on a large area previously destroyed by strip mining for coal on the north bank of the Illinois River just south of Ottawa, Illinois.[5] The gullies and spoil pits were filled and sculpted with bulldozers and heavy landscaping equipment, ultimately creating five stylized zoomorphic mounds in the shapes of a snake, water strider, frog, catfish, and turtle that sprawled over 224 acres. Heizer's project drew on specific artistic concerns, his political beliefs, and his awareness of Native American traditions.

In part, Heizer's artworks and those of other contemporary earth artists such as Robert Smithson, Walter de Maria, and Richard Long, among many others, were efforts to extract artistic practice from galleries and museums and to create works that demanded a more protracted interaction than the glancing appreciations of paintings on a wall or of sculptures surrounded by protective barriers.[6] Further, Heizer's earth art responded to the convulsions of the Vietnam War; as he wrote, "I started making this stuff in the middle of the Vietnam War . . . It looked like the world was coming to an end, at least for me."[7] Finally, Heizer's *Effigy Tumuli* also reflected historical events in North America: "The Native American tradition of mound building absolutely pervades the whole place, mystically and historically and in every sense. These mounds are part of a global, human dialogue of art, and I thought it would be worthwhile to reactivate that dialogue . . . It will be reminiscent of that native American history."[8] *Effigy Tumuli* simultaneously drew on Native American traditions and acknowledged the disruptions and dislocations of that experience. (It is sad but important to recall that when Ephraim Squier and Edwin Davis published their 1848 *Ancient Monuments of the Mississippi Valley: Comprising the Results of Extensive Original Surveys and Exploration*, they assumed that such monumental mounds had been built by earlier and more sophisticated cultures unrelated to the region's Native Americans.) As Heizer stated, the *Effigy Tumuli* acknowledges this past as "an untapped source of information and thematic material . . . It's a beautiful tradition, and it's fully neglected."[9]

Just as Heizer's *Effigy Tumuli* was a mid-twentieth-century response to earlier cultural creations and was shaped by the politics and economics of his era, the same is true of other monuments, including the enormous mounds at Sechin Alto. Although the specific sets of concerns undoubtedly differed between second-millennium BC builders in northern Peru and a late-twentieth-century construction in Illinois, some of the issues and contexts must have been similar: What is the purpose of the project? How can necessary resources be obtained, and how will the project be seen through to conclusion? Is it designed to even have a conclusion, or does the mound have an extended existence? None of these questions is readily answered; none can be ignored. The challenge we face as archaeologists is to try to understand the contexts that gave piles of dirt the meanings of monuments. Some of the challenges and complexities are suggested by the meanings of mounds built by the Mapuche of Chile.

⊓

The original homeland of the Araucanians, known today as the Mapuche, was central and south-central Chile, although they also spread into western Argentina in the early historic period.[10] Today, an estimated 700,000–800,000 Mapuche live in Chile, another 30,000 live in western Argentina, and they are the most numerous indigenous group in southern South America.[11]

The Araucanians of south-central Chile resisted European domination longer than any other Native American society, unconquered and independent until they were subdued by Chilean troops in 1897. Known as the *el pueblo indómito*, the Araucanians had remained outside the control of the Inca Empire, forming coalitions of communities that the Spaniards dubbed *los estados*. Rather than centralized "states," the Araucanian estados were alliances between large and independent regional federations of smaller territorial units known as *levos*. These complex mosaics of political alliances were integrated by networks of patrilineal kinship, historical memories, and ancestor veneration anchored and embodied by mounds.

The individual mounds, *kuel*, are burial mounds for important leaders from nearby communities. Kuel are animate monuments. Araucanian leaders and priestly shamans communicated with and learned from these mounds. Beginning around AD 1200 and continuing into the nineteenth century, the archaeologist Tom Dillehay writes, Araucanian political and religious leaders "learned how to interact with and learn

from the *kuel* in order to link community goals to ancestral history, to establish a new identity, and to reorganize themselves through guiding cosmological principles to become active compatriots in a new social order. *Mound literacy* . . . was, in effect, a social contract between *kuel*, deities, ancestors, and the living community that enabled a new kind of society to develop and to resist outside intrusion."[12] Kuel are not inert piles of soil but are perceived by the Araucanians "as living kindred who participate in public ceremony, converse with priestly shamans about the well-being and future of the community, and thus have powerful influence over people."[13]

Although it covers the grave of an important chief or shaman (*machi*), the kuel is more than a burial mound. Rather, there are two sets of events created on the earth: (1) placement of the chiefly tomb (*eltun*) (2) and the raising of the mound through regular "earth-capping" rites (*cueltun*) conducted by kinfolk and neighbors of the deceased.[14] In the years after the leader's death, kinfolk, friends, and allies participate in the cueltun ceremony, enacting a complex referential cosmology that links people, mounds, and landscape. Families living west of the kuel deposit earth on the mound's west side, and families from the east fill the eastern slope, in both cases often transporting soil from their home territories. The mound's shape reflects the changes over time in the influence of the deceased. The base of the mound is broad, just as the recently dead leader's network of kin and allies once was wide. Over time, the circumference of the conical mound shrinks, as the deceased ruler progresses upward into the realm of true ancestors and the network of kinfolk and supporters decreases. The mound itself is shaped by these changing social fields. As the earth-capping rites physically raise the height of the mound, the cueltun simultaneously lifts the spirit of the corpse into the realm of the ancestors, translating a sentient human into an authentic ancestor. In the process, the connections between the living and the dead are maintained and instantiated with layers of earth.

The mounds have names that hint at the linkages among kinfolk, landscape, environmental features, and human action.[15] Some names appear prosaic, identifying natural resources: *Maicoyakuel*: "a mound with ten oaks," or *Rapahuekuel*: "a mound where there is black clay." Other names denote mythic histories, such as *Hueichahuekeul*: "the mound where they carried out war," or *TrenTrenkuel*: "the mound where the good snake of the origin tale resides." Other names denote places of human action, such as *Ñachekuel*: "a mound where blood is sacrificed," *Huitranlehue*: "the mound that is a great meeting place," or—intriguingly—*Porenchedakuel*: "a place where ritual medicine is found in human excrement and where people climb to the top of the mound to carry out sanctifying ceremonies." Other names indicate the animate nature of these piles of soil, such as *Tremefquenkuel*: "the mound that slowly moves its head up and down," or *Nechekuel*: "a mound that is observant or vigilant; it has a human eye."

The mound complexes, *rehuekuel*, consist of a modified hilltop or leveled ridge (*nichi*) on top of which two or more kuel are built. The rehuekuel are the locations of ceremonies, preeminently the *nguillatun* fertility ceremony attended by hundreds of Mapuche and unifying distinct patrilineages from different communities.[16] A ceremony to ensure agricultural fertility, the nguillatun is held on a large, flat field, a sacred space that has never been plowed and is near a body of water. The field is either U-shaped or a three-sided square with the opening oriented to the east. The ceremony attracts families from multiple lineages, and each lineage and its families have defined locations along the three sides of the field where they build brush-covered ramadas. The east side is open and unoccupied, as this forms the wide portal through which the ancestors arrive to join the nguillatun ceremony.

Dillehay reports, "Informants explain that the *nguillatun* field is physically and metaphorically structured to accommodate the relationship between the living members of the Nag Mapu space and the ancestors and deities of the Wenumapu space. The living participate in ceremony through ritual belief and behavior while the ancestors and deities are brought into ceremonial participation by *machi*."[17]

This unification among Mapuche lineages, the ancestors, and the deities leaves physical traces on the surface of the mound.[18] The kuel still used in nguillatun ceremonies and other rituals are crisscrossed with trails 1 m to 2 m wide, connective routes between the kuel and the communities who gather there, a web of movement between patrilineages' home spaces and the collective's sacred space. The kuel sits by a nichi platform where dancers circle around the mound during the rituals. A ramp corkscrews around the sides of the kuel, a spiral path to the top of the mound. On the east flank of the summit, two deep holes serve as conduits for offerings of chicha (a traditional Andean beer often made from maize), llama or cattle blood, and a special blend of blood—often made from chickens—and chile peppers that each family blends at home and brings to the mound. Every family member sips from the mixture of spicy blood before handing the remaining liquid to the machi, who pours it into the mound where the ancestors and deities can drink.

This deeply affective landscape is anchored by mounds, cultural practice, and memory. Dillehay states, "Informants believe that there is a strong 'pull' or sense of obligation and desire to walk by or over *kuel*, to acknowledge their presence, and to gaze at them. It is said that gazing at *kuel* provides a sense of comfort and relief and an identity to the history of the area . . . Sighting the mounds from elevated points across the landscape gives orientation, according to several informants. People receive greater comfort and solace from places, such as the Tren

Tren *kuel*, where there is a wide viewshed to multiple mounds, and living communities."[19]

Dillehay asserts, "The Araucanian's religious ideology is associated with a cognitive map or imagery of sacred routes and places . . . that connects historically meaningful landscapes and spiritual locations of the real physical world and the spiritual or esoteric worlds, that is, other regions of levels of the cosmos . . . Taken together, *kuel* and *rehuekeul* form a social and aesthetic physical arrangement of spaces, pathways, meanings, and objects that keep alive the memories of those individuals and lineages that make Araucanian history."[20]

This richly endowed landscape of mounds, dance fields, and pathways recursively reflects and creates Mapuche existence and worldview. The intricacies discussed above would be very difficult—in many instances impossible—to discern from the material traces of archaeological sites. In fact, it is only through the informants' voices and historical accounts that such detailed relationships and valences can be conveyed to us outsiders. And yet, the richness of the Mapuche worldview should give us pause before we conclude that a mound is simply a pile of earth.

Ⅱ

Now, years later, rereading my field notes from our excavations in Santa Rosa, I see the creeping uncertainty as the excavations failed to expose the archaeological site I had imagined. On the second day of excavations I began to revise my ideas, posing that instead of a simple four-walled compound, perhaps there were actually interior rooms built along the compound walls. The absence of artifacts further complicated matters. There were few sherds from utilitarian pottery, the types of ceramics that should be most common. We saw none of the cooking pots, grater bowls, plates, or other pots for daily use that we knew from other Tumbes sites. And there was a final, curious observation in my notes on April 2, 2007: "Sherds are found on the high points of the site."

While all team members documented their specific excavations with notes, drawings, and photos, my own notes—as the project director—included each day's goals (a daily "to do" list), overall observations, and efforts to synthesize the excavation's progress. It is my practice to variously title these paragraphs "Objectives," "Observations," "Ideas," and so on, to distinguish between them, but on April 2, 2007, a new category appeared in my field notes labeled "Confusions."

There were several, numbered points of uncertainty:

1. Where are the walls?
2. Where is the other material re. subsistence and other activities?
3. What is the relationship between upper "walls" and lower burned area?

Santa Rosa was the most complex site I have excavated, and those complexities reflected the intense attraction this place had for prehistoric people. After more than ten weeks' digging, we understood that Santa Rosa had been reoccupied over the centuries for very different reasons. Sometime between 3650 and 3500 BC Santa Rosa was a camp or a settlement, as indicated by a gray, ashy midden that contained shellfish collected from the mangroves and lagoons, whitetail deer and dog bones, a few flaked and ground stone tools—but no pottery.

In the next centuries, Santa Rosa was settled by two or more families who lived in large, roughly circular dwellings, probably pole and thatch constructions, that were about 13 m × 12 m in size. I think these houses dated to about 3490–3100 BC, and again, no pottery was found in the dwellings. At approximately this same time, the people of Santa Rosa built a very curious feature: a circular hearth in a well-made basin 2.2 m across. When we found it, the hearth was intact and undisturbed, with a layer of gray ash compacted and hard as pumice. Under the ash layer was a dense lens of fire-reddened earth and charred wood dating to between 3350 and 2910 BC. Unlike cooking hearths, the circular hearth was not a jumble of charcoal and ash but rather discrete layers of ash-reddened earth/charcoal undisturbed after its last firing.

Sometime after these dwellings and the unique hearth were abandoned, Santa Rosa was occupied by folks who lived in a very different kind of house built from adobe walls on top of stone foundations. We only uncovered a portion of one house in our excavations, and subsequent ground-penetrating radar and magnetometer studies have not found evidence for other rectangular adobe and cobblestone buildings in Santa Rosa.[21] Although we could not find a good sample for radiocarbon dating, the pottery appeared to be late styles dating to between approximately AD 900 and 1450. The foundation stones were in some cases very large cobbles and boulders set in mud mortar, with a few traces of adobes still in place because the building had been extensively remodeled or salvaged, the foundations stones moved, and the adobes torn down.

At some point, the meanings of place changed at Santa Rosa. I don't fully understand the transformations or values that became associated with the site, but it was no longer a dwelling place. Santa Rosa became a sacred place, a *wak'a*.

The first trace of this transformation was the creation of a chalk-white floor in the southern portion of the site. The floor was fragile and thin, less than a centimeter thick. It may have been made by mixing water and ash and pouring the mix on the ground. This floor had not been exposed to the elements; a single rainy season would have washed it away. We saw patches of this floor near the large circular hearth and under the mound built on the southern end of Santa Rosa.

The mound was a curious construction; I know of no other mound quite like it from Tumbes or elsewhere in South America. The mound was 2 m tall and consisted of carefully placed, alternating layers of fire-reddened earth and gray clay. In one profile we counted twenty-two alternating red-and-gray bands of color, like the stripes of a candy cane. The interfaces between these strata were un-weathered and precise, suggesting that the layers were placed in relatively quick succession. The soil had not been burned on the mound; there was no charcoal in the layers. The fire-reddened earth may have come from hearths like the large ceremonial hearth, although this is far from certain. People reshaped Santa Rosa, moving boulders, mounding fired earth and clay, and transforming the site into a sacred space.

Nearby, prehistoric people built small cairns of cobblestones about a meter in diameter and less than a meter tall, stones set in mud mortar.

While the mortar was still wet, *Spondylus* shells were shoved hinge-first into the mud. Small pieces of sheet copper or copper needles were placed in the cairns, as were human teeth and small fragments of burned bones, suggesting these mounds were places for secondary burials.

But at the larger, bi-chromatic mound, another form of burial occurred when shaft tombs were carefully dug into the mound. The

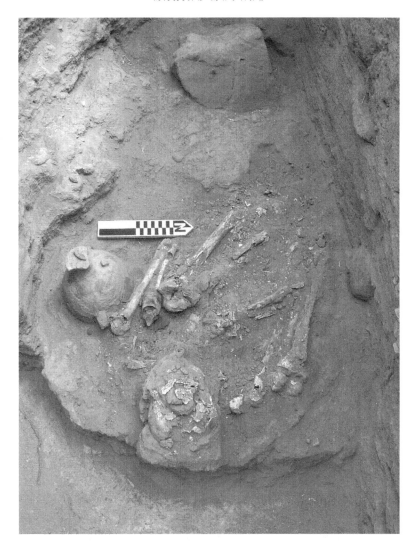

main shaft was about 1.3–1.8 m deep, with a larger chamber at its base—a form archaeologists unimaginatively refer to as a "boot tomb." The sides of the shaft had been stabilized with a mud coat. The tomb pits cut through the fragile white floor. At the bottom of the shaft were the skeletons of three people. Their bones were fragmented, fragile, and decayed—but unburned. Two adults were buried together in one tomb; another adult was buried separately but nearby. The burials had occurred at different times. The mouths of the tombs were at different depths, and the single individual had been buried first, the tomb filled and sealed with a layer of cobbles, and then several more layers of fire-reddened earth and gray clay were added to the mound before the second tomb was bored into it.

The body faced west. The single adult had been wrapped in a cotton shroud, although time and decay had reduced the wrappings to fragments smaller than a thumbnail. The person had a copper bracelet on its left arm, which was folded across the person's chest. There was a miniature redware jar on the left side of the body, a tiny Inca-style vessel with an out-flaring spout. On the right side of the skeleton we found a small disk of gourd rind, a couple of copper beads, and a *Spondylus* shell. About 20 cm to the north of the body were two other ceramic vessels. One was a redware jar, single-handled like a pitcher with the spout shaped into a bird beak flanked by a pair of nubbin eyes. Next to it was a press-molded blackware vessel, its surface decorated with rows of small dots and raised welts—a motif known as goose skin (*piel de ganso*) from its similarity to a plucked fowl. These three pots implied that the burials dated to after the Inca conquest of the North Coast of Peru, as they included both Inca and Chimú-Inka styles.

In the second shaft tomb, the bones of the two adults were fragmented, a jumble, although it was possible to note that the skulls had once faced each other. The bodies were flexed when lowered into the tomb. It is possible that the two bodies were placed on separate occasions, with one burial disturbing the other, or perhaps additional offerings were made after the bodies were in the tomb. The offerings included a Chimú-Inka blackware stirrup-spout bottle, three small orange-colored jars, a small redware olla, and a whole *Spondylus* shell. There were no traces of metal or cloth, but numerous small beads were found among the shattered bones.

After the burials, the tomb was sealed. Large adobe bricks were placed in the shaft, mortared with mud, and capped with cobblestones. Then the alternating layers of fire-reddened earth and gray clay resumed. Ironically, the source of these layers seems to have been

ancient hearths burned millennia before. We obtained a radiocarbon sample from the uppermost layers of the mound, strata that sealed the provincial Inca shaft tombs, which dated to 3520–3090 BC—in other words, contemporary with the large ceremonial hearth and pre-dating the tombs by more than 4,500 years. Clearly, the fill layers were salvaged from earlier deposits, not randomly but as carefully composed gestures in red and gray.

Yet I cannot claim to understand the meanings and gestures reflected by the material record of Santa Rosa. Despite our months of excavations, I suspect there are many more hidden and subtle discoveries waiting to be made. I want to return to Tumbes and explore again the wak'a at Santa Rosa, to journey to far northern Peru and explore this complex site. I want to understand how this apparently nondescript place, today abandoned and covered with trash, was physically transformed from an area where people lived and died 4,000–5,000 years ago to a place that seems to have anchored complex meanings and delicate gestures of faith. There is much yet to learn about how these mounds were made, as mounds are rarely as obvious as they might seem.

NOTES

1. Jerry Moore and Carolina Maria Vílchez, "Spondylus and the Inka Empire on the Far North Coast of Peru: Recent Excavations at the Taller Conchales, Cabeza de Vaca, Tumbes," in *Making Value, Making Meaning: Techné in Pre-Columbian Mesoamerica and Andean South America*, edited by Cathy Costin, 221–51 (Washington DC: Dumbarton Oaks, 2016).

2. Thomas Jefferson, *Notes on the State of Virginia*, Query 11 (1787), accessed March 17, 2016, http://xroads.virginia.edu/~hyper/jefferson/ch11.html.

3. Sarah C. Sherwood and Tristram R. Kidder, "The DaVincis of Dirt: Geoarchaeological Perspectives on Native American Mound Building in the Mississippi River Basin," *Journal of Anthropological Archaeology* 30 (2011): 69–87, at 69.

4. Thomas Pozorski and Shelia Pozorski, "Preceramic and Initial Period Monumentality within the Casma Valley of Peru," in *Early New World Monumentality*, edited by Richard Burger and Robert Rosenswig, 364–98 (Gainesville: University Press of Florida, 2012).

5. Michael Heizer and Douglas McGill, *Effigy Tumuli: The Re-emergence of Ancient Mound Building* (New York: Harry N. Abrams, 1990).

6. For an extended and insightful exploration of this topic, see Lucy Lippard, *Overlay: Contemporary Art and the Art of Prehistory* (New York: Pantheon Books, 1983).

7. Heizer and McGill, *Effigy Tumuli*, 11.

8. Ibid., 22–23.

9. Ibid., 11.

10. This discussion relies on the decades of research Tom Dillehay has conducted on the Mapuche and the Araucanian estado. In addition to the sources cited below, see "Cuel: Observacioes y comentarios sobre los túmulos en la cultura

Mapuche," *Chungara: Revista de Antropologia Chilena* 16–17 (1986): 181–93; "Mapuche Ceremonial Landscape: Social Recruitment and Resource Rights," *World Archaeology* 22, no. 2 (1990): 223–41; *The Teleoscopic Polity: Andean Patriarchy and Materiality* (New York: Springer Science and Business Media, 2014).

11. Dillehay, *Teleoscopic Polity*, 8.

12. Tom Dillehay, *Monuments, Empires, and Resistance: The Araucanian Polity and Ritual Narratives* (Cambridge: Cambridge University Press, 2007), 22, original emphasis.

13. Ibid., 1.

14. Tom Dillehay, "Mounds of Social Death: Araucanian Funerary Rites and Political Succession," in *Tombs for the Living: Andean Mortuary Practices*, edited by Tom Dillehay, 281–313 (Washington, DC: Dumbarton Oaks, 1995), 296.

15. Dillehay, *Monuments, Empires, and Resistance*, 220–23.

16. Ibid., 182–98.

17. Ibid., 197.

18. The following is based on ibid., 224–25.

19. Ibid.

20. Ibid., 42.

21. See Jerry Moore, "Making a Huaca: Memory and Praxis in Prehispanic Far Northern Peru," *Journal of Social Archaeology* 10, no. 3 (2010): 531–55; and "Architecture, Settlement, and Formative Developments in the Equatorial Andes: New Discoveries in the Department of Tumbes, Peru," *Latin American Antiquity* 21, no. 2 (2010): 147–72.

CHAPTER THREE

La Caminata

IN JUNE 2005 I STOOD IN A CROWD among the foundation stones of the site of Pumapungo in the city of Cuenca in southern Ecuador. There were about 300 of us. Many of us had never met. I knew no one. We milled about, standing among traces of what had been the birthplace of Huayna Capac, the last Inca to govern a unified empire.

Cuenca was originally known as Tomebamba—"the field of knives"—and this valley and its surrounding hills were settings for conquests. Originally, this place was one of the principal towns of the Cañaris, an indigenous nation the Incas conquered in the late 1400s. The conquest came at great cost. The northward expansion of the Inca Empire was led by Topa Inca. The Incas were fiercely resisted by the Cañaris and other Ecuadorean ethnic groups.[1] The northern conquests occurred over a period of twenty years and consisted of six to eight major military campaigns. The Spanish soldier and historian Pedro Cieza de Leon claimed that the Inca fielded enormous armies of 200,000 soldiers—probably an exaggeration but certainly one of the largest forces ever assembled in

pre-Columbian South America.[2] Inca soldiers were drafted from distant provinces, and many soldiers never returned home. A Colonial account from the province of Chucuito, located on the western shores of Lake Titicaca nearly 2,000 km south of Tomebamba, stated that Chucuito's towns and villages had sent 6,000 soldiers to the northern wars; 5,000 died. In a single engagement, 2,000 Chucuito soldiers went into battle on the Inca's behalf. One thousand were slain.

The bloodshed did not end with the Inca conquest of the northern Andes. When Huayna Capac died unexpectedly from smallpox in 1528, his two sons—the half-brothers Huascar and Atahualpa—plunged the Inca Empire into civil war. These rivals split the empire into two major factions, between the armies led by Huascar based in Cusco and the forces led by Atahualpa from his base in Quito. Atahualpa claimed his father's throne. Learning of the northern rebellion, Huascar rapidly sent an advance guard of 2,000 experienced Inca captains and soldiers to Ecuador, where they were joined by 30,000 troops loyal to Cusco, including the kuraka of Tomebamba. Atahualpa's army and Huascar's forces fought for three days on the plains and hillsides near Tomebamba, but ultimately Huascar's forces triumphed and Atahualpa was captured and imprisoned in a *tambo* at Tomebamba.

The sixteenth-century chronicler Augustin de Zárate recorded the legend:

> But while Huascar's men were celebrating their victory with a great drunken feast, Atahualpa broke through the thick wall of the tambo with a copper bar, which a woman had given him, and fled to Quito, about seventy leagues away. Collecting his people, he told them that his father had transformed him into a snake, which enabled him to creep out through a small hole, and that he had promised him victory if he would return to the fight. Thus inspired, his followers fell on the enemy, fought them, defeated and routed them, many being killed on both sides in this battle also, so many indeed that great piles of bone still lie scattered on the battlefield.

Marching south, Atahualpa attacked the Cañaris "and killed sixty thousand of the army who had fought him, destroying with fire and sword the very large town of Tumibamba."[3]

At this same moment, Francisco Pizarro landed on the coast of Peru, and the Spanish conquest of the Andes was set in motion. Atahualpa's destruction was followed by the Spaniards' occupation of Tomebamba, razing the vestiges of the town and building the city of Cuenca over them. Very few traces of Tomebamba's glory remain, except the foundation stones at Pumapungo where we stood.

We gathered among those stones to walk in a winter solstice procession, a *caminata del solsticio*, organized by the Museum of the Banco Central del Ecuador, the National Institute of Cultural Patrimony, and other cultural institutions in Cuenca. A small, colorful brochure for the event stated that such processions "provide an alternative tourism that at the same time allows us to know the majestic Andean heights, integral parts of our daily lives, and allows us to understand the cultural values our ancestors attributed to these places. It is necessary to interconnect with and take possession of what is ours, so we will be part of our surroundings and cultural reality."[4]

At the center of the crowd was a Huaroani shaman from the Amazonian lowlands. Wearing an immaculate long white shirt, loose cotton pants, and a tumble of shell bead and feather necklaces, he walked with a spear tipped with a foot-long metal blade. He was accompanied by another Huaroani man who wore an orange headband with a single macaw tail feather. His earlobes were extended with plugs the size of poker chips, and he wore an Adidas windbreaker and jeans.

There were numerous Cañaris, distinctive in their narrow-brimmed white felt bowlers worn by men, women, and children alike. Many Cañari men wore scarlet ponchos. There was a group of four boys from the town of Paccha, wearing horsehair wigs and dressed in headscarves, shawls, and skirts improvised from handkerchiefs. The boys were led by a man who beat a flat drum and blew a three-note whistle. The boys from Paccha carried wooden swords and batons and had strings of small globular bells tied around their ankles that tinkled as they walked.

A middle-aged woman from Cuenca was dressed in a beige pantsuit topped by a tie-dyed shawl and was wearing a felt fedora; she walked carrying a sword and a seashell. Most members of the crowd were middle-class Ecuadoreans, dressed in windbreakers, jeans, and sensible shoes, but there was a sprinkling of American undergraduates on a study abroad program from Lewis and Clark College in Portland, Oregon. There was a woman from Madrid; when I asked her why she was there she simply said, "I like to walk."

I was there to watch and learn from this diverse group of strangers who gathered in southern Ecuador, pilgrims walking to the sacred lake of Kituiña at the base of Cerro Guagualzhumi.

Ⅲ

The Andes are covered with sacred places, ancient and modern, places where the sacred surfaces on the landscape. These are *hierophanies*, as Mircea Eliade called them, "irruptions of the sacred . . . that result in detaching a territory from the surrounding cosmic milieu and making it qualitatively different."[5] Eliade observed, "For religious man, space is not homogeneous; he experiences interruptions, breaks in it; some parts of space are qualitatively different from others."[6] Such sacred places occur on all continents, and the sacred is deeply embedded in the landscape of the Andes.

Perhaps it is because of the volatility of the Andes. Earthquakes rumble. Volcanoes spew ash and rivers of lava. Drenching rains from El Niños are followed by decades of drought. On the coast of Peru, I have heard sand dunes groan at night. It is easy to conclude that the Andean landscape is alive. Traditional Andean people weave complex explanations of the world around them, extensive metaphors and tropes that enmesh the landscape and guide human actions.

Writing about the Quechua-speaking Qollahuayas of highland Bolivia, the anthropologist Joseph Bastien describes the intricacies of such worlds. A group famous as herbalists and spiritual healers who live northeast of Lake Titicaca, the Qollahuayas are recognized across the southern Andes as "curers (*curanderos*) who cure with natural remedies and diviners (*yachaj*) who not only cure with supernatural remedies but also arrange tables [mesas] to feed the earth."[7] The Qollahuayas of Kaata live on the eastern slopes of Mount Kaata, and they and their neighbors think of Mount Kaata as like a human body. Bastien writes, "Kaatans look to their own bodies for an understanding of the mountain. How they see themselves is how they see the mountain." The mountain corresponds to the different parts of the human body and, similarly, is organically integrated. The Kaatans do not believe in a mind-body dichotomy, and their ritual world is indivisible from the landscape where they dwell. Bastien writes, "Kaatan religion is not conceptual nor does it contain a world of spirits, but is a metaphorical relationship with their land. Kaatans do not pray to the mountain to appease its spirit; rather, they feed the mountain blood and fat to vitalize and empower it. Ritual involves them physically with the mountain. The mountain is their land and their divinity."[8]

Mount Kaata is a living landscape. The Kaatans are curers and diviners because they live on the central slopes of Mount Kaata, among the heart and viscera of the peak, where they can feed the mountain with blood (*yawar*) and fat (*wira*), recharging essential cycles of life and energy. Blood embodies life. "There are different bloods," Bastien writes, "strong, weak, frightened, and exhausted."[9] Blood is pumped by the heart (*sonqo*); the "heart is thought, intention, and emotions"; and hearts may be "sad, happy, and sick."[10] Fat is energy. Fat is produced in the bowels: stomach, intestines, liver, pancreas, and kidneys. These circulatory systems link other regions of Mount Kaata; none exists apart. The upper reaches of Mount Kaata are the head, and the highland lakes are the eyes of the mountain. Just as in humans, the inner self enters and exits through the head; dead souls navigate subterranean rivers to the eyes of the mountain, where they emerge again into the land of the living. The waters of highland lakes mirror the last beams of Andean sunsets: "The sun dies into these eyes of the highlands, but from the reflections within the lake come all living creatures. The lake's reflections (*illa*) are the animals and people returning from inside the earth."[11] For the people of Mount Kaata, "Death is ecliptic, hiding the dead within the earth where they journey with the movements of the sun, the seasons, and the land."[12]

The lower slopes of Mount Kaata are watered by rivers that run from the highland lakes down to the lowland jungle. These slopes are the lower limbs of the mountain. The warmer lower fields produce maize, which is brewed into a corn beer, *chicha*. Chicha is drunk at all rituals and ceremonies on Mount Kaata, and highland herders bring llamas and Kaatan diviners bring blood and fat for the maize-planting ceremonies on these lower fields. A trip from the lower limbs of Mount Kaata to its ocular highland lakes is a full day's journey. When ceremonies are involved, the movements of people over Mount Kaata become processions.

The New Earth ceremony is one of a trio of rituals that gradually awaken slumbering fields from fallow and revitalize the land. Directed by a profoundly respected and charismatic ritual leader, the ceremony advances in stages participated in by scores of individuals with different roles and responsibilities as they move across the landscape. Community leaders (*secretarios*) are usually middle-aged men who have ascended through a series of progressively more important and demanding offices. The secretarios consult with the ritual leader, who sets the dates for the New Earth ceremony. A week before the event, the secretarios begin preparations: slaughtering llamas, baking bread, contributing chicha or cane alcohol (*trago*), and collecting contributions from each family—a tithe of a guinea pig, a half kilo of coca leaves, a half kilo of llama fat, and a pint of trago.

Just after midnight on the first day of the ceremony, the secretarios, their wives, and the ritual leader meet in a community building where they eat a meal of soup and llama meat. They chew coca, drink chicha and trago, and prepare offerings for each of the thirteen earth shrines on Mount Kaata. The ritual leader eats thirteen plates of soup and llama meat—one for each of the shrines—feeding the mountain as he feeds himself because he embodies the mountain. With the first light of dawn, the participants stagger outside to begin the process of feeding the earth shrines. Half of the participants face the dawn, looking at the birth of the sun. Half of the participants face west, where the sun dies. Four emissaries carry offerings of coca, llama fat, and other sacred objects: two depart for the high reaches where the sun is born; two descend to the lowlands where the sun is entombed. Other emissaries march toward the earth shrines across the slopes of Mount Kaata, carrying fluttering flags made from bundles of rhea feathers.

Arriving at the earth shrines, the emissaries place offerings at the mouth of the shrine, a hole in the mountain the size of a basketball. Nearby, a ritual *mesa* is laid out, a tablecloth on which twenty-six seashells cup offerings of coca leaves, incense, llama fat, blood, and carnations. Children chosen from hardworking families begin to till the field in front of the shrine, digging into the earth with foot plows. Musicians play a four-note melody on flutes, the rhythm beaten on a drum.

A sacrificial llama is hobbled near the mouth of the shrine. The participants embrace and kiss the llama, sprinkling the animal with drops of trago. The llama's head is twisted toward the sunrise, his throat is cut, and a knife plunges into his chest and the still-beating heart is removed. Blood sprays around the mouth of the earth shrine. Small chunks of the llama's heart are placed in each shell on the mesa, and these offerings are fed to the mouth of the shrine.

After the shrine has been fed, chicha is poured and the musicians dance around the newly plowed field. "They danced in their slow east-to-west spiral," Bastien observed, "which every so often reversed its direction and retraced its steps, until finally at the point of completion, the dancers turned and marched from the small field toward Kaata . . . As mysteriously as a sun being constantly reborn or a circle revolving in upon itself, the chain of musicians moved toward Kaata to the staccato beat of the drum and the four recurring notes of the flute."[13]

We began to walk at about 8:45 a.m., leaving Pumapungo and descending onto the streets of Cuenca. Traffic cops stopped cars as we walked through the city, passing through the suburbs and following the Río Tomebamba before turning east into the countryside. We were escorted by an ambulance and five civilian defense workers in day-glow orange jumpsuits. For the first mile or so, two young men on stilts inexplicably led the procession, drumming as they walked.

Four men carried an altar on a platform litter built from planks, like a patient on a stretcher. The altar consisted of a trapezoidal chunk of white limestone surrounded by a ceramic brazier, seven ears of white corn, a plastic bag of coca leaves, and a green calabash—all tied to the platform with baling wire. The brazier smoked with smoldering pine resin, and it was tended by a young Latina who wore a scarlet shawl.

A man armed with a sheaf of large bottle rockets ran ahead of

the procession, periodically launching the fireworks into the sky. The explosions set off car alarms. Dogs ran from their houses, barking and snapping as we walked through the streets of Cuenca. When we passed the large windows of a storefront, I caught a glimpse of my reflection: a tall, gray-haired, middle-aged gringo with a large blood and russet bruise on his cheek.

We left the paved streets and turned onto a dirt road toward the small town of Rayoloma. On the outskirts of the town, an enterprising woman sold roasted guinea pigs spitted on sticks. We halted in the center of Rayoloma, and the altar was set down in the middle of the basketball court in front of the church. More incense was fed to the smoking brazier, and the various ritual leaders—the Huaroani shamans, the Cañari ritualist, the woman from Cuenca in fedora and shawl, and various other people carrying decorative staffs and spears—all gathered around the altar.

The long-haired Cañari ritualist began the orations: "Thank you Pachamama, thank you Father Inti, for the water, for the earth, for this shared humanity." His sermon trailed off into further thanksgivings

and entreaties that I could not hear over the murmurs of the crowd. As he spoke, the Cañari paused to puff on a cigar, blowing smoke toward the altar and waving the cigar through the clouds of incense as he concluded his speech. Following him, each of the leaders made a short speech, puffing on cigars and waving the smoke through the incense, after which everyone shouted in approval. When all had spoken, the altar bearers picked up the wooden platform, and we continued on our pilgrimage.

Across the ancient Americas, public rituals occurred outdoors. Even when these ceremonies occurred on constructed landscapes—on artificial mounds, monumental staircases, causeways, or plazas—rituals meant to be seen were held outside. In prehispanic South America, outdoor rites—especially those expressed in pilgrimages and processions—were dynamic displays that engaged with landscape.

We have a particularly rich record about traditional notions of sacred landscape from the Andes, largely the by-product of intense efforts by Catholic priests to eliminate native beliefs and indigenous worldviews. In 1621 the extirpator of idolatry, Father Pablo José de Arriaga, wrote about native gestures of veneration for rivers: "When they have to cross a river they take a little water in their hands, and as they drink it they talk to the river, asking it to let them cross over without being carried away. They call this ceremony *mayuchulla*, and the fishermen do the same when they go fishing."[14]

Native Andeans worshipped the sun, the moon, and the constellation we know as the Pleiades. Lightning was also worshipped. Land and sea were adored. Arriaga wrote, "They invoke Mamacocha, or the sea . . . and they come down from the sierra to the lowlands to call upon it. They ask it especially to keep them from sickness and to let them return home from the errand in health and with profit. All of them do this, even the very small children. They also reverence the earth as Mamapacha," the extirpator reported, "especially the women at seed time. They talk to it and ask for a good harvest and pour out chicha and corn meal, either by themselves or through the intermediary of a sorcerer."[15]

The natives worshipped freshwater streams and springs, "especially when water is scarce, begging them not to dry up."[16] Continuing this litany of idolatry, Arriaga wrote, "They also worship and reverence the high hills and mountains and huge stones. They have names for them and numerous fables about their changes and metamorphoses, saying they were once men who have been changed to stone."[17]

Snow-capped peaks were venerated, as they were the homes of the *apu*, the mountain deities. The ruins of ancient sites were revered as the homes of the *huaris*, giants who were the first occupants of the Andes. Andean people worshipped the *pacarinas*, places of origin— the hills, rivers and streams, lagoons and lakes—from which their ancestors emerged. The only way to eradicate these beliefs, Arriaga argued, was to show these native peoples the error of such superstitions: "These are all the huacas that they worship as gods, and since they cannot be removed from their sight because they are fixed and immobile, we must try to root them out of their hearts, showing them truth and disabusing them of error."[18] Despite five centuries of proselytizing effort, many of these ideas still reside in the Andean landscape and in the hearts of the people.

Ritual processions are dynamic corollaries of these beliefs. If Mamacocha is the object of worship, then one must travel to the sea. If snow-capped peaks are the places where lightning is born, then that is where lightning must be worshipped. If highland lakes are the eyes of the mountain from which dead souls emerge from their subterranean sojourns into the realm of the living, then a journey to those highland lakes is required. If the Andean landscape is pocked with hierophanies and they are the places where reverence must be paid, then the faithful must walk in pilgrimage to holy places.

I got the bruise a few days earlier in a bus accident in which three people were killed.

In the last dark before dawn, I left my hotel in Tumbes, Peru, and went to the bus station to travel across the border to Ecuador. The waiting room was neon-lighted and scented with insecticide. The morning news program blasted from a television mounted high on the wall. If the morning news in the United States is bubble-headed brightness, in Peru (at least that morning) it was a litany of horrors. At a small fiesta celebrating the birth of a child, fireworks blew the hands off people attending the party. Illegal horse meat was confiscated at the Huancayo market in central Peru. In the foothills east of Lima, a small girl drowned in a fast-flowing open channel of a sewer; her body was found 2 km downstream among twisted debris. Story after horrific story of assaults, bloody accidents, and deaths. Amazingly, all this was presented in less than fifteen minutes, as my bus arrived on time and we headed north.

The landscape around Tumbes is covered with dry thorn-scrub forest, but once across the border, the countryside is quickly covered in green. There is significantly more rainfall in southern Ecuador, and cornfields and pasturelands gave way to extensive banana plantations as we headed north.

We arrived in Machala, Ecuador, at 8:30 a.m., and I walked around the corner to the terminal of the Azuay Lines whose bus for Cuenca was about to depart. I climbed onboard with my backpack and settled into a seat behind the driver where there was more room for my legs. We drove south for a few kilometers and turned eastward and inland at the large junction of El Cambio, where the Pan-American Highway connects with Ecuador's Route 80 that climbs into the Andes to Cuenca. The vegetation grew lush and tropical. Every day, moisture from the Gulf of Guayaquil collects on the western foothills of the mountains, and enormous ferns and the elephant-ear leaves of philodendrons line the hills. The soil is rich, the moisture abundant, but hillsides are steep and every slip of flat land is farmed. We had just passed slowly through the foothill community of Pasaje, crossing the bridge over a fast-flowing river and carefully edging over the speed bumps on the outskirts of town. I was looking across the bus to my right, amazed by a tiny cornfield tended on the soft shoulder of the road, the tassels on the tall stalks golden in the sunlight, when I heard the bus driver shout "*hombre*" and we slammed into another vehicle.

I was thrown forward and hit my face on the seat in front of me. My side of the bus had torqued from the impact, and the windows shattered in a cascade of glass. A woman behind me was cut, bleeding, and screaming. Everyone was frightened and dazed. We grabbed our things and stumbled out the door.

The driver of a red Nissan pickup had swerved across the road and hit us head-on. The front of the bus was mangled, but the red pickup was crumpled, its frame bent, and the front cab collapsed. Like many pickups in South America, its rear bed was built up with wooden sides. A passenger standing up in the rear bed of the truck was thrown into the air and landed on the highway, dying instantly. The other truck passengers were seriously injured. The driver and two other people riding in front could barely be extracted from the crushed cab. Passers-by put the pickup driver and the other injured riders into the back of another truck and hurried to the closest hospital. The injured people moaned and held compresses to their wounds. Later, two more passengers died.

The dead man leaked blood onto the asphalt. At one point, a gentleman leaned over with a handkerchief and wiped blood from the dead man's face, a beautiful and futile gesture. The blood flowed down the road, mixing with pools of brake fluid before curling into the gutter on the side of the road.

Passengers called for help on their cell phones. As traffic backed up on both sides of the wreckage, fifteen men manhandled the red truck off the road to clear a lane. In the commotion, our bus driver slipped into the cornfields. We never saw him again.

Firemen and police arrived. The police began taking statements, but they learned little because the pickup driver had been taken to the hospital, the bus driver had run away, and the rest of us could only state the obvious: there was an accident and people died. The firemen took away the dead man on a stretcher, the corpse covered with a black plastic tarp.

Another Azuay Lines bus headed for Cuenca pulled up. We retrieved our luggage and climbed onboard, standing in the aisles as we continued on to Cuenca. As we pulled away, I glanced at the cornfield on the edge of the road I had been looking at just before the accident. The tall maize stalks were trampled flat.

Пilgrimages are just one of the rites we use to understand and influence a mysterious and often tragic cosmos. Pilgrimages are, in turn, a subset of processions, what Richard Schechner has called "natural" theater in which "usually a procession moves towards a goal: the funeral to the grave, the political march to the speakers' stand, the circus parade to the big top, the pilgrimage to the shrine. The event performed at the goal of the procession . . . is well planned for, rehearsed, ritualized."[19] Today across South America, there is an amazing array of processions: the whirling colors and shimmering bodies dancing at Carnival, military parades commemorating the establishment of nation-states or pivotal battles, and religious processions in which the faithful shoulder heavy images of saints. Writing of pilgrimages in the modern Andes, the ethnographer David Sallnow observes that such processions create "a totemic topography" and "a kinesthetic mapping of space."[20]

Similarly, archaeologists have documented a range of processions in prehispanic South America. At different times and places, pilgrimage centers emerged in the Andes, exerting a magnetic field that drew the faithful from far reaches. In the early 1600s, Antonio Vasquez de Espinosa wrote about the Central Andean ruins at the site of Chavín de Huántar, Peru: "Near this village of Chavín there is a large building of huge stone blocks very well wrought; it was a guaca, and one of the most famous of the heathen sanctuaries, like Rome or Jerusalem with us; the Indians used to come and make their offerings and sacrifices, for the Devil pronounced many oracles for them here, and so they repaired here from all over the kingdom."[21] Chavín de Huántar may have asserted its prestige as a pilgrimage center as early as 1500–500 BC and retained vestiges of veneration over millennia.

In the Rimac Valley on the central coast of Peru, the site of Pachacamac originated as a shrine to a local deity at about AD 500–600.[22] When the Wari Empire conquered the Peruvian coast, the shrine at Pachacamac was venerated and expanded. Members of a highland state that ruled between AD 550/600 and 1000, the Wari built the elaborate Templo Pintado, a multi-level construction whose base was larger than a football field. The outside walls of the Templo Pintado were painted scarlet and covered with complex imagery depicting crops, fish, and anthropomorphic figures. When the Wari abandoned the coast at around AD 1000, Pachacamac's prestige grew as the shrine became affiliated with the god Ychsma, who was simultaneously the "creator of the world, oracle, healer and master of earthquakes," a powerful deity who ruled over fertility and death.[23] When the Incas conquered the coast, they co-opted the oracle of Pachacamac, consulting its priests on the fate of their empire. Major shrines like Chavín de Huántar and Pachacamac had tremendous influence over broad swathes of the Andes.

Other shrine sites cast more localized gravitational fields. On the south coast of Peru, Nasca culture developed from about 200–150 BC until AD 600–640 along the slender valleys watered by the unreliable tributaries of the Nasca and Ica Rivers.[24] The largest Nasca site, Cahuachi—a sprawling square-mile complex of plazas, cemeteries, and mounds—apparently only had a small permanent population but periodically drew the faithful to worship. Many of the famous Nasca lines were also were pilgrims' routes, the lines in the sand leading the devout to the sacred, the very act of walking an act of reverence.

Other processions were less pacific or benign. Between approximately AD 450 and 900 on the North Coast of Peru, Moche artisans produced elegant pottery with complex depictions of selected aspects of life, including processions. A particularly gruesome procession culminates in what Christopher Donnan and Donna McClelland called the "Warrior Narrative" and the "Sacrifice Ceremony." Moche warriors—resplendent in elaborate headdresses, tunics, and jewelry—parade their leashed captives who are naked, bleeding, and wide-eyed in terror. In the final phases of the procession, the bound prisoners are presented to the Moche ruler, and their throats are cut. Donnan and McClelland write, "The great number of Warrior Narrative paintings clearly demonstrates that warriors and the treatment of captives were subjects of intense interest," bloody ancient finales akin to twenty-first-century images of Islamic extremists beheading hostages or American jailers posing with bound and humiliated prisoners at Abu Ghraib.[25]

Just before we left Rayoloma, the pilgrimage leaders asked a group of musicians from Paccha to play. The musicians broke into a *huayno*, the Andean songs whose 4/4 rhythms loop around a melody line. The Cañari shaman and the Latina from Cuenca danced and twirled in the middle of the crowd. The band consisted of a fiddler and an accordionist who had decorated his squeeze box with cutout paper letters that spelled "AMOR" and "FE." A guitarist was joined by a man playing a *charango*, a ten-string Andean lute with a sound box made from an armadillo shell. The fiddler's violin had a white paper tag dangling from its neck on which was printed in English "Guarantee of authenticity_____." A trumpeter played a horn made from an eight-foot-long white PVC pipe two inches in diameter, with a mouthpiece fashioned from an elbow joint of copper pipe attached to the PVC with wrappings of black electrician's tape. This was an inventive version of the *bocina*, a traditional Andean version of an alpenhorn made from a long cane tube and a blowpiece fashioned from the curving swirl of a bull's

horn. When the Paccha trumpeter blew his homemade instrument, it sounded deep bass notes like a foghorn at sea.

We left Rayoloma and walked into the countryside. Batches of onlookers watched from their houses and applauded people they knew in the procession. Our march was herded by staff from the Museo del Banco Central equipped with walkie-talkies and bullhorns, which, mercifully, were seldom used. There were three pools of sound along the procession's straggle. Near the front of the procession was the man from Paccha and the boys in horsehair wigs. The man played his flute and drummed, accompanied by the untimed tinklings of bells tied to the boys' legs. Further back was the band of five musicians: guitar, charango, violin, accordion, and PVC bocina. At the rear of the march were the acrobats who played *quena* and *tambor* as they walked along the dirt road, having relegated their stilts to a pickup truck.

We were a crowd of very hot and tired people when we arrived at Paccha just after noon. We gathered in the small town square in front of the church, a plaza that doubled as a basketball court and miniature soccer field. A small ceremony was held, with the leaders of the solstice procession giving speeches, asking for blessings, and waving cigar smoke.

This was followed by a raucous *folklorico* performance accompanied by a nine-man brass band. Four couples danced to the music, the women wearing multi-layered skirts of orange and turquoise cloth, the men with multi-colored striped ponchos and fuzzy chaps made from long wool tied over their pants. They twirled and twined in an Andean reel. When the band stopped, recorded music filled the void, pounding from enormous loudspeakers set around the plaza. Entrepreneurial women had set up food stands around the square, selling guinea pig, corn on the cob, fried potatoes, *seco de pollo*, and sausages. The entire event was "*alegre*" rather than somber or still.

The following stage of the pilgrimage was announced over a scratchy loudspeaker: those who wished could wait here at Paccha while the others continued on to the sacred lake and holy mountain. Those who stayed behind could catch free buses back to Cuenca; later, buses would be available for the pilgrims who continued on. Most people decided to walk on. The next segment of the route was steep, climbing 400 m in a little more than 2 km on a hot and dusty road. The march of pilgrims slowed and straggled.

We crested the ridge and dropped into a basin near a small lake named Cunshucocha. In Quechua, *cocha*—sometimes spelled *ccocha* or *qocha*—often means lake, but its meanings may be more broadly hydraulic. A 1608 dictionary by the Jesuit Diego Gonçalez Holguin, for example, lists a series of concepts surrounding ccocha.[26] *Mama ccocha* is "the sea" from which all waters originate in the vast hydraulic cycle

linking rain, lakes and rivers, and the ocean. *Ccocha ppochiquen* are "the living waters of the sea, the waves." *Ccocho puma* (literally, "water puma") is the name for a sea lion. *Ccochallayan* is "to dam or divert the water that runs in a canal or river and scatter it." Unable to resist the urge to proselytize, Gonçalez Holguin added *Ccochayan ccochaya-manan allincay niycuna*: "I am lacking in virtues because I have not been well watered with sermons, etc." So cocha means "water," but only in a rather fluid and flowing way.

Cunshu is, if anything, more elusive. On those rare occasions when the word occurs, it pops up in cookbooks for traditional Ecuadorean cuisine, where it may refer to "crumbs" like those fallen from a cake. More important, cunshu refers to the dregs produced from boiling maize or from fermenting *chicha de maíz*.[27] Cunshu can be used as a starter for brewing new batches of chicha, an indispensable beverage in traditional Andean lives, and at Lago Cunshucocha we walked past the lake of the waters where chicha began.

Our trail passed through a eucalyptus grove and crossed boggy grassland before climbing a steep slope of loose cobblestones. The white rock altar was transferred to a small pickup truck, its rear wheels spinning for traction. Finally, we breached the ridge and descended to the sacred lake, Kituiña, at the foot of Cerro Guagualzhumi. If the meaning of Cunshucocha is obscure, the definition of "Guagualzhumi" is nearly impossible to capture. According to the cautious explanation in the brochure prepared by the Museo del Banco Central, "The different versions of the toponym Guagualzhumi have different meanings that can give us some reference about its origin and correct form of pronunciation." The pamphlet suggested various cognate words and possible meanings, ranging from "the child's breast," a tree species, or a "hard rock," before suggesting, "Arguably the best candidate is Guagalrumi, which combines the Cañari word for sacred feline (*guagal*) with the Quechua word for stone (*rumi*), resulting in 'stone in the form of a sacred feline.'"

Ultimately, though, these fine points of nomenclature matter little. Lake Kituiña and Cerro Guagualzhumi are sacred places because people have said they are. They become sacred through human acts of reverence and pilgrimage.

⯃

One of the most fascinating and blood-chilling discoveries involving South American pilgrimages relates to the Inca ceremony of *capac-cocha*. Once again, the etymology links back to water, but this was a royal (*capac*) water (*cocha*) ceremony, arguably "the most important of Inca religious ceremonies: that involving a human sacrifice and its accompanying sumptuary offerings."[28] Human sacrifice was relatively common in prehispanic South America and well-documented from the ancient Andes. Across ancient South America, elites were often accompanied into the afterlife by sacrificed retainers or wives. Not only do fine-line portraits on Moche ceramics illustrate gruesome scenes of human torture and sacrifice, but these images of agony are corroborated by the cut marks and traumatic fractures on Moche skeletons. In the Nasca culture, beheading was common: victims' heads were dried in the desert sun, a hole was drilled through the forehead, and a rope was threaded through so the trophy head could be worn dangling from the killer's belt.

But of all these forms of human sacrifice, the capaccocha was different: children were sacrificed at select shrines on specific occasions. As a father, I lose my scholarly distance when I think about sacrificing children. There is no other arena of ancient South American prehistory that I find so foreign.

The sixteenth-century chronicler Juan de Betanzos—the most respected translator of Quechua in Colonial Peru—described how the Inca ruler Inca Yupanqui established the Temple of the Sun, the holiest shrine in Cusco:

> Next, Inca Yupanque ordered the lords of Cuzco to have ready within ten days provisions of maize, sheep [llamas], and lambs along with fine garments and a certain number of boys and girls whom they call *capac-*

cocha, all of which was for making a sacrifice to the Sun. When the ten days elapsed and everything was gathered, Inca Yupanque ordered that a big fire be built into which, after having the heads cut off of the sheep and lambs [i.e., llamas and alpacas], he ordered them thrown along with the garments and maize as a sacrifice to the Sun. The boys and girls whom they had brought together were well dressed and adorned. He ordered them to be buried alive in that temple which was especially made where the statue of the Sun was.[29]

The Incas sacrificed children at especially grave moments, such as upon the death of a ruler or to placate cosmic forces in the aftermath of natural disasters. Father Bernabe Cobo described the shrines in Cusco and the surrounding region, the reasons for the shrines' sacredness, and the items given as offerings. In front of the Temple of the Sun was a square named Chuquipampa, or "plain of gold." It was the place, Cobo wrote, "where they said that the earthquake was formed. At it they made sacrifices so that it would not quake, and they were very solemn ones, because when the earth quaked children were killed."[30] At another sacred place, on top of a high hill, three stones represented the Creator, Thunder, and the Sun: "On this hill, universal sacrifice was made of boys and girls and figurines of the same made of gold; and clothing and sheep were burned because this was considered to be a very solemn shrine."[31]

The sacrifice of children triggered Cobo to write a scathing indictment. The subjects of the Inca Empire, Cobo wrote, "were kept in very severe servitude by the ambition and tyranny of their princes, and nevertheless, if that were the extent of the oppression and misery in which they lived, it could be tolerated. But besides the tributes already mentioned, another was added; willingly or by force, the people were compelled to contribute their own children, who were killed in their abominable sacrifices. This cruel act was progressively more inhumane in proportion to the innocence of the youngsters, who least deserved such treatment."[32]

Particularly elaborate capaccocha ceremonies culminated on the highest summits in the Andes, the places of the apu. More than 100 shrine sites are known from mountain peaks between 5,200 m and 6,700 m above sea level in the cordilleras of southern Peru, Bolivia, Argentina, and Chile. High-elevation capaccocha sites have been studied by various archaeologists, among whom are the American climber-scholar Johan Reinhard and the Argentine *andenista* and archaeologist Constanza Ceruti.

In these journeys to the summit shrines, Reinhard and Ceruti write, "the Incas undertook some of the longest pilgrimages known in the Americas," adding that "reaching distant sacred mountains would require months of travel at distances of more than a thousand kilometers."[33] Colonial sources describe these processions. The marchers were led by somber priests who walked with heads lowered, eyes straight ahead. The young victim was carried in a litter by bearers, sometimes accompanied by the parents. Other assistants carried supplies and offerings, including pots of llama blood. The pilgrimage was joined by people from each province, who accompanied the procession to the edge of their home territory where a new group of people took their place. En route, the pilgrims worshipped at sacred places, and local shrines received offerings in the name of the Inca. Music and dances occurred along the journey, but the capaccocha pilgrimage was a solemn march. When the procession passed through a village or town, local residents were forbidden to watch and commanded to lay prostrate on the ground, their faces in the dirt.

Arriving at the base of the sacred peak, the pilgrims began the ascent, which took three or four days. At this stage the procession shrunk to ten to fifteen people—priests, assistants, and the children—who slept in windbreaks and way-stations that sheltered the pilgrims from nights scraped by high, cold winds.

The sanctuary was perched on the summit. On some capaccocha peaks, sanctuaries and a funeral platform were built before the pilgrims arrived. On rare occasions, a hut was constructed just below the summit where the priests and victims passed the night before the ceremony at dawn. In most places, however, the ceremonial buildings at the summits were rustic and modest, unimpressive compared to the enormous vistas and exquisite objects that accompanied the sac-rificed children.

At the capacocha site at Mount Llullaillaco, a 6,739-m summit on the Chile-Argentina border studied by Reinhard and Ceruti, three children were sacrificed: a girl age six, a boy about seven, and a young woman about fifteen years of age known as "the Maiden." In the weeks of pilgrimage, the children were well fed, and they were plied with rich foods and drink in the hours before their death. These children may have been buried alive, although probably in a deep slumber or uncon-scious from alcohol. Their bodies portray no evidence of trauma, no bashed-in bones or rope burns from garroting. Their skins are leath-ered by the dry Andean sky.

The boy wore a red tunic wrapped in a scarlet outer mantle, and he sat on a folded black mantle. He wore a pair of leather moccasins and anklets of white fur. He was buried with two extra pairs of sandals for his journey into the afterlife. The boy's body was surrounded by rare offerings from distant places: two figurines carved from *Spondylus* shells, a small gold statue of an Inca noble, three small llama figurines made from silver, miniature versions of bell-spouted Inca jugs. The boy faced east.

The young girl was placed in a narrow niche in the summit's bedrock. She wore a sleeveless dress and a shawl. Her leather moccasins were trail-scuffed and worn. Surrounding her were miniature ceramic pots, a small wooden tankard, and tiny bags filled with maize kernels and dried llama meat. She also had a small bag of coca leaves, the bag dec-orated with the scarlet and yellow feathers of tropical birds. Her hands were crossed. The young girl wore a distinctive metal plaque, threaded into the hair on top of her head. Sometime after her death, a bolt of lightning found this plaque and the crackling light burned a cloth cov-ering her face, charring her skin. She faced west.

The Maiden wore a sleeveless dress and a shawl fastened with gold pins. She wore leather moccasins. Her hair was braided into numer-ous fine strands, a hairstyle common in the Bolivian highlands, possi-bly the Maiden's home. Her face was powdered with red pigment. She wore a magnificent white crescent headdress of snow-white feathers. The maiden was surrounded by more than two dozen offerings: a small male figurine of solid gold, elaborately dressed with a plumed headdress of orange feathers; two female figurines made from gold and two female figurines made from silver; a silver miniature llama; tiny jugs, pots, plates, and bowls; small bags woven from llama wool containing coca leaves, peanuts, dried potato, maize kernels, and dried llama meat. The Maiden faced northeast.

Although it is impossible to be certain, these three children may have been sacrificed at the same time. The careful arrays of offerings seem undisturbed, their mummies unmoved. The priests retreated down the mountain. The children remained behind. With their deaths, these children transited directly into other worlds. The long pilgrimage of their brief lives was over, and they entered the realm of the gods.

꣠

We arrived at Lago Kituiña around 2:30 in the afternoon. Many of the pilgrims flopped down on the grass, but the leaders quickly went to work. The Latina who had tended the brazier during the entire trek carried the smoldering censer to the edge of the lake and stirred embers to smoke. The white stone, the white ears of maize, and other objects were unwired from the wooden carrying platform and carefully placed nearby. Bathed in incense, the white stone sat upright like a small snow-capped peak. White maize cobs were arrayed around it, tassles pointing to the stone and framed by a curved span of sugarcane. The Cañari shaman sat next to these items, chewed coca leaves, and looked into the waters of the lake.

The Huaroani man who had walked with a spear shoved its shaft into the turf, its blade pointing to the sky. This was joined by the beribboned staffs of other leaders, ceremonial swords stuck into the ground, and bastones—staffs of authority carved from the dark hardwood of chonta palm carried by traditional leaders. The staffs, swords, and bastones formed a loose picket of ceremonial staves between the crowd and the

lake, and on the other side ponchos were laid like tablecloths, forming a "mesa." Bouquets of white carnations were laid out to form a cross, each end a bright cluster of white. Bottles of cane alcohol and other beverages were placed on the mesa along with offerings of fruit, tobacco, and ears of purple and red corn. A white Cañari bowler hat was placed upside down, and two miniature jugs were set inside. A platter held a small mound of red and white carnations.

The various religious leaders formed a circle and offered prayers and invocations in turn. The Huaroani shaman and his wife, her cheeks reddened with achiote, chanted a duet. Another leader said we need to learn from our ancestors because they could cure and purify and treat disease incurable by modern medicine. The long-haired Cañari leader brought this phase of the ceremony to a close with a long speech and then said that anyone who wished could be spiritually healed and cleansed with lake water.

The crowd surged forward. Using a large conch shell as a funnel, the Cañari leader poured lake water onto peoples' heads, bathing them with the waters of Lake Kituiña. A Saraguro healer massaged peoples' heads and faces and then spat a fine mist of perfumed water into the believers' faces.

Another man, his arms outstretched and smiling broadly, shouted to me and all the other pilgrims: "The lake knew we were coming."

NOTES

1. Jaime Idrovo Uriguen, "Tomebamba: Primera Fase de Conquista Incasica en los Andes Septentrionales: Los Cañaris y La Conquista Incasica del Austro Ecuatoriano," in *La Frontera del Estado Inca*, edited by Tom Dillehay and Patricia Netherly, 71–84 (Quito: Fundación Alexander von Humboldt, 1998), 77.

2. Pedro Cieza de Leon, *La Crónica del Perú* (Lima: Ediciones Peisa, 1984 [1553]), 121–26.

3. Agustin de Zárate, *The Discovery and Conquest of Peru*, translated by J. Cohen (London: Folio Society, 1981 [1555]), 59–60.

4. Brochure, "Caminata del Solsticio Hasta los Santuarios Andinos de Altura: Pumapungo—Paccha—Guagualzhumi Sábado 11 de junio 2005," 2005, translation mine.

5. Mircea Eliade, *The Sacred and Profane* (New York: Harcourt, Brace, and Jovanovitch, 1968), 26.

6. Ibid., 20.

7. Joseph Bastien, *Mountain of the Condor: Metaphor and Ritual in an Andean Ayllu* (Prospect Heights, IL: Waveland, 1985), 9.

8. Ibid., 43–45.

9. Ibid., 45.

10. Ibid., 46.

11. Ibid., 47.

12. Ibid., 178.

13. Ibid., 77.

14. Pablo José de Arriaga, *The Extirpation of Idolatry in Peru*, translated by L. Clark Keating (Lexington: University of Kentucky Press, 1968 [1621]), 23.

15. Ibid.

16. Ibid.

17. Ibid., 23–24.

18. Ibid., 24.

19. Richard Schechner, *Performance Theory* (New York: Routledge, 1988), 159–60.

20. David Sallnow, *Pilgrims of the Andes: Regional Cults in Cusco* (Washington, DC: Smithsonian Institution Press, 1987), 96, 184.

21. Antonio Vasquez de Espinoza, *Description of the Indies*, trans. Charles Clark, Smithsonian Miscellaneous Collections, vol. 102 (Washington, DC: Smithsonian Institution Press, 1968 [ca. 1620]), 491.

22. Peter Eeckhout, "Change and Permanency on the Coast of Ancient Peru: The Religious Site of Pachacamac," *World Archaeology* 45, no. 1 (2013): 137–60. For a recent bioarchaeological study of a Pachacamac cemetery, see Lawrence S. Owens and Peter Eeckhout, "To the God of Death, Disease and Healing: Social Bioarchaeology of Cemetery I at Pachacamac," in *Funerary Practices and Models in the Ancient Andes: The Return of the Living Dead*, edited by Peter Eeckhout and Lawrence S. Owens (New York: Cambridge University Press, 2015), 158–85.

23. Eeckhout, "Change and Permanency," 147. See also Helaine Silverman, "The Archaeological Identification of an Ancient Peruvian Pilgrimage Center," *World Archaeology* 26, no. 1 (1994): 1–18.

24. For an overview of Nasca, see Helaine Silverman and Donald Proulx, *The Nasca* (Malden, MA: John Wiley and Sons, 2008).

25. Christopher Donnan and Donna McClelland, *Moche Fineline Painting: Its Evolution and Its Artists* (Los Angeles: UCLA Fowler Museum of Culture History, 1999), 135.

26. Diego Gonçalez Holguin, *Vocabulario de la Lengua General de Todo el Peru llamada Lengua Qquichuia o del Inca* (Lima: Universidad Nacional Mayor de San Marcos, 1952 [1608]).

27. Thesaurus: Boletin del Instituto Caro y Cuervo, Tomo LI, Número 1: Dialectos del Español de Colombia Caracterización Léxica de los subdialectos Andino-Sureño y Caucano-Vallundo, 10, accessed September 15, 2015, http://cvc .cervantes.es/lengua/thesaurus/pdf/51/TH_51_001_009_0.pdf.

28. Johan Reinhard and Constanza Ceruti, *Inca Rituals and Sacred Mountains: A Study of the World's Highest Archaeological Sites* (Los Angeles: Cotsen Institute of Archaeology, University of California, 2010), 6.

29. Juan de Betanzos, *Narrative of the Incas*, translated and edited by Roland Hamilton and Dana Buchanan (Austin: University of Texas Press, 1996 [1576]), 45–46.

30. Bernabe Cobo, *Inca Religion and Customs*, translated and edited by Roland Hamilton (Austin: University of Texas Press, 1990 [1653]), 54.

31. Ibid., 57.

32. Bernabe Cobo, *History of the Inca Empire*, translated and edited by Roland Hamilton (Austin: University of Texas Press, 1983 [1653]), 235.

33. The following discussion is based on Reinhard and Ceruti, *Inca Rituals and Sacred Mountains*, quote from 89.

CHAPTER FOUR

River of Paintings

In nine months of a man's life he can think a lot of things, from the
loftiest meditations on philosophy to the most desperate longing
for a bowl of soup . . . And if, at the same time, he's somewhat of an
adventurer, he might live through episodes of interest to other people and his haphazard record might read something like these notes.

ERNESTO GUEVARA, *Motorcycle Diaries*[1]

HAIL SHOT FROM CHARCOAL CLOUDS AS WE DROVE across the pampas
southwest of Buenos Aires. I slowed the rental car onto the dirt shoulder and under the shelter of a roadside tree, scant protection but saving
the vehicle from damage. The roadway was silver. The parked car shud-
dered as the storm blew past. The sun broke through. The hail melted
and puddled. The wind still blew. I started the car, and we continued on
our way to Patagonia. We had begun our journey of 2,500 miles to the
River of Paintings to see the Cave of Hands.

The route tracked southwest across the wet pampas, a landscape of
low hills and hummocks pocked with small ponds and streams. The

farmlands looked like the rolling fields of Iowa or Kansas: corn and wheat, green and russet. Two chains of low mountains, the Sierra de Tandil and the Sierra de Ventanilla, border the wet pampas. The sierras are mountains of magmatic rocks that once formed the southern margin of Western Gondwana, sharing an ancient geological heritage with the Elsmere Range in Antarctica and the Cape granites of South Africa, immigrant ranges of granite, diorite, and gneiss—hard stones that resist water and wind. As we traveled further, the country became drier and flatter. The highway left the wet pampas and tacked due west and into the wind. Wisps of red clay drifted across the blacktop.

At the small town of Chimpay on the north bank of the Río Negro, snapping banners flagged a shrine. A sign proclaimed ¡*Nosostros creemos en Ceferino Namuncurá*! "We believe in Ceferino Namuncurá!" Ceferino Namuncurá is the only Argentine-born saint, a Mapuche Indian whose mother was a creole captive and whose father was an Indian war chief who resisted the Argentines and was one of the last native leaders to surrender. As a young boy, Ceferino converted to Catholicism and studied with the Salesian priests in Buenos Aires. Ceferino traveled to Italy to study for the priesthood, where he died of tuberculosis in 1905 at age eighteen. Decades later, his bones were returned to Argentina and his birthplace at Chimpay became a shrine. In 2000 it was determined that a young woman was miraculously cured of uterine cancer through her prayers to Ceferino, and Pope Benedict XVI beatified him in 2007. Ceferino is known as the "Santo Aborigen." The snapping banners at this shrine marked the complex histories of migration and expatriation, movement and permanence, conflict and place that characterize Patagonia, where so much seems driven by the wind.

One cannot travel in Patagonia uninfluenced by Bruce Chatwin. *In Patagonia* is a travel narrative constructed as Cubist vignettes, in which Chatwin portrayed Patagonia as a landscape of impermanence, a region of wind-blown steppe sparsely inhabited by displaced lives. Chatwin explained the thesis of his book: "Patagonia is the farthest place to which man walked from his place of origins. It is therefore a symbol of his restlessness."[2] Chatwin wrote of an immigrant from the Rhineland, who settled in Patagonia after the Great War and raised blue lupines that reminded him of Germany. At a sheep ranch, Chatwin met a Scottish rancher who wore a kilt and had carved his own bag- pipes during the long Patagonian winter. Displaced Boers lived near Sarmiento. A toothless Lithuanian pilot still flew at age eighty-five. A homesick Canary Islander remembered the warm winds of Tenerife.[3] In the words of the elderly English gardener Miss Nita Starling, who had traveled the world but ended up tending flowers on a Patagonian *estancia*, "You never know where you'll end up."[4]

In January 2014, I ended up in Patagonia with the archaeologist Andrew Stewart. We have been friends for more than thirty years, hav- ing met as graduate students in the 1980s at UC Santa Barbara. Andrew lives in Toronto and conducts research on geoarchaeology and Inuit ethnoarchaeology in the region around Hudson Bay. He is an accom- plished traveler and a wealth of information on the geologies shaped by rivers. The plan for our journey to the Río de las Pinturas and La Cueva de las Manos was simple, although the product of nearly a year's planning. Andrew and I rendezvoused in Buenos Aires, meeting in a hotel across the plaza from the Recoleta Cemetery, where Eva Peron and other Argentine luminaries are interred. More important for our immediate interests, the hotel was next to an outstanding microbrew- ery, and it was a fine thing to sip ales and porters while people-watching in the summer twilight.

Since we would be traveling on paved or good gravel roads, there was no need for a 4-wheel-drive vehicle. We rented a small four-door Renault. There was enough room for our gear: notebooks, clothes, cam- eras, maps, books, boots, and spare bottles of Malbec. One special bag contained our backup equipment: a two-man tent, sleeping bags and pads, a Leatherman™, a roll of Gorilla tape, a backpacking stove, a small kettle, and a collapsible entrenching tool. On my road trips, I always travel with an entrenching tool. I have never actually used it, so it has become an indispensable talisman.

We drove six days from Buenos Aires to arrive at the Río de Pinturas. After a night in Bahía Blanca, we crossed the Río Negro and Río Colorado, the northern border of Patagonia, and spent a night in Neuquén, the capital of the province of Patagonia—a city of few charms but great commercial bustle, with large numbers of auto dealers and distributors of farm machinery.

We left Neuquén early the next morning, slamming into a 40 mph headwind on the outskirts of town. The wind blew huge pillars of yellow dust across the loessic landscape. The landscape was arid, covered with scraps of flinching bunchgrass. White plumes from alkali pans spiraled into the sky. In an exchange with the Argentine journalist Uki Goni, Chatwin claimed that the profiles of *In Patagonia* were simply a matter of discovery: "At every place I came to it wasn't a question of hunting for the story it was a question of the story coming at you . . . I also think the wind had something possibly to do with it."[5]

∏

Humans first occupied the pampas and Patagonia sometime between 13,000 and 12,000 years ago.[6] Based on current evidence, people crossed the Río Negro into Patagonia at the end of the Pleistocene, about 12,800–12,000 years ago. Swirls of controversy surround these deceptively simple sentences. For decades, archaeologists argued that people first migrated into North America sometime between 11,500 and 11,000 years ago and gradually moved south, perhaps arriving in southern South America 1,000 or 2,000 years later.[7] Recent recalibrations of radiocarbon dates from early sites in North and South America indicate that many of these sites are coeval or separated by only a few centuries. These early dates from both hemispheres suggest that either people were already in South America or that human expansion through the Americas was extremely rapid compared with other parts of the globe. (In contrast, it is estimated that 300–400 generations—approximately

7,000 to 10,000 years—passed before fully modern humans expanded from the Near East and occupied most of Europe).[8]

After millennia of complex cultural developments across South America, fundamental changes occurred in the fourteenth and fifteenth centuries and intensified in the post-Colombian world.[9] These changes reflected other events in the Andes, such as political dislocations caused by the southern expansion of the Inca Empire into what are today northern Chile and northwestern Argentina and the development of complex military and political alliances among clusters of Araucanian communities, which the Spaniards would later incorrectly call *estados*. People who spoke Araucanian languages, Mapuche in the north and Tehuelche in the south, crossed the Andes and moved into the pampas. As if blown eastward by the wind, these immigrants encountered the native peoples of the pampas just as Tupi-Guarani speakers living along the Atlantic Coast were retreating into the interior away from the first Spanish explorers and settlers.

Compared with other areas of the Americas, the European conquest of the pampas and Patagonia occurred late. In the late 1700s, Europeans and creoles only held a very narrow strip of coastal Argentina. Most of the pampas were controlled by native groups who were transformed— but not immediately devastated—by European contact. By the early

1700s native people had obtained horses through purchase or theft or by capturing mustangs. Instead of remaining limited to the pace of a human jog and having only dogs as beasts of burden, the Tehuelche and Mapuche became mobile hunters who ranged across Patagonia on horseback. In 1869 a young British naval officer and traveler, George Musters, traveled with the Tehuelches[10] for nearly a year, a journey he described in his book *At Home with the Patagonians: A Year's Wanderings over Untrodden Ground from the Straits of Magellan to the Rio Negro*. Musters was a perceptive and sympathetic observer who provided a wealth of detail about Tehuelche life.[11] By the mid-nineteenth century, all the native groups of the pampas had horses; only the coastal hunters of Tierra del Fuego traveled by foot and canoe. Smaller than most Europeans' mounts, Musters observed, the Patagonian horses were "of great speed and endurance."[12]

This led to other changes. The chipped stone points that once tipped darts and arrows grew into large blades hafted on long-shafted lances. Small hide-covered huts developed into larger multi-chamber *toldos*, a complex and heavy tent of poles and guanaco hides carried on packhorses. The Tehuelche hunted guanacos and rheas using bolas, a weapon made from weighted cords. Some bolas had three thongs tied to rocks the size of apricots, designed to entangle a fleeing guanaco's

hind legs. Another bola had a single stone, swung overhead like a lasso and thrown at a rhea's head, killing the bird instantly. As a Tehuelche band moved to the next night's camp, men rode out and hunted, stampeding game into a surround of galloping hunters. The men also killed pumas with their lances, the large cats occupying the savannas like their distant African cousins. Even in the late 1800s, pumas occupied the pampas "in surprising great number."[13]

The horse dramatically increased the Tehuelches' range over territory they knew, revered, but did not settle. The horse also increased their ability to raid and rustle. The Argentine government (itself a fractured assortment of provincial and national governments incompletely unified until the 1880s) made various attempts to curtail native threats. The pampas were an untameable landscape, but a stunning effort to restrain it was the *zanja de Alsina*, or "Alsina's ditch." Adolfo Alsina, minister of war and the navy in 1874–77, designed a massive defensive moat to protect the Argentines from Indian attacks from the pampas, a ditch 2 m deep and 3 m wide bordered by a meter-tall rampart. The original plan called for a line 600 km long; this was never achieved, but a staggering 376 km were dug by soldiers and peons in the 1870s.[14] The zanja was fortified with 6 garrisons placed at strategic positions and another 109 smaller outposts (*fortines*) consisting of a watchtower, a small barracks, and eight or ten conscripted soldiers forcibly drafted from frontier communities.

Alsina's ditch failed to contain marauding Mapuches and Tehuelches, who were subjugated only after six years of sustained attacks by the Argentine army, an 1878–84 war that slaughtered thousands of Indians and displaced thousands more. This genocidal project was led by the general and future president Julio Argentino Roca (1843–1914), who declared, "Our self-respect as a virile people obliges us to put down as soon as possible, by reason or by force, this handful of savages who destroy our wealth and prevent us from definitely occupying, in the name of law, progress and our own security, the richest and most fertile lands of the Republic."[15] The military campaigns were called the "Conquest of the Desert," as if all that was being conquered were unoccupied lands. The Conquest of the Desert extended Argentina's control to Patagonia, and it is still celebrated and depicted on the back of the 100 peso bill.

Our road dropped into a small valley, and we drove through the town of Piedra de Aguila, sheltered at the base of an escarpment. In the valley bottom, apple orchards were planted in fields edged by pleached rows of poplar trees, pruned to create overlapping sheets of leafy branches that sheltered the fruit trees from the wind. The road climbed back onto the pampas and headed southwest as we began to gain the forested slopes of the eastern Andes near San Carlos de Bariloche, where we joined La Ruta 40.

La Ruta 40 runs for 5,300 km along the base of the Andes. Like the Silk Road, the Via Appia, and Route 66, La Ruta 40 is a legendary highway, connecting distant towns and isolated estancias and entwining different strands of history and fiction. La Ruta 40 begins in the northwest corner of Argentina in the high, dry valleys near Juyjuy and Salta and runs south, brushing the glaciers and mountain lakes of Tierra del Fuego. Until recently, it was a rough track of gravel and riprap, dusty and jolting in the summer and slick and boggish in the winter. La Ruta 40 is braided from ancient trails and recent roadbeds. The northern span follows the network of Inca roads that flowed south from Bolivia, hugging river valleys and dashing across arid pampas. In northwestern Argentina the Inca road was a complex web of trails, with multiple north-south routes tied by lateral roads crossing high passes in the Andes. La Ruta 40 twines these routes into a firm but flexible north-south path.

From Potosi, Bolivia, La Ruta 40 passes the small border town of Pumahuasi (Quechua for "Puma House"), past San Antonio de los Cobres and the ruins of Quilmes (whose native residents were conquered and forcibly resettled near Buenos Aires in 1668) before continuing another 1,100 km south to Mendoza. In this northern one-third of the road, La Ruta 40 sinuously parallels modern highways connecting the major cities of Salta, San Miguel de Tucuman, and Cordoba.

Before his continental road trip recorded in *The Motorcycle Diaries* (which only briefly intersected with La Ruta 40 at San Carlos de Bariloche), Ernesto "Che" Guevara traveled through northwest Argentina in 1950 on a bicycle equipped with a small motor, the tires repeatedly punctured by the riprap.

La Ruta 40 parallels the rails of La Trochita, the Old Patagonian Express, the narrow-gauge railroad constructed between 1916 and 1935. La Ruta 40 passes through the broad meadowlands near Cholila, where

the famous North American train robbers, Butch Cassidy and the Sundance Kid, settled on a 15,000-acre ranch between 1901 and 1905. Using the alias James or Santiago Ryan, Cassidy signed receipts for cattle purchases, which are on display at the Museo Leleque.

The Museo Leleque is an improbable institution, created from the intersection of two very different lives: those of the Italian textile magnate Carlos Benetton and a relatively obscure Ukrainian naturalist and amateur archaeologist, Pablo S. Korschenewski.

Benetton Group, the Italian garment manufacturer, was drawn to Patagonia as a source of wool and in 1991 purchased the Southern Argentine Land Company, which produces 2.9 million pounds of wool each year.[16] The family-run Benetton Group became Patagonia's single largest private landowner, acquiring 2.2 million acres as well as having extensive landholdings elsewhere in Argentina. Benetton has been criticized for dispossessing indigenous families, since the vast estancias of the Southern Argentine Land Company (originally British-owned) were created after the Conquest of the Desert when the Tehuelche and Mapuche inhabitants were killed or driven out.

The Benetton decision to fund the Museo Leleque has been criticized as little more than an empty public relations gesture. Carlos
Benetton described his motives in more romantic terms, writing: "To
me, Patagonia represents an ideal place, an enchanted remote site by
the end of the earth. From the very first time I set eyes here, the magic
sequence of limitless tableland, mountains, blue lakes, rivers, glaciers
and scrub deserts made me feel at home."[17]

Pablo Korschenewski's archaeological collections are the core of the
Museo Leleque. Korschenewski was a quintessentially Chatwinesque
character. Born in Odessa, Ukraine, in 1925, Korschenewski survived
the Holodomor, or "Hunger Extermination," of 1932–33, in which Josef
Stalin cordoned off the Ukraine in response to the peasants' resistance
to collectivization and stirrings of Ukrainian nationalism, destroying
food supplies and starving to death 3.5 million to 7 million Ukrainians,
"a famine organized as a genocidal act of state policy."[18] Korschenewski
lived through the Nazis' 1941–42 invasion of the Ukraine, in which
another 9 million Ukrainians died before the war's end. Against the
odds, Korschenewski survived these horrors.

Pablo Korschenewski arrived in Buenos Aires in 1948 with his
father and brother; his mother, separated from her family at the end
of the war, was reunited with them in 1952. The Korschenewskis initially were housed in the Hotel de Inmigrantes—a government-run
dormitory and kitchen located near the North Docks of Buenos Aires,
where 3,000 immigrants could be sheltered, fed, and assisted with
finding work.[19] In 1953 Korschenewski began working as an electrical
mechanic in the massive coal mine at Río Turbio, in the southwest
corner of Patagonia. Korschenewski nurtured intellectual interests
that he shared with a close group of friends who established a small
museum and library. Korschenewski's initial interests in the history
of late-nineteenth- and early-twentieth-century Patagonia ultimately
led to archaeological explorations.

Korschenewski was not the only scholar interested in Patagonia's
past. Between 1932 and 1937, the North American archaeologist Junius
Bird (1907–82) conducted a total of four years of archaeological survey

and excavations along the coasts of Tierra del Fuego and the Beagle Channel, with additional sorties into the steppe of southernmost Patagonia.[20] In 1938 Bird published a brief synopsis of his research, outlining a relative sequence of five archaeological complexes whose precise ages were unknown. Further, this tentative sequence was primarily relevant for Tierra del Fuego, as Bird noted, because "Argentine Patagonia has no stratigraphic studies for comparison with those made in the south."[21] In the late 1930s, no deep middens were known from Patagonia, only surface artifacts from briefly occupied sites. Bird admitted that his estimates for the antiquity of human presence in Tierra del Fuego and Patagonia "are given for what they are worth—a few degrees better than an outright guess."[22]

Less cautious archaeological conclusions were made by the expatriate Austrian archaeologist Oswald Menghin (1888–1973). A European prehistorian who was appointed rector of the University of Vienna in 1935–36, Menghin embodied the *kulturkreise* (culture circles) school of German social science, which envisioned a people, a language, and a culture as unified domains. Cultures changed—the theory held—through migration or diffusion as either a distinctive complex of people/language/culture spread out from its place of origin or as traits originally developed elsewhere were adopted subsequently by neighboring peoples. In his archaeological writings, Menghin argued that in the deepest, most ancient eras of human prehistory, "there was a greater correspondence between race, language, and culture,"[23] a conviction that led him to propose a universal history of the Paleolithic and to argue for strong connections between the Old and New Worlds.

Further, Menghin argued that archaeology could inform the "Jewish Question." As a conservative, anti-Semitic Catholic, Menghin contended that the Jewish presence was a contaminating influence on "the" German people, writing that "every people has not only the right but also the moral duty to defend its nationality."[24] Yiddish-speaking urban Jews corrupted Germany's language and culture, especially those of the German rural peasantry who were uniquely connected to the soils of the Fatherland. Menghin argued that Jews should be expelled to Palestine because race, culture, language, and place were linked and should remain pure.

Initially listed as a war criminal but never charged with war crimes, Menghin was allowed to immigrate to Argentina, where he became professor of archaeology at the University of Buenos Aires in 1948. Menghin soon began fieldwork in the Sierra de Tandil southwest of Buenos Aires, excavating at La Gruta del Oro with the physical anthropologist Marcelo Bórmida, an Italian immigrant to Argentina.[25] The archaeologist Gustavo Politis has written, "After a few days of shovel excavation with local rural workers, he [Menghin] recovered a handful of lithic material which he correlated with Bird's findings in southern Patagonia" but whose roots lay in East Asia.[26]

Menghin "insisted that all humanity took part in the same universal world-historical process," Philip Kohl and José Antonio Pérez Gollán write, "while at the same time maintaining an almost religious belief in the existence of three fundamental culture circles or *Kulturkreise*. He traced these three traditions—blade, bone, and hand-axe—to the beginnings of the Palaeolithic and saw them as corresponding respectively to the three basic races of humanity, white, yellow, and black."[27] Emphasizing the derivative origins of prehistoric South American cultures, Menghin interpreted two Patagonian stone tool industries, the "Epiprotolithic" and "Mio-Protolithic" as similar to the Lower/Middle Paleolithic and the Upper Paleolithic of Eurasia, remnants of cultures originally from Europe and Asia.[28] Even in prehistory, Menghin believed, Patagonia had been occupied by immigrants, its culture derived from elsewhere.

I do not know if these issues mattered to Pablo Korschenewski. Seemingly, he was content to wander, to look, and to collect. (His only scientific publications were of ornithological observations along the Patagonian coast, with a special interest in penguins.) Korschenewski was invited to help establish a museum at the Atlantic coastal city of Puerto Madryn, and he moved there in the mid-1960s. Over the next years he made repeated journeys across Patagonia, collecting spear points, bola stones, and other artifacts. Ultimately, Korschenewski amassed a collection of nearly 15,000 artifacts, and unlike most amateur collectors, he carefully noted the locations of the archaeological sites. Bola stones and projectile points were found across the breadth of Patagonia, durable remains from ancient hunts.

Flaked stone scrapers were used to make *quillangos*, a warm cloak made from stretched guanaco hides. The sixteenth-century Spanish navigator and historian Pedro Sarmiento de Gamboa wrote that the Patagonians "wear as garments cloaks made of skins, well matched and sewn."[29] The soft hides from juvenile guanacos were highly desired, and as many as thirteen hides were stitched to make a cloak. The quillangos were worn with the fur inside and were elaborately decorated on the outside, including with distinctive motifs that also appear on rock art. One design was the labyrinth motif, an element in a style of rock art Menghin called *estilo greca*, a term denoting a fretwork motif created by repeating lines as if they were visual echoes. The labyrinth motif is a complex, stepped cross in which the outline of the cross is repeated with a diamond shape at its center. The labyrinth motif is still used today, depicted on the flat drums used by Mapuche shamans. Like most symbols, the labyrinth motif conveyed multiple meanings: the interlocking chains of kinfolk and ancestors but also, according to the anthropologist Rodolfo Casamiquela, a tortuous road that the spirits of the dead must journey to join their ancestors in the world of the dead. The complex interweavings of the *laberinto*, according to Casamiquela, form "the symbol par excellence of the difficult route to the Beyond."[30]

⬚

We have tended to exercise an imaginative bias against flatlands: moor, tundra, heath, prairie, bog and steppe . . . They seem to return the eye's enquiries unanswered, or swallow all attempts at interpretation. They confront us with the problem of purchase: how to anchor perception in context of vastness, how to make such a place *mean*.

ROBERT MACFARLANE, *The Wild Places*, 78

At the end of the Pleistocene, Patagonia was a different landscape. About 12,700 to 11,500 years ago, Patagonia was warmer and wetter than today, a broad sweep of luxuriant grasslands instead of today's drier steppe.[31] This wetter period was followed by an inconstant trend toward greater aridity, largely caused by fluctuations in the location and intensity of a massive belt of wind that flows around the Earth, the Southern Westerly Wind (SWW).[32] The normal position of the SWW is between 50°–55° latitudes South, sweeping around Antarctica and touching the tip of Tierra del Fuego but otherwise flowing around the Earth unimpeded by continents. However, the position of this raging river of wind changes throughout the year and over millennia, creating stronger winds during the austral summer as the air currents are forced together, producing a nearly constant wind that blows 30–40 km per hour. Approximately 12,500 years ago, windier and wetter conditions existed, which were particularly damp on the western slopes of the Andes but also supported more extensive grasslands in Patagonia.[33] This wetter era 12,500 to 8,500 years ago was followed by fluctuating climates between 8,500 to 5,500 years ago and then by weaker westerlies that blew less moisture across the Andes, creating the drier shrub-covered steppe of Patagonia.

Humans moved into this changing, challenging environment. As a team of researchers recently wrote, "Early inhabitants of southern Patagonia, east of the Andes, had to face an unstable climate that led to discontinuous use of most areas."[34] The Argentine archaeologist Luis Alberto Borrero, an expert on the peopling of Patagonia, has proposed that people moved into Patagonia in a halting but adventurous way, facing an unstable environment of changing habitats and dispersed pockets of key resources. Borrero writes, "Humans had to adjust to changing sets of circumstances, which would require different adaptations."[35] This gradual settlement of Patagonia progressed as people confronted certain pressures and overcame specific obstacles. People moved into new territories, Borrero proposes, as they gradually extended the range of their day's hunting, when social conflicts caused band communities to fracture, or because of "starvation, curiosity, and other causes, principal among them the simple act of living within a variable home range."[36]

The earliest colonizers of Patagonia faced imperfectly known challenges, but the greatest was finding freshwater. "Although there were changes in the availability of water through time, as well as regional differences," Borrero writes, "it is difficult to visualize a Patagonian archaeological period when water was not a critical resource."[37] Limited water and patchy resources meant the people of Patagonia moved across the landscape in relatively small groups, following river valleys whenever possible, striking out across dry deserts to known waterholes when necessary, but leaving vast areas either "sparsely populated or . . . not used at all."[38]

The oldest archaeological sites currently known from Patagonia come from a vast region of volcanic geology known as the Deseado Massif, a region that extends south and east from Perito Moreno to the Atlantic Coast, a staircase of geological formations that drop in elevation as they reach the coastline. The Deseado Massif is cut by river drainages that run from the base of the Andes to the sea. The formation contained resources of interest to human hunters-and-gatherers. The bedrock was pocked with caves that made excellent rockshelters. The rocky outcrops contained high-quality stone for tool making: chalcedony, quartz, and rare but highly prized obsidian. In addition to the rivers, the hard strata of the Deseado Massif trapped freshwater in basins and channeled underground water to surface streams.

The region was covered with grasslands that fed vast herds of game. At the end of the Pleistocene, the pampas grasslands supported an impressive array of large mammals, including the American horse (*Hippidion saldiasi*), the extinct gigantic armadillo (*Eutatus seguini*), and ground sloths (*Mylodon darwinii*). (A scrap of preserved ground sloth hide sent by a distant relative to England and displayed in his grandmother's dining room was the talisman that prompted Bruce Chatwin to go to Patagonia.) These extinct animals' bones are found across the pampas. In his journal from the voyage of HMS *Beagle* the young Charles Darwin wrote, "Besides those which I found during my short excursions, I heard of many others, and the origin of such names as 'the stream of the animal,' 'the hill of the giant,' is obvious. At other times I heard of the marvelous property of certain rivers, which had the power of changing small bones into large; or, as some maintained, the bones themselves grew . . . We may conclude that the whole area of the Pampas is one wide sepulcher of these extinct gigantic quadrupeds."[39]

In the pampas just north of Patagonia, Gustavo Martinez and colleagues have excavated at two deeply buried archaeological sites, Paso Otero 5 and Paso Otero 4, located between the Sierra de Tandil and the Sierra de Ventanilla.[40] The sites are exposed in the banks of the Río Quenquen Grande. Paso Otero 5 is the older site, dating to about 12,600–11,350 years ago, while Paso Otero 4 dates to approximately 10,670–7,980 years ago. At Paso Otero 5, remains of a dozen genera of animals were found, ten of them now extinct; only one species of extinct llama showed any evidence of human use. In contrast, twenty-three different types of animals were identified at Paso Otero 4; eleven classes of fauna showed evidence of human use: butchering cut marks, fractures, or fire-burning. These fauna include a large number of rhea eggshells and the butcher-etched scutes of the extinct giant armadillo.

The gigantic quadrupeds died off at the end of the Ice Age, although human complicity in their demise is uncertain. To date, there is no archaeological evidence for massacres of game. Sites with butchered or burned remains of extinct fauna have evidence of only one or two individuals that were killed, not slaughtered herds. Some animals, such as the gigantic ground sloth, may have become extinct just before humans entered the pampas, while animals that *were* hunted—such as guanacos and rheas—did *not* become extinct. Humans may have contributed to these extinctions—perhaps through burning grasslands or hunting—but they were not the principal cause.

Perhaps these species became extinct as they were caught between the changing environments at the end of the Ice Age and their inability to quickly modify their behaviors. It is possible that these large animals failed to become more mobile or to venture into previously unexplored habitats—the essential human strategy for moving across the pampas and into Patagonia. The first human explorations into Patagonia were neither aimless forays nor wind-blown wanderings but initial sorties followed by careful acquisition of knowledge about water, shelter, and food. In that process, humans made place.

Ⅱ

Traveling south, La Ruta 40 leaves the forested hills and moves out onto the steppe. Hundreds of kilometers stretch between the towns: Esquel, Tekla, General San Martin, and Río Dos de Mayo. For 120 km, Andrew and I drove slowly as La Ruta devolved into loose gravel and gray dust, and it was late afternoon when we finally arrived at the town of Perito Moreno.

Named for an Argentine explorer, archaeologist, and booster of Patagonia, Francisco Moreno (1852–1919)—*perito* is an honorific meaning "expert"—Perito Moreno straddles a main street with three stoplights and a dividing verge planted with Italian pines. There are a couple of cafés and a mini-mart. A dry goods store built in the 1910s has been converted into a small tourist center with a bar that serves cold Quilmes beer. The only public artworks were a few lines of graffiti inscribed on walls by a group known as Acción Poética. And even here, among the streets lined by pollarded stumps of cottonwoods and in the sheltering lee of concrete buildings, the wind slashed through Perito Moreno as if determined to push us east again from where we came. Andrew and I considered setting up a tent in the municipal campground, but the wind blew us toward the Hotel Americano on a darkening afternoon. The El Viejo Bar served a passable *churasco* and salad, improved by a bottle of Malbec. The bar was a modest place of Formica tables with tablecloths covered by protective polyvinyl sheets. Most of the walls were a simple bone white, but the bar itself, built from rough stonework, was painted an otherworldly reddish-tangerine in defiance of the dun and sage of the surrounding landscapes.

The next morning we woke early, quickly downed coffee and breads, and left Perito Moreno by 8 a.m. The winds were strong, pushing the

Renault across the lanes of asphalt. La Ruta 40 curved southward over the hills and down into arroyos when suddenly we saw our first guanacos, their long, elegant necks peering like periscopes above the ridge crest. After about 40 km we left La Ruta 40 and turned onto the gravel road that leads to the River of Paintings.

The River of Paintings lies south of the Phoenix River and below the headwaters of the River of Desire. The Río Pinturas cuts through mesas, carving steep-walled canyons 200 m into thick blocks of basalt flows. Leaving La Ruta 40, Andrew and I drove 28 km on a good gravel road to the interpretive center that consisted of a minuscule museum, quarters for the site guards and guides, and a small parking lot. Eighty archaeological sites are known from this immediate stretch of the Río Pinturas, with four major complexes of rock paintings. When we arrived, about twenty other people were waiting to be guided to the site, a necessary precaution to protect the fragile rock art.

The Cueva de las Manos sits about 88 m above the Río Pinturas. The cave is a broad but shallow overhang that runs for 48 m, with a single large chamber, 27.4 m deep and 9.5 m wide, that bores into the mountain. Layers of midden and sediment form a narrow shelf fronting the mouth of the cave. The archaeological deposit was about 95 cm at its thickest and contained layers of charcoal, cultural materials, and a cap of rock spall that separated lower and upper levels. These caves were used over thousands of years, as people took shelter and watched for guanaco to come down from the mesetas to drink and browse along the river. Sitting by campfires, ancient people made tools, butchered game, and built lives. And, of course, they made paintings.

The earliest levels are over 9,000 years old and contain abundant stone flakes, bones, and charcoal. Most of the stone tools were scrapers and flake blades made from chalcedony and chert, with rare fragments of obsidian and basalt. There was a piece of a bola stone. Only two projectile points were found, rough triangles made from obsidian. Patches of charcoal and burned earth marked ancient hearths. A medley of animal bones, particularly from guanacos, was found in the cave; many bones had cut marks and intentional fractures. The earliest layers also held numerous chunks of red, ochre, and white mineral pigments and a fragment of fallen cave stone with traces of yellowish-brown paint.

The uppermost levels were deposited more that 8,500 years later, and the artifacts were significantly different. Dating to AD 370–600, these layers held more projectile points (although they were still rare), particularly small, finely worked triangular points. There were more bolas, grinding stones, and various bone awls and tools. Sometime later in this region, even smaller points marked the arrival of the bow and arrow, and the potsherds signaled the introduction of pottery, a cultural complex associated with the pre-contact Tehuelches.

The rock art is sheltered from the wind by overhanging rock ledges along the canyon walls. The paintings were made with mineral pigments—iron oxides, kaolin, manganese oxide, natrojarosite, and copper oxide—to create figures in red, white, black, yellow, and green. (The rare green copper oxide came from a source 150 km away.) The porous surface of the buff-colored rock allowed the pigments to penetrate the stone, and the images are surprisingly vivid thousands of years after they were made.

The earliest paintings are thought to date to 13,000–9,300 years ago. Excavations in the floor of the Cueva de las Manos in the 1970s,

directed by Carlos Gradin, uncovered small fragments of rock spall covered with red and yellow pigments in layers radiocarbon dated to 8700–8300 BC.[41] Even earlier layers underlie these dated strata.

Some of the rock art allows for basic and obvious interpretations; other motifs are profoundly obscure. The oldest images depict guanacos and human hands. Unlike the slender camelids Andrew and I have seen, the guanaco are shown as sway-bellied and full. Some are swollen in pregnancy, and an X-ray-like image appears to show an enwombed fetus. A solid white disk may depict a full moon, and it is said that guanacos give birth near the full moon.

There are numerous hunting scenes, dynamic chases of guanacos by people running and twirling bolas. Bolas are shown as dots of paint with trailing, wind-whipped lines. Herds of guanaco walk across the cave stone. A few stylized human figures, shown in frontal view, seem to carry ropes. Other motifs—some geometric, some zoomorphic— are painted in solid forms. Later, rock art became increasingly geometric—a red chain of triangles or a circle filled with dots—and schematic, such as a pair of raised but disembodied human arms.

The previous paragraph is filled with conjecture; most writing about prehistoric rock art is. Whether painted pictographs or pecked petroglyphs, prehistoric rock art is indisputably human and utterly mysterious at the same time. A glance at these images of guanacos and disks, squiggled lines and painted dots, is enough to identify these motifs as human creations, but no archaeologist can know the symbols' complete and fundamental meanings.

Look, for example, at the human hands. Hands are the most distinctive human feature; the images are indisputable creations of human intention. Some of the oldest known rock art shows human hands, such as at the Spanish cave site of El Castillo, where stenciled hands outlined in red ochre have been dated to 37,500 years ago.[42] Hand motifs have been found on rock art panels on every continent occupied by ancient humans, literally from Australia to Arizona and from Borneo to Baja California. Hand motifs are rarely isolated and often occur by the hundreds. In Australia, for example, hand stencils were signs of territorial membership: people who had a special relationship with a specific area would mark that right with a handprint or by identifying the handprints of specific ancestors.[43]

At Cueva de las Manos, the majority of the hand motifs are stenciled, made by blowing ground pigment through a bird-bone tube creating the negative imprint of the hand (and occasionally the forearm). Of the 829 hand motifs recorded by Gradin and colleagues, only 31 were of right hands, suggesting that a mere 3.7 percent of the people who

visited and lived at Cueva de las Manos were left-handed—of course, assuming that artist and subject were the same person.[44] Some of the hand stencils were made with variously colored pigments, and the care and precision of the negative outlines suggest that the subject/artist had to hold the left hand in place for at least five to ten minutes, with all the pigments ground and mixed with some binder and a blow tube comfortably within reach. All this is readily inferred at a glance.

Most hands are of adults, although a few, smaller hands of children are preserved on the cave walls, but this does not suggest an initiation ceremony. Even the larger hands vary in size, suggesting men and women left their marks on these stones.

But what do these images *mean*?

Despite the careful excavations and the detailed analyses of images, no archaeologist has a firm understanding of the rock art on Cueva de las Manos—or for the vast majority of rock art sites. We can identify stylistic changes and variations in techniques, but we always confront the elusive nature of meaning. We will never hear the stories that accompanied ancient art or be certain of the tales that wrapped around image. Yet here in Patagonia, after thousands of miles of travel, I look carefully at these cave walls and strain to hear their message above the sound of the wind:

"We were here."

NOTES

1. Ernesto Guevara, *Motorcycle Diaries: Notes on a Latin American Journey*, translated by Alexandra Keeble (New York: Ocean, 2003), 31.

2. Quoted by Nicholas Shakespeare, "*In Patagonia*: An Introduction," in *In Patagonia*, by Bruce Chatwin (New York: Penguin, 2003), ix.

3. Quoted in Nicholas Shakespeare, *Bruce Chatwin* (New York: Nan A. Talese/Doubleday, 1999), 306.

4. Chatwin, *In Patagonia*, 119.

5. Ibid.

6. Luis Borrero, "Early Occupations in the Southern Cone," in *The Handbook of South American Archaeology*, edited by Helaine Silverman and William Isbell, 59–77 (New York: Springer, 2008).

7. Vance Holliday and D. Shane Miller have recently written that Clovis points in North America were significantly older: "The generalized 'Classic Clovis' design (well-crafted lanceolate point partially fluted on both faces and usually made of high-quality raw material) dates to ~13.4k–12.7k cal yr BP (~11,600–10,800 14C yr BP)"; see "The Clovis Landscape," in *PaleoAmerican Odyssey*, edited by Kelly E. Graf, Caroline V. Ketron, and Michael R. Waters, 221–45 (College Station: Texas A&M University Press, 2013), 222.

8. Mathias Currat and Laurent Excoffier, "Modern Humans Did Not Admix with Neanderthals during Their Range Expansion into Europe," *PLoS Biol* 2, no. 12 (2004): e421.

9. For an overview, see Jerry Moore, *A Prehistory of South America: Ancient Cultural Diversity on the Least Known Continent* (Boulder: University Press of Colorado, 2014).

10. Tom Dillehay, *Monuments, Empires, and Resistance: The Araucanian Polity and Ritual Narratives* (Cambridge: Cambridge University Press, 2007).

11. Fernanda Peñaloza, "The Ethnographic Imagination and the Tehuelches," in *Across the Great Divide Conference: Selected Papers from the IV Symbiosis Conference* (Edinburgh: Scotland's Transatlantic Relations Project [STAR], University of Edinburgh, April 2004).

12. George Chaworth Musters, *At Home with the Patagonians: A Year's Wanderings over Untrodden Ground from the Straits of Magellan to the Rio Negro* (London: John Murray, 1871), 132.

13. This is a rough paraphrase from Musters.

14. Laura Oliva Gerstner, "La Linea de Frontera entre 'Bárbaros' y 'Civilizados' en la Argentiga del Siglo XIX: El Caso de la Zanja de Alsina," *Ar@cne: Revista Electrónica de Recursos en Internet Sobre Geografía y Ciencias Sociales* (2010), accessed March 18, 2016, http://www.ub.edu/geocrit/aracne/aracne-138.htm.

15. Quoted in David Maybury-Lewis, "Genocide against Indigenous Peoples," in *Annihilating Difference: The Anthropology of Genocide*, edited by Alexander Hinton, 43–53 (Berkeley: University of California Press, 2002), 45. For an intriguing and polemical discussion of the narratives and images surrounding the Conquest of the Desert, see Jens Andersen "Argentine Literature and the 'Conquest of the Desert,' 1872–1896," accessed July 19, 2014, http://www.bbk.ac.uk/ibamuseum/texts/Andermann02.htm.

16. Daniel Helft and Eliana Raszewski, "Mapuche Tribe Fights to Remove Benetton from Homeland (Update 1)," *Bloomberg News*, November 21, 2005, accessed March 18, 2016, http://unpo.org/article/3357; see also Veronica Smink, "Benetton, uno de los 'dueños' de la Patagonia argentina," BBC Mundo, Argentina, Jueves, 9 de junio de 2011, accessed March 18, 2016, http://www.bbc.co.uk/mundo/noticias/2011/06/110603_argentina_ley_tierra_extranjeros_vs.shtml; Julio Vezub, "Le musée Leleque et le groupe Benetton en Patagonie," *Gradhiva: Revue de Anthropologie e Histoire des Arts*, no. 4 (2006): 53–69, accessed March 18, 2016, https://gradhiva.revues.org/612.

17. See the Museo Leleque website, accessed October 16, 2016, http://web.archive.org/web/20120417193949/http://www.elmaiten.com.ar/museo/htm.

18. Norman Davies, *Europe: A History* (New York: HarperCollins, 1996), 965; see also Robert Conquest, *The Harvest of Sorrow: Soviet Collectivization and the Terror-Famine* (Oxford: Oxford University Press, 1986).

19. Now Argentina's Museo de la Immigración, accessed October 16, 2016, http://untref.edu.ar/muntref/museo-de-la-immigracion.

20. Junius Bird (1907–82) had a long and illustrious career, contributing to a range of topics in South American prehistory. For his work in the tip of South America during the 1930s, see the engrossing account *Travels and Archaeology in South Chile*, edited by John Hyslop (Iowa City: University of Iowa Press, 1988).

21. Junius Bird, "Archaeology of Patagonia," in *Handbook of South American Indians*, vol. 1: *The Marginal Tribes*, edited by Julian Steward, Bulletin 143, 17–24 (Washington, DC: Smithsonian Institution Press, 1944), 22.

22. Junius Bird, "Antiquity and Migrations of the Early Inhabitants of Patagonia," *Geographical Review* 28, no. 2 (1938): 250–75, 275.

23. Philip Kohl and José Antonio Pérez Gollán, "Religion, Politics, and Prehistory: Reassessing the Lingering Legacy of Oswald Menghin," *Current Anthropology* 43, no. 4 (2002): 561–86, 564.

24. Ibid., 563.

25. For a critical review of Bórmida's ideas regarding race, see Rolando Silla, "Raza, raciología y racismo en la obra de Marcelo Bórmida," *Revista del Museo de Antropología* 5 (2012): 65–76.

26. Gustavo Politis, "Comments," *Current Anthropology* 43, no. 4 (2002): 580–81, 581.

27. Kohl and Pérez Gollán, "Religion, Politics, and Prehistory," 564.

28. See Luis Orquera, "Advances in the Archaeology of the Pampa and Patagonia," *Journal of World Archaeology* 1, no. 4 (1987): 333–413.

29. Quoted in Alfredo Prieto, "Patagonian Painted Cloaks: An Ancient Puzzle," in *Patagonia: Natural History, Prehistory, and Ethnography at the Uttermost End of the Earth*, edited by Colin McEwan, Luis Borrero, and Alfredo Prieto, 173–85 (Princeton, NJ: Princeton University Press, 1997), 179.

30. Rodolfo Casamiquela, "Aspectos Históricos II," in *Patagonia: Un Lugar en el Viento*, edited by Marcos Zimmerman, 163–69 (Buenos Aires: Marcos Zimmerman Ediciones, 1988), 167, my translation.

31. George Brook, M. Virginia Mancini, Nora Franco, Florencia Bamonte, and Paulo Ambrústolo, "An Examination of Possible Relationships between Paleoenvironmental Conditions during the Pleistocene-Holocene Transition and Human Occupation of Southern Patagonia (Argentina) East of the Andes, between 46° and 52° S," *Quaternary International* 305 (2013): 104–18.

32. Frank Lamy, Rolf Kilian, Helge W. Arz, Jean-Pierre Francois, Jérôme Kaiser, Matthias Prange, and Tatjana Steinke, "Holocene Changes in the Position and Intensity of the Southern Westerly Wind Belt," *Nature: Geoscience* 3, no. 10 (2010): 695–99, 95, accessed November 11, 2016, http://www.nature.com/ngeo/journal/v3/n10/full/ngeo959.html#auth-7.

33. Ibid., 696.

34. Brook et al., "Examination of Possible Relationships," 109.

35. Luis Alberto Borrero, "The Prehistoric Exploration and Colonization of Fuego-Patagonia," *Journal of World Prehistory* 13, no. 3 (1999): 321–55, 345.

36. Luis Alberto Borrero, "Moving: Hunter-Gatherers and the Cultural Geography of South America," *Quaternary International* (2014): 2, accessed July 8, 2014, http://www.sciencedirect.com/science/article/pii/S1040618214001487.

37. Luis Alberto Borrero, "The Archaeology of the Patagonian Deserts: Hunter-Gatherers in a Cold Desert," in *Desert Peoples: Archaeological Perspectives*, edited

by Peter Veth, Mike Smith, and Peter Hiscock, 142–58 (New York: Wiley-Blackwell, 2005), 144.

38. Ibid., 154.

39. Charles Darwin, *The Voyage of the Beagle* (New York: Barnes and Noble, 2004), 130–31.

40. Gustavo Martinez, Maria Gutiérrez, and Eduardo Tonni, "Paleoenvironments and Faunal Extinctions: Analysis of the Archaeological Assemblages at the Paso Otero Locality (Argentina) during the Late Pleistocene–Early Holocene," *Quaternary International* 299 (2013): 53–63.

41. Carlos J. Gradin, Carlos Aschero, and Ana M. Aguerre, "Arqueología del Área Río Pinturas (Santa Cruz)," *Relaciones de la Sociedad Argentina de Antropología* 13 (1979): 183–227; Carlos J. Gradin, Carlos Aschero, and Ana M. Aguerre, "Primeros niveles culturales en el Area Río Pinturas (provincia de Santa Cruz, Argentina)," *Estudios Atacameños* 8 (1987): 118–41.

42. Alistair Pike, Dirk L. Hoffmann, Marcos Garcia-Diez, Paul B. Pettitt, Jose Alcolea, Rodrigo de Balbin, César Gonzalez-Sainz, Carmen de las Heras, C. José Lasheras, Ramón Montes, and Joao Zilhao, "U-Series Dating of Paleolithic Art in 11 Caves in Spain," *Science* 336, no. 6087 (2012): 1409–13.

43. Robert G. Gunn, "Hand Sizes in Rock Art: Interpreting the Measurements of Hand Stencils and Prints," *Rock Art Research* 23, no. 1 (2006): 97–112.

44. Gradin, Aschero, and Aguerre, "Arqueología del Área Río Pinturas," 198; for discussions of handedness among traditional societies, see Charlotte Faurie, Wulf Schiefenhövel, Sylvie le Bomin, Sylvain Billiard, and Michel Raymond, "Variation in the Frequency of Left-handedness in Traditional Societies," *Current Anthropology* 46, no. 1 (2005): 142–47; left-handedness varied in the four ethnographic cases from 3.3 percent to 26.9 percent. For an analysis of handedness in Upper Paleolithic rock art from France and Spain, see Charlotte Faurie and Michel Raymond, "Handedness Frequency over More Than 10,000 Years," *Proceedings of the Royal Society of London* B271 (2004): S43–S45, where analysis of 343 unambiguous images of hands identified 79 right negative hands for an estimate of 23 percent left-handers. See also Jean-Michel Chazine, "Some Clues from Borneo for Deciphering Hand Stencils," in *International Federation of Rock Art Organizations 2013 Proceedings, American Indian Rock Art* 40: 363–72 (Glendale, AZ: American Rock Art Association, 2013); Dean Snow, "Sexual Dimorphism in Upper Palaeolithic Hand Stencils," *Antiquity* 80 (2006): 390–404.

CHAPTER FIVE

Land Lines

Arid plains do not dream.

RAÚL ZURITA, *The Desert of Atacama VI*

THE ATACAMA DESERT IS THE DRIEST DESERT IN THE WORLD. Parts of the Atacama have not been splashed by a raindrop in recorded history. Northern Chile is particularly arid. Away from a few narrow river valleys, the landscape is barren of vegetation and nearly empty of life. In portions of the Atacama, soil samples are absolutely lifeless even at the microbial level, the only place on Earth where this is true.[1] The wind scrapes. The gravelly sand is gray. The distant hills are slate, and the deep-blue sky is fringed by a fog bank climbing from the Pacific Ocean to the west. There are few traces of human lives, except for the lines on the land that brought me to this desolate place thousands of miles from my home.

It is October 2009, and I am here with my friend, the poet and essayist Bill Fox. Bill's thirteen non-fiction books and innumerable essays orbit around issues of how people make sense of landscape, an intentionally broad topic he has explored in such different places as the Great Basin, the Central Desert of Australia, and Antarctica. Seven years before, Bill and I met as fellows at the Getty Research Institute, where we immediately realized that we had a lot to talk about. Our divergent interests intersect at many points, and those conversations have continued over the last fifteen years.

Which is why we were in Chile. We flew north 1,100 km from Santiago to the port and mining center of Antofagasta, where I had reserved a 4×4 Chevrolet pickup at the airport. We stopped at a mini-mart and bought four gallons of drinking water. I traveled with a duffle bag packed with duct tape, vise grips, a Leatherman™, a machete, an entrenching tool, and other stuff for emergency repairs. We left Antofagasta following the coast, drove east through a coastal chain of hills before joining the Pan-American Highway, and traveled south about 40 km where we turned off the pavement and headed southwest into an unnamed arroyo. Using my Garmin GPS, Bill and I calculated our route, tracing a graded gravel road past nitrate test borings and tailing piles. We followed our bearings and best guesses to the south until we spotted a small triangular dry lake bed, shimmering alkaline in the desert sun, which we recognized from our Google Earth research. I turned off the engine and let the truck roll to a stop. We were enveloped in dry silence. Just north of us, we saw low berms and broad, shallow trenches bulldozed into the desert.

We were at the location of the longest poem in the world. It is a four-word poem that stretches over 3 km, the creation of the Chilean poet Raúl Zurita. The poem in its entirety reads, "*ni pena, ni miedo*," or "without pain, without fear." Born in 1951, Zurita was swept up in the repression that followed the 1973 overthrow of Salvador Allende and the dictatorship of Augusto Pinochet. Initially imprisoned with hundreds of other political prisoners in the pitch-black hold of a ship, after his release Zurita used his art as a tool of resistance. This geoglyph is one result.

"Geoglyph" is an elastic term, stretched to cover a wide variety of human-made works on the ground: figures, ritual pathways, labyrinths, intaglios, and other forms. As with so many inscriptions on the landscape—whether mounds, rock art, roadbeds, or tombs—most geoglyphs are simultaneously obviously human and profoundly unknowable. Ironically, this remote poem carved into the Atacama Desert is the most literal and oddly accessible example of a geoglyph I have ever seen. In Zurita's case, we know about the contexts surrounding this work: the tortures and disappearances during the seventeen years of the Pinochet regime, the response and resistance that poetry reflects, and the capacity for works of art to respond profoundly to human events of enormous scale—whether genocides or broken hearts. Of his poetry in general, Zurita commented, "Art draws attention to things of this magnitude. Poetry is something like the hope for that which has no hope."[2]

Yet with all of the available information about this poem inscribed in the Atacama Desert, neither Bill nor I anticipated the physical beauty and sculptural impact of Zurita's poem.[3] The letters are carved in an elegant cursive script flowing through the sand. The stems and arcs of each letter are formed by broad flat trenches, about 40–60 cm deep and 6–8 m wide and flanked by crisp berms about a meter tall. The work is surprisingly sculptural in execution, and it is deeply affecting. The berm edges are spiked with evenly spaced stakes that once guided the grunts and cuts of the bulldozer, undoubtedly driven by a man more accustomed to carving roadbeds and causeways than cursive letters but whose pragmatic expertise was brilliantly turned to art.

Bill stepped over a berm and into the broad shaft of the first "n" and began walking the poem, later writing, "The land turns to prose under my feet."[4] I climbed a small hill to the south to look at the poem. The wind ruffled softly. At the distant edge of the playa, an intense mirage shimmered blue, echoing the Pacific Ocean further west. Other than the poem itself, there were few signs of human action. Rare footpaths headed toward the ocean. I find the base walls of a three-sided windbreak with a sawed cow bone from an encampment sometime in the recent past. The sun-dried carcass of a horned toad baked on a stone. These were the only signs of life: except—of course—for Bill, me, and the poem.

Along much of the west coast of South America, ancient humans sculpted the earth. From northern Chile to far northern Peru, geoglyphs are found over a stretch of more than 2,600 km along the Pacific Coast.[5] These creations are often on desert pavements where sand layers are capped by a layer of pebbles or cobbles coated with a thin layer of clay and iron or manganese known as "desert varnish." The geoglyphs were made in one of two ways: either by scraping away the desert pavement to expose the lighter soils underneath or by gathering together the overlying stones to create forms. That much is clear. Beyond that, a great deal remains unknown.

Some geoglyphs have astronomical alignments, but the vast majority are lines untethered to stars, including depictions of humans, animals, and other undecipherable beings. For example, in the Santa Valley on the North Coast of Peru, the archaeologist David Wilson recorded two groups of geoglyphs, one set in the lower valley about 19 km inland and another set about 35 km inland in the upper valley.[6] Both groups

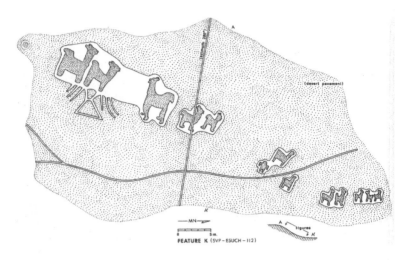

FEATURE K (SVP–ESUCH–112)

were made on hillsides and were created by removing desert pavement to expose the lighter sediments beneath (although with the additional touch of adding small stones to clearly define the edges of the exposures) and by mounding stones together. The problems of understanding geoglyphs become clear just by looking at the two groups of geoglyphs in the lower Santa Valley.

One group spreads over 130 m and depicts a man with a herd of llamas. The man and llamas were made by piling stones to form the figures, leaving surrounding fields of exposed soil. The figures are interpretable at a glance—but then, less obvious points emerge. For example, most of the llamas are "naturalistic" (their backs and bellies sway), but the man and the two llamas nearby are more geometric and angular. Were the llamas and man all made at once or at different times? It is impossible to know. A long, sinuous line trails between the llamas and the man. Does this depict a road to the highlands? Again, impossible to know. A straight, cleared line less than 50 cm wide cuts across the sinuous line and the central pair of llamas, approximately aligned with the transit of the sun; the line was clearly made after the llama it crosses, but what does it mean? To conclude with a final enigma, the largest group of llamas was created on top of an earlier geoglyph, destroying it except for

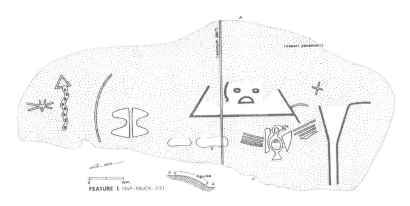

FEATURE L (SVP-ESUCH-112)

what appear to be a set of tail feathers and wingtips, possibly a depiction of a condor. Was this an intentional act of destruction, an ancient iconoclastic gesture, or simply a matter of neglect and disregard? We do not know.

Similar uncertainties become even more prominent when we look at another set of Santa Valley geoglyphs made by both removing and mounding desert pavement but with very different results. Covering about 120 m × 20 m, this group of geoglyphs also has the overlain straight path oriented to the sun's passage. An avian figure interpreted as a condor is similar to the triangular tail feathers in the other group of geoglyphs. But at this point, the images dissolve into doubts. What is the Y-shaped alignment of stones so carefully cleared at the south end of the group? What are those traces of eyes and downturned mouth in the incomplete triangle? What is the significance of the bi-lobed and mirrored cleared forms? Are the cross and starburst representations of constellations? What are the blobs that look like incomplete speech balloons in a cartoon or the two elegant and incomplete curves? And what is the triangular-headed, snake-like line that is 16 m long, spotted with mounded piles of stone? To describe this group of geoglyphs as "enigmatic" is unduly precise.

Most archaeologists would contend that such efforts at interpreting the forms of geoglyphs are misguided—unless other sources of information are available, such as historical accounts or ethnographic records. Even "obvious" forms might have hidden implications, such as in the geoglyphs depicting the man and llamas.

An alternative approach is to try to understand the people who made the geoglyphs and uncover how those creations were incorporated into their lives. This approach has been used by archaeologists working in the Atacama Desert in far northern Chile. Geoglyphs have been recorded in the region since the early nineteenth century. In 1826 the British antiquarian and geologist William Bollaert recorded

> curious ancient Indian remains called "Pintados," or Indian Pictography, found in the province of Tarapaca . . . consisting of representations of Indians, llamas, dogs, and other forms, on the side of the desert ravine, some of the figures being thirty feet or more in height, cut, or rather scraped out in the sandy soil, the lines being twelve to eighteen inches broad, and six to eight inches deep. I was then informed they were the work of "Indios Gentiles," or old pagan Indians, and I thought that the Pintados had been done by ancient and modern Indians for amusement; but I have now reason to believe, that some of them mark burial places, places of worship, and to preserve memorials of the past.[7]

Since these early observations, more than 5,000 geoglyphs have been recorded in the deserts between Antofagasta and Chile's border with Peru, especially in the provinces of Tarapacá and Antofagasta. Extraordinarily difficult to date, the earliest geoglyphs may date to approximately 400 BC, although most seem to have been created between AD 900 and 1450.[8] Although some are isolated, most geoglyphs are associated with ancient roads traveled by people herding caravans of llamas—some on trading journeys or migrations to pasturage and others perhaps on pilgrimage.

Networks of ancient roads crisscrossed northern Chile, with many routes between the Pacific Ocean and the Andes that connected the arid coastal deserts to the high, treeless puna. Other roads ran north-south, anchored by river valleys and oases that were sources of water and pasturage. Knowledge of the locations of these vital resources was key to survival in the Atacama Desert, and the geoglyphs indicate this

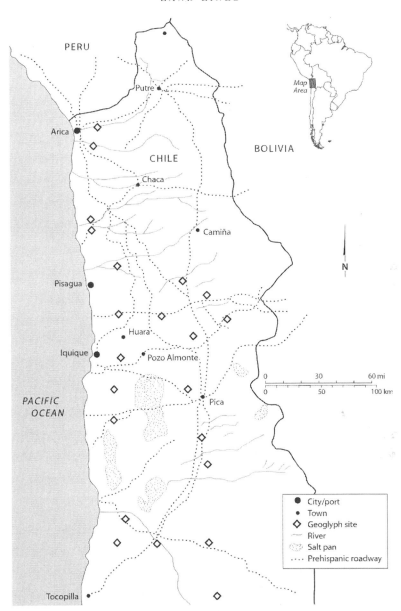

perception and understanding of the harsh environment. The Chilean archaeologist Luis Briones observes that all the geoglyphs are next to roads and campsites, accompanied by other features made from stones:

windbreaks, corrals, *markas* (stone cairns on the horizon marking the route), and *apachetas* (large piles of rocks on mountain passes or route junctions where travelers add stones in gestures of thanksgiving or atonement).[9] The geoglyphs themselves have different forms. Many are geometric motifs reminiscent of shapes seen in ancient textiles and pottery: circles, dots, lines, and spirals. A notable geometric motif is a "stepped rhombus," also known as the Andean cross, or *chakana*, as variants of this shape were used by various Andean cultures including the Chimú, the Tiwanaku, and the Incas; it is also similar to the labyrinth motif on Mapuche shamans' drums and is found in Patagonian rock art as a symbol for the path to Paradise.

Distinct motifs are found in different portions of the landscape. Circle motifs are generally found on terraces and other flat surfaces above 1,500 m, while arrows are found on open, flat sectors of the desert. Other motifs are zoomorphic and anthropomorphic. The zoomorphs are often quite detailed and recognizable from a "bird's-eye" view. Not surprisingly, geoglyphs depict llama caravans, some with as many as eighty animals in a line. The lizard is prominently depicted, with one reptilian geoglyph stretching over 50 m. A surprising number of the animals are associated with water or the sea, including flamingos, seagulls, dolphins, toads, and sharks, while other geoglyphs portray eagles, foxes, monkeys, and dogs. The anthropomorphic motifs are often sketchy and stylized. Some of the human figures stand with arms raised as if in adoration or greeting, while others are engaged in hunting, fishing, or sex. Yet the vast majority of these motifs are static, whether depicting animals or people, and only the geoglyphs of llama caravans are regularly shown as dynamic.

Briones argues that these geoglyphs were an integral part of prehistoric people's adaptations to the Atacama Desert: "From the first explorations of the Atacama desert, humans were forced to adopt careful solutions for survival."[10] With the domestication of the llama as a pack animal, "They were able to increase their knowledge of the regional geography and its various extreme environments like the

puna, cordilleras, gullies, pampas and salt flats, and to reach points that were both remote and difficult."[11] Based on their knowledge about the location and dependability of water and pasturage, the people of the Atacama Desert created "a complex *network of paths* . . . that crossed the different geographical regions of the desert. In the face of this challenging reality, people frequently turned naturally to religion, and laid down messages, memories and rites related to it."[12] In short, these geoglyphs were not simply *placed* on the landscape; they were creations that *became* the landscape of the Atacama Desert.

Ⅱ

In his engaging and innovative book *Lines: A Brief History*, the anthropologist Tim Ingold distinguishes between two types of movement across landscape: *transport* and *wayfaring*. "Transport," Ingold writes, "is destination oriented. It is not so much a development along a way of life as a carrying across, from location to location, of people and goods in such a way as to leave their basic natures unaffected."[13] Transport is what occurs when goods are loaded into container vessels and shipped from Shanghai to the port of Los Angeles or (to use another Southern California example) when I get in my car and drive on LA freeways, arriving at my destination unchanged except for my elevated blood pressure. As Ingold describes, "The transported traveler becomes a passenger, who does not himself move but is rather moved from place to place."[14]

Wayfaring is different. "The wayfarer is continually on the move," Ingold writes. "More strictly, he is his movement."[15] The wayfarer moves across a landscape of experience, not simply a progression from one spatial coordinate to another but rather a movement through the world. Borrowing the concept of *meshwork* from Henri Lefebrve's *The Social Production of Space*, Ingold writes, "While on the trail the wayfarer is always somewhere, yet every 'somewhere' is on the way to somewhere else. The inhabited world is a reticulate meshwork of such trails, which is continually being woven as life goes on along them."[16]

Ingold cites ethnographer Benjamin Orlove's beautiful book *Lines in the Water: Nature and Culture in Lake Titicaca*. Orlove writes, "It was not on the first or second look through my photographs, but only much later, that I noticed how frequently paths and roads appeared in them. My position as an outsider and my work . . . led me to travel more than many people do in the altiplano, but the paths and roads, I realized, form an integral part of the landscape for the villagers as well as for a foreign anthropologist."[17] The pathways and roads surrounding Lake Tititcaca, "thousands of kilometers of them, form a network that covers the altiplano: a web of lines on the land. Most of them are barely a meter wide, beaten or trodden by the feet of animals and men and women, and also of children, who, by the age of three or four, trot along uncomplainingly to keep up with the adults, whether for a short walk to a relative's house or a field, or for half a day's hike to a distant pasture or market. Some of the lines are quite literally drawn in the earth by villagers working with picks and shovels."[18] More than merely conduits for transport, "As lines on the land along which people walk, paths have a material existence," Orlove writes. "Their physicality and their unbreakable association with movement and travel allow them to stand for other, less tangible lines and movement. One can think of metaphorical paths as lines through time rather than space: paths as sequences, not of places, or, more precisely, not only of places, but of the events and phases that mark an individual's life."[19]

Moving across these paths and routes, the wayfarer—according to Ingold—"is a being who, in following a path of life, negotiates or improvises a passage as he goes *along*. In his movement as in life, his concern is to seek a way through: not to reach a specific destination or terminus but to keep on going."[20] This suggests that our efforts to decipher the meaning of the geoglyphs in the Santa Valley are probably misplaced. Looking at those creations made by sweeping and piling stones as if they were symbols encoding stable meanings (like the words in this sentence) only contributes to our confusions because it extracts the geoglyphs from the lives and landscapes in which they were made. It is a well-worn adage in archaeology that "context is everything," and this is no less true for artifacts and sites than it is for lines on the land.

Ancient South Americans not only made lines in deserts, but some of the most intriguing geoglyphs on the continent come from recent discoveries in Amazonia. Initially spotted in the late 1990s by the geographer Alceu Ranzi, who was flying in a small plane above his farm in the state of Acre, Brazil, these geoglyphs consist of trenches in geometric shapes, such as circles or squares.[21] The Amazonian geoglyphs were discovered as the jungle was cleared for farming and ranching. Similarly, the long trenches must have been dug when the area had been at least partially cleared of trees, although it is unknown whether this was a result of human deforestation or climate change. But as the pace of modern deforestation has increased and as satellite imagery has become more accessible with Google Earth, the number of known Amazonian earthworks has grown. For example, 200 sites with 210 earthworks have been recorded from an area of about 250 km^2 in western Brazil. Similar

geoglyphs are recorded from the adjacent regions of lowland Bolivia, making a total of approximately 300 geometric earthworks. Since only about 10 percent of this area has been cleared, many more geoglyphs probably exist in the region. In turn, this strongly implies that the prehistoric population of Amazonia—a vast region once thought to be largely unoccupied by ancient humans—was much greater than previously estimated.[22]

Most earthwork trenches are about 11 m wide and 1 m to 3 m deep, and they are bordered by berms up to a meter high. The circular earthworks have diameters of 90 m to 300 m. A circular geoglyph 200 m in diameter would require moving 8,000 m³ of soil, a task that would occupy eighty people for several months.[23] The oldest known earthworks are about 3,000 years old, and they continued to be constructed into the fourteenth century AD, suggesting the existence of "a continuous, collective regional tradition."[24] In turn, many of these earthworks are associated with roads and causeways that link specific sites, constructions that point to the movements and interconnections of people.

And yet, no one is quite certain what these geoglyphs *are*. The areas enclosed by earthworks lack traces of dwellings and have scant evidence of human occupation. Unlike other areas of Amazonia where ring villages were enclosed by defensive palisades, the enclosures in Acre do not contain dense deposits of potsherds, middens, or dwellings.[25] Instead, excavations in western Amazonia earthworks found only a few potsherds, fragments of stone tools, and chunks of burned clay—and these were in the bases of the trenches and not in the central open space—and no palisades or fortifications like those at tropical sites across South America.[26] Another intriguing bit of evidence: at the Fazenda Atlântica site, the archaeologist Sanna Saunaluoma excavated a small mound that had been built on one side of a 250 m × 250 m rectangular enclosure. The mound was less than 1.6 m tall and only 15 m in diameter, but it was made by intentionally heaping layers of dark soil and sherd-filled midden. Before the mound was built, an "offering" was made consisting of a large bowl, the uncharred but very fragmented bones of an agouti and other unidentified animals, and some chunks of burned clay. These items were intentionally placed, but their purpose and meaning are utterly obscure.

The geoglyphs of western Amazonia are more numerous and extensive than previously imagined. They were built at various times over three millennia, probably by speakers of different languages and members of different ethnic groups who nonetheless had this as a common tradition. The specific purposes of the enclosures remain unclear. They do not seem to have an astronomical function. Unlike the Atacama geoglyphs, the geometric earthworks are not associated with major transportation routes, and many of the sites are far from navigable rivers. There is little evidence that the enclosures were densely inhabited and no evidence that they were fortified. Essentially, the geoglyphs are interpreted by default as ceremonial or ritual structures.

Saunaluoma and the ethnographer Pirjo Kristiina Virtanen observe, "In contemporary Amazonian indigenous villages, infrastructure construction, such as arranging and maintaining plazas used for public meetings, rituals, and sportive events, is a communal undertaking. We believe that building geometric enclosures was a collective effort requiring a certain amount of persons, but in contrast to contemporary communities, [it] certainly involved a firmly organized social unit larger than a few families."[27] Given the size of the geometric enclosures, a hundred or more people probably dug the ditches and built the mounds, their work carefully planned to form elegant, precise shapes. In turn, these workers undoubtedly belonged to dozens of families, so a large community was directly and indirectly involved in the effort. This much seems clear. Perhaps the large geometric earthworks were special fields for dances, ceremonies, or competitive games—enclosed areas swept clean of debris.

But Virtanen suggests another intriguing, although unproven, idea. Across Amazonia, *ayahuasca* is a hallucinogenic brew commonly used by shamans—as well as by tourists on "spiritual drug vacations"—made from the psychoactive vine *Banisteriopsis caapi* and other ingredients. Some indigenous communities living in Acre state that ayahuasca produces geometric hallucinations associated with deities or ancestors. Virtanen reports that a young Manchineri man drew an image he had seen in an ayahuasca vision; it was strikingly similar to a satellite image of a geometric earthwork. The young man interpreted the photo of the earthwork as "the 'vehicle' of a palm spirit." "According to the Manchineri people," Virtanen writes, "the shamanic visions come from entities such as palm spirits, one of the most powerful non-human beings in Manchineri sociocosmology. These visions, similar to dreams, provide an important source of knowledge from non-human beings. The visions allow transformation through the interaction with non-humans whose real nature and forms are expressed. They are experienced at a very personal level and represent a totalizing image of the world."[28] The Manchineri see a close relationship between palm trees and the origins of humans and non-humans; the connection between palms and forest spirits is revealed by ayahuasca. These are accompanied by the appearance of geometric designs—circles, squares, and triangles—that "become visible only when the person interacts with non-human beings."[29] Although the Manchineri do not construct geometric earthworks, they do use geometric motifs on cotton cloth, pottery, and body paint. Circles are related to celestial bodies, while squares "are associated with resistance or sameness," with squares more prominent among the Manchineri and circles more significant to Apuriná to the north—a pattern also seen in the spatial distribution of geoglyphs.[30]

Currently, the meanings and purposes of the geoglyphs in western Amazonia are unknown. Archaeological research into the geoglyphs is just beginning; fewer than a dozen geoglyphs have been excavated. It may be that we will never fully understand the meanings and significances of these creations. Even after extensive studies, some geoglyphs seem to resist interpretation, including the most famous South American geoglyphs: the Nasca lines.

Deserts, like all landscapes, have their own languages that archaeologists must master.

CLIVE RUGGLES AND NICHOLAS SAUNDERS, "DESERT LABYRINTH," 1138.

On June 8, 2015, I stand on a low hill just west of the Pan-Americana Sur in the middle of the Pampa de Nasca in southern Peru. Less than

2 km to the east is a chain of naked stone mountains of gray and rust. The Pacific Ocean is 45 km to the west, but the low relief of the pampa appears to stretch to infinity. The pampa is covered by a layer of rocks, tinted with iron oxides and ranging from russet to coal black. Underneath the stones is an ashen deposit of sand.

As I climb the hill, I see a small segment of order just a few stones long, but as I ascend the line resolves with greater precision. It is a narrow vector of swept stones only 30 cm wide, slicing northeast across the pampa in a perfect straight line to the base of a ridgeline, running 3.3

km at a precise azimuth of 355° before breaching the ridge and dropping into the Ingenio Valley, one of several small rivers that allowed
people to live in a desert without rain. As I look around more, I realize
that numerous prehistoric lines run to and from this small hill. None
meander. All are intentional and elegant. Some of the lines continue for
11 km. The prehistoric lines lack indecision. They are specific, careful,
and made.

The Pampa de Nasca contains one of the largest concentrations of
geoglyphs on Earth. The pampa covers about 500 km². Most geoglyphs
were made between 200 and 150 BC and AD 600–640.[31] Over 1,500
geoglyphs have been recorded, including several hundred recently discovered. The most famous geoglyphs depict animals and other creatures: the Hummingbird, the Monkey, and the Condor, among others.
Some geoglyphs were made by removing stones and exposing the
light-covered desert floor; other images were created by piling rocks
together or creating fields of stones. And here is another point, easily
overlooked: although it is frequently stated that the Nasca geoglyphs
are only visible from the air, this is not true. The lines are visible from
higher ground—like the hill where I stand—and they were also visible
at ground level: as paths, routes, and vectors. These lines were made
not only to be *seen* but to be *experienced*, linking people from the various river valleys to the enormous ceremonial center at Cahuachi, the
largest and most elaborate Nasca site located on the Río Nasca, consisting of elite residences, mounds, and cemeteries sprawling over 150
hectares.[32] Not all geoglyphs had the same purpose, shared the same
form, or were made in the same manner. Later geoglyphs crosscut and
partially destroyed earlier lines. Yet they have this point in common:
people inscribed the desert surface with their actions and movements
across the Pampa de Nasca.

The archaeologists Clive Ruggles and Nicholas Saunders reconstructed one segment of geoglyphs not from the air but from the ground
by walking a specific set of lines. They self-deprecatingly refer to their
research as "a piece of straightforward brilliance on the part of our
authors: get down on the ground, where the original users were, and

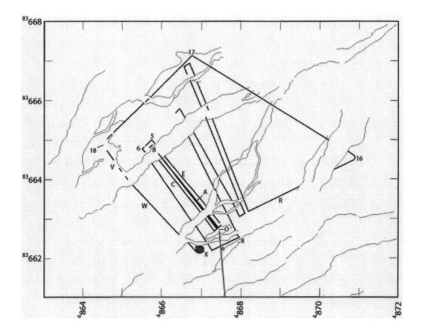

see where your feet lead you."[33] Ruggles and Saunders identified an odd combination of connected lines anchored to a small hill, a line center where many other geoglyphs intersect. Beginning as a 5.5-m-wide path to the northwest, the first segment continues for 280 m—narrowing to only 1.1 m, doubling back to the southeast, and paralleling the initial segment before reversing directions once again and returning to the southeast. At ground level, each turn establishes a new and unexpected vector. At this point the labyrinth becomes two sets of roughly parallel paths each 350 m long that run northwest-southeast before hiking east for almost 300 m, turning northwest for half a kilometer, making a left turn to the southwest for 325 m and then a final left turn to the southeast for another 350 m, only to culminate in a tight spiral whose coils are only 50 cm wide. Having walked approximately 4 km, the pilgrim ends up only 60 m from the start.

Several important—and somewhat obvious—inferences can be made. First, this geoglyph is not obviously representative. Unlike the famous Hummingbird or other zoomorphic geoglyphs on the Nasca plain, this labyrinthine set of paths was not meant to be visualized from above or imaginatively reconstructed as a "bird's-eye" view. Second, the lines are not oriented to astronomical events or distant mountain peaks, nor do they lead from one valley to another; this geoglyph is determinedly internal, meant to be walked and experienced rather than referencing something else. Third, this geoglyph is labyrinth but not a maze. It has no dead-ends or cul-de-sacs. It is not designed to mislead. Finally, the pathways may have been walked by groups of people, but the final segments could only be transited by people moving in single file.

Not all the Nasca lines are like this apparent labyrinth, but all were designed to be seen and experienced from ground level. Although it is claimed that the lines were first noticed by pilots carrying mail between Lima and Santiago, the first documented study was in 1927 by the Peruvian archaeologist Toribio Mejia Xesspe (1896–1983), who spotted the lines while hiking in the hills east of the pampa. The American historian Paul Kosok (1896–1959) is usually credited with initiating scientific research into the lines, research that was continued for five decades by Maria Reiche (1903–98). Kosok and Reiche interpreted the Nasca lines as linked to astronomical events, such as solstices or the appearance of particular constellations. Subsequent research suggests that although some lines may have astronomical associations, the vast majority do not. The archaeologist Johan Reinhard has argued that some of the geoglyphs point to distant mountain peaks, the source of precious water and the dwellings of the *apu*.[34] Again, some of the glyphs may have been linked to water rituals, but others have no obvious connection.

A more recent explanation by the archaeologist Masato Sakai is based on his ongoing research.[35] Since 2007, Sakai and his team have discovered 198 new lines and 149 line centers on the Pampa de Nasca using satellite imagery and in some cases enhanced with 3-D imagery to capture subtle surface traces. Combined with existing data on geoglyphs, Sakai proposes that some of the geoglyphs are associated with distinct pilgrimage routes that link different portions of the Nasca

Valley and the Ingenio Valley to the north. These geoglyphs were made in two ways, either by removing stones from the body of the geoglyph but using them to mark eyes or mouths (Type A) or by piling stones to make the form of the geoglyphs (Type B). These geoglyphs depicted various animals and were placed on hillsides that were highly visible, designed to be seen from ritual paths between the upper Ingenio and Nasca Valleys. As Cahuachi developed into the most prominent ritual center in the region, the pilgrimage routes shifted to the west on the Nasca Plain, and the functions of the geoglyphs may have changed. If the earlier geoglyphs were meant to be seen by passing pilgrims, the later geoglyphs became places of worship as devotees walked the lines and made offerings of elegant polychrome pottery at line centers, intentionally smashing jars on the stones. Many of the best-known Nasca geoglyphs were made during Cahuachi's ascendancy—images portraying enormous hummingbirds, killer whales, condors, and other mythological figures. And while these figures were meant to be experienced at ground level, I—like thousands of other tourists—wanted to see them from the air.

Π

The Nasca airport is named for Maria Reiche, and the terminal is about the size of a laundromat. No international or domestic flights land there, and it exclusively serves the half-dozen tour agencies that fly small planes over the Nasca lines. Flights leave in the morning before the thermal updrafts develop. I was at the AeroParacas counter by 8 a.m. and paid for my half-hour flight. Despite its size, the terminal was exceedingly chaotic as booking agents scurried around trying to fill flights, shifting passengers from one agency to another so every plane had a minimum of five tourists. For unknown reasons, I was repeatedly asked to present my passport—when I bought my ticket, which was normal, and three more times as my name was checked against the passenger manifest; as I moved from the general waiting room to a smaller "security" zone; and as I boarded the flight. (I had to show my passport more times to fly over the Nasca lines than I did to enter Peru.) The airport's disorder was underscored by three television monitors showing the same video, *Nasca Lines: The Buried Secrets,* a National Geographic Society film that highlights the research of the archaeologist and my friend, Dr. Christina Conlee. The video is actually quite good, but the three monitors were slightly unsynchronized, so the airport had three overlapping fields of the echoing dialogue "Living in a harsh desert environment . . . Living in a harsh desert environment . . . Living in a harsh desert environment" or of Christina intoning "Taking a human head is a powerful act . . . Taking a human head is a powerful act . . . Taking a human head is a powerful act." This all contributed to a sense of vertigo even before I left *terra firma.*

This vertiginous feeling was underscored as four tourists from Japan and Germany and I folded ourselves into the Cessna and the co-pilot asked, "None of you ate breakfast, did you?" I admitted to having had a bread roll and a cup of coffee. "Oh well" the co-pilot shook her head. "There are barf bags in front of you." This was duly noted.

We taxied to the end of the runway and took off into the west and over the irrigated fields bordering the Río Nasca before banking over the vast desert. As has happened to me elsewhere and before, there are moments in my journeys when I visit a well-known and much-photographed archaeological site or landscape—for example, Machu Picchu or the Amazon River—yet seeing it with my own eyes is a profoundly exciting moment. As much as I have looked at satellite images and photographs of the Nasca lines, I was still deeply moved by their scale and beauty.

The desert is bare except for small clumps of leafless ephedra that grow in the long-dry washes that scroll down from the mountains. The pampa seems infinite. The pilot flies on a choreographed route, a "greatest hits" tour of the most famous geoglyphs: the Monkey, the Hummingbird, the Condor, the Llama, and the "Spaceman" (an anthropomorphic with bulbous, helmet-like head). Our cameras snap. As we fly above each figure, the pilot alternately turns the Cessna into tight corkscrews—first left, then right—so tourists sitting on both sides of the plane can take unobstructed pictures of the lines. Thus the barf bags.

I am enchanted by the huge figures, but I am intrigued by two other sets of geoglyphs: the long, straight footpaths and triangular and rect-angular areas cleared of stones. The footpaths are unnecessarily straight, as if plotted with an enormous ruler across the pampas. This rigid lin-earity contrasts with more recent trails and roads that snake across the desert. Simply navigating the landscape does not require such undevi-ating rigidity. The roan and black hilltops flanking the pampa are highly visible landmarks, and the location of the Nasca Valley is marked by the enormous Cerro Blanco, which at more than 2,000 m in elevation is claimed to be the tallest sand dune in the world. It would be very dif-ficult to get lost in this desert. The long, straight lines were not simply a matter of way-finding but rather a gesture of place-making.

And so were the large areas cleared of stones, geoglyphs that are nei-ther figurative nor footpaths. Some of the cleared areas are enormous triangles and trapezoids that merge into broad vectors. Among the largest is a rectangular area 858 m long and averaging 95 m wide that runs ENE × WSW.[36] The rectangle is edged with a border of stones that cuts over earlier lines, including one of the most famous geoglyphs, the

Condor, whose tail feathers were clipped by the rectangle's edge. At the west end of the rectangle is a large pile of stones about 8 m in diameter, which looks like an apacheta but fundamentally resists interpretation.

These lines, these indisputably human creations, have been the subjects of rampant interpretation, but some points seem clear. Some of the geoglyphs predate the emergence of Nasca culture, while some of the motifs etched into the ground—such as the Killer Whale—are also found on Nasca pottery. The offerings of Nasca pottery at line centers point to the use of some of the lines as ritual paths and labyrinths, and the shifts in the orientations of the lines occurred as Cahuachi became the prominent ceremonial center in the region. When Cahuachi declined as a result of environmental degradation—possibly by overpopulation, deforestation, and El Niño flooding—and when the Wari Empire expanded into the region, new lines were made across the desert, at least for a while. But here is an interesting point: at some point the practice of making these geoglyphs was abandoned. For example, the Incas did not made geoglyphs in Nasca, despite being a culture deeply engaged in the creation of lines and profoundly interested in ritual and landscape. The lines were known but misunderstood. In 1553 the Spanish chronicler Pedro Cieza de Leon wrote of "the beautiful and great road of the Incas" that passed through Nasca, observing that "on some of the sand dunes are seen signs that indicate the road" for travelers.[37] The lines crisscrossing the plains of Nasca remained in the desert, unseen and silent.

In his book *Aereality*, Bill Fox discusses the process and assumptions involved in viewing landscape from above. Although the bird's-eye view has become commonplace since the twentieth-century development of commercial flight, Fox writes, "aerial images are now more important than ever to study as aesthetic objects within the broader range of visual culture, precisely because they are so widespread in their use and influence," requiring that we "understand why and how we accord such authority to views elevated literally and figuratively above all others."[38] Although the aerial perspective may have proliferated in the twentieth century, it long predates the development of aircraft. As

Fox notes, the aerial perspective is present in the famous mural from the Turkish site of Çatalhöyük dating to 6,200±97 BC, in which the settlement is shown from above and the eruption of the Hasan Dağı volcano is shown in profile (an interpretation confirmed in 2014 by geological evidence).[39] Numerous non-Western traditions incorporate an aerial perspective, from Australian aboriginal art to navigational "stick-maps" used by Pacific Islanders.[40] As Tim Ingold observes, "The vast majority of maps that have ever been drawn by human beings have scarcely survived the immediate contexts of their production," yet there are sufficient examples to indicate the universality and chronological depth of the bird's-eye view.[41] This aerial perspective, Fox suggests, is "actually a normative one, something we [do] all the time without necessarily being conscious of it."[42]

In the preface to his collection of elegant images of the Nasca lines taken over the last thirty years, the American photographer and Andeanist Edward Ranney writes:

In spite of the information provided by aerial views, it seems to me there is still much to be gained by seeing and experiencing the lines on ground level, as their creators did. Since I first made photographs of the pampa some thirty years ago, one of my particular interests has been to explore how geoglyphs in different areas of the coastal desert occupy and alter space on ground level. In addition to their perceptual qualities, the lines can be seen as a form of mapping, marking reference points and connections within the landscape, thereby transforming a harsh natural environment into an understandable, even intimate cultural space . . . It is unlikely that we will ever definitively know what the geoglyphs meant to their creators. But what is clear is they mark places—and times—of significance. This minimal landscape continues to reveal to us a fragile record of its human occupation. It is a record of elusive meaning, a unique equivocation of the inalterable connection between humans and nature.[43]

The aerial perspective reflected in ancient South American geoglyphs—whether in the Atacama Desert, western Amazonia, or the plains of Nasca—are not really about a breakthrough in seeing the Earth from above. What these images represent are human inscriptions that transformed space into place, land into landscape.

NOTES

1. William Fox, "Re: Marking the Land: Excerpted Notes from the Atacama," in *Incubo: The Atacama Lab*, 49–95 (Santiago, Chile: Incubo, 2008), 51.

2. Daniel Borutsky, "Today or a Million Years Ago: An Interview with Raúl Zurita," in *Harriet: A Poetry Blog* (2015), accessed July 7, 2015, http://www.poetry foundation.org/harriet/2015/03/today-or-a-million-years-ago-an-interview-with -raul-zurita/. See also Daniel Borutsky, "Written on the Sky: Chilean Poet Raúl Zurita Talks about Life after Pinochet," *Poetry Foundation* (2010), accessed July 7, 2015, http://www.poetryfoundation.org/article/239920.

3. The poem can be seen on GoogleEarth at S24° 02'42" (latitude) W 70°26'42" (longitude).

4. William Fox, "In the Desert of Redemption," *Volume* 31 (2012): 106–11, 109.

5. Aurelio Rodríguez Rodríguez, *Los campos de geoglifos en la costa central del Perú*, Cuadernos de Investigación 2 (Lima: Pontificia Universidad Católica, Instituto Riva-Agüero, 1997).

6. David Wilson, "Desert Ground Drawings in the Lower Santa Valley, North Coast of Peru," *American Antiquity* 53, no. 4 (1988): 794–804.

7. William Bollaert, *Antiquarian, Ethnological, and Other Researches in New Granada, Equador, Peru and Chili, with Observations on the pre-Incarial, Incarial and Other Monuments of Peruvian Nations* (London: Trübner, 1860), 157–58, accessed October 16, 2016, https://catalog.hathitrust.org/Record/008586598.

8. Luis Briones, Lautaro Núñez, and Vivien G. Standen, "Geoglifos y tráfico prehispánico de caravanas de llamas en el desierto de Atacama (norte de Chile)," *Chungara, Revista de Antropología Chilena* 37 (2005): 195–223, 196.

9. Luis Briones, "The Geoglyphs of the North Chilean Desert: An Archaeological and Artistic Perspective," *Antiquity* 80, no. 1 (2006): 9–24.

10. Ibid., 10.

11. Ibid.

12. Ibid., original emphasis.

13. Tim Ingold, *Lines: A Brief History* (London: Routledge, 2007), 77.

14. Ibid., 78.

15. Ibid., 75.

16. Ibid., 81–85.

17. Benjamin Orlove, *Lines in the Water: Nature and Culture at Lake Titicaca* (Berkeley: University of California Press, 2002), 209.

18. Ibid., 210.

19. Ibid.

20. Tim Ingold, "Footprints through the Weather-World: Walking, Breathing, Knowing," *Journal of the Royal Anthropological Institute* S121–S139 (2010): S126, original emphasis.

21. Martti Pärssinen, Denise Schaan, and Alceu Ranzi, "Pre-Columbian Geometric Earthworks in the Upper Purús: A Complex Society in Western Amazonia," *Antiquity* 83 (2010): 1084–95.

22. For recent overviews on archaeology in Amazonia and other tropical regions in South America, see Michael Heckenberger, *The Ecology of Power: Culture, Place, and Personhood in the Southern Amazon, AD 1000–2000* (New York: Routledge, 2005); Michael Heckenberger, "Tropical Garden Cities: Archaeology and Memory in the Southern Amazon," *Revista Cadernos do Ceom* 26, no. 38 (2013): 185–207; Michael Heckenberger and Eduardo Neves, "Amazonian Archaeology," *Annual Reviews in Anthropology* 38 (2009): 251–66; Eduardo Neves, "Ecology, Ceramic Chronology and Distribution, Long-Term History, and Political Change in the Amazonian Floodplain," in *Handbook of South American Archaeology*, edited by Helaine Silverman and William Isbell, 359–79 (New York: Springer, 2008); Denise Schaan, "The Camutins Chiefdom: The Rise and Development of Social Complexity on Marajó Island, Brazilian Amazon" (PhD dissertation, University of Pittsburgh, 2004); Denise Schaan, "The Nonagricultural Chiefdoms of Marajó Island," in *Handbook of South American Archaeology*, edited by Helaine Silverman and William Isbell (New York: Springer, 2008), 339–57; Denise Schaan, *Cultura Marajoara* (Rio de Janeiro: Senac Nacional, 2009); Denise Schaan, "Long-Term Human Induced Impacts on Marajó Island Landscapes, Amazon Estuary," *Diversity* 2 (2010): 182–206; Charles Spencer and Elsa Redmond, *A Pre-Hispanic Chiefdom in Barinas, Venezuela: Excavations at Gaván-Complex Sites*, Anthropological Papers 100 (New York: American Museum of Natural History, 2014).

23. Sanna Saunaluoma and Pirjo Kristiina Virtanen, "Variable Models for Organization of Earthworking Communities in Upper Purus, Southwestern Amazonia: Archaeological and Ethnographic Perspectives," *Tipití: Journal of the Society for the Anthropology of Lowland South America* 13, no. 1 (2015): 23–43.

24. Sanna Saunaluoma, "Geometric Earthworks in the State of Acre, Brazil: Excavations at the Fazenda Atlântica and Quinauá Sites," *Latin American Antiquity* 23, no. 4 (2012): 565–83, 566.

25. Heckenberger, "Tropical Garden Cities."

26. For examples, see Spencer and Redmond, *Pre-Hispanic Chiefdom*.

27. Saunaluoma and Virtanen, "Variable Models for Organization," 27.

28. Pirjo Kristiina Virtanen, "Constancy in Continuity? Native Oral History, Iconography, and Earthworks in the Upper Purús River," in *Ethnicity in Ancient Amazonia: Reconstructing Past Identities from Archaeology, Linguistics, and Ethnohistory*, edited by Alf Hornburg and Jonathan Hill, 279–96 (Boulder: University Press of Colorado, 2011), 279.

29. Ibid., 287.

30. Ibid., 288.

31. An extensive literature exists regarding different aspects of Nasca society. A comprehensive and clear overview is Helaine Silverman and Donald Proulx, *The Nasca* (Malden, MA: Blackwell, 2002). Also see Donald Proulx, "Paracas and Nasca: Regional Cultures on the South Coast of Peru," in *Handbook of South American Archaeology*, edited by Helaine Silverman and William Isbell, 563–85 (New York: Springer, 2008).

32. For descriptions of Cahuachi, see Helaine Silverman, *Cahuachi in the Ancient Nasca World* (Iowa City: University of Iowa Press, 1993); Helaine Silverman, *Ancient Nasca Settlement and Society* (University of Iowa Press: Iowa City: University of Iowa Press, 2002); Giuseppe Orefici, ed., *Nasca: El Desierto de los Dioses de Cahuachi / Nasca: The Desert of the Cahuachi Divinities* (San Isidro, Peru: Graph Ediciones, 2009); Giuseppe Orefici, ed., *Cahuachi: Capital Teocrática Nasca* (Lima: Universidad de San Martin de Porras, 2012).

33. Clive Ruggles and Nicholas Saunders, "Desert Labyrinth: Lines, Landscape and Meaning at Nasca, Peru," *Antiquity* 86 (2012): 1126–40, 1126.

34. Johan Reinhard, "Interpreting the Nasca Lines," in *The Ancient Americas: Art from Sacred Landscapes*, edited by Richard Townsend, 291–302 (Chicago: Art Institute of Chicago, 1992). *Apu* are powerful mountain-dwelling deities.

35. Masato Sakai, Jorge Olano, Yoichi Watanabe, and Kaoru Honda, "Nasca Lines, Ceramic Sherds, and Social Changes: Recent Investigation at the Nasca Pampas, Southern Coast of Peru," paper presented at the Society for American Archaeology Annual Meeting, April 16, 2015, San Francisco, CA.

36. Measurements based on GoogleEarth; the orientation is AZ 248.97°.

37. Pedro Cieza de León, *La Crónica del Perú* (Lima: PEISA, 1553), 185, translation mine.

38. William L. Fox, *Aereality: On the World from Above* (Berkeley: Counterpoint, 2009), 15.

39. Axel K. Schmitt, Martin Danišík, Erkan Aydar, Erdal Şen, İnan Ulusoy, and Oscar M. Lovera, "Identifying the Volcanic Eruption Depicted in a Neolithic Painting at Çatalhöyük, Central Anatolia, Turkey," *PLoS ONE* 9, no. 1 (2014): e84711, doi:10.1371/journal.pone.0084711.

40. Donald Wise, "Primitive Cartography in the Marshall Islands," *Cartographica: The International Journal for Geographic Information and Geovisualization* 13, no. 1 (1976): 11–20.

41. Ingold, *Lines*, 84.

42. Fox, *Aereality*, 101.

43. Edward Ranney, *The Lines* (New Haven, CT: Yale University Press, 2014), no page number.

CHAPTER SIX

To the Lost City

When I rode my mule along a knife-edge ridge in Colombia, I felt self-conscious—as if I had inadvertently wandered into a movie by Werner Herzog. The sun-baked green slopes of coffee, cacao, and pasturage slipped northward toward the Caribbean. By two in the afternoon, sweat-drenched clothes shrink-wrapped my body. I sank into the dull stupidity of dehydration. My guide swatted the mule's shanks with a switch, shouting *mula! mula! mula!* to keep the beast climbing up the deep ruts of the slick gray trail. I held the pommel with both hands as the mule lurched.

I was on my way to the Lost City. I was here to chase a dream. The dream was this: the cosmos is shaped like an egg.

"Ciudad Perdida" is an archaeological complex of spectacular ridge-top circular plazas and stone-faced terraces that cling to hillsides. Known locally as "Teyuna"—the hummingbird—the site was built around AD 800 and was associated with the Tairona chiefdom, one of the dozens of chiefly societies that flourished in South America just as

Europe devolved into the Middle Ages.[1] In the northern Andes, different chiefdoms staked out their territories in the broad river valleys and forested mountain ranges of what is now Colombia.[2] The fertile volcanic soils supported abundant crops of maize. The enormous Magdalena River, which runs for more than 1,500 km from Colombia's southern frontier to the Caribbean Sea, served as a nautical highway connecting the Andes and the coast. Trade enriched these ancient societies. Some of these societies created great works of art. At San Agustin, more than 500 stone sculptures portray men with massive fanged heads, probably shamans in the act of metamorphosis into spirits. One anthropologist wrote that this art depicted "a complex system of ideas related to shamanism," forming "a consistent and articulated complex of shamanic art, with transformation as the unifying theme."[3] And the native chiefdoms of Colombia had gold.

In ancient Colombia, gold was fashioned into elegant objects imbued with deep meanings, often small and intimate objects, shimmering symbols of personal identity. From northern Colombia came the legend of a great king whose coronation involved offerings of gold and jewels to the sacred Lake Guatavita. The Spanish chronicler Juan Rodriquez Frayle wrote in 1636, "The new king they stripped to his skin, and anointed him with a sticky earth on which they placed gold dust so that he was completely covered with this metal. They placed him on the raft . . . and at his feet they placed a great heap of gold and emeralds for him to offer to his god. With this ceremony the new ruler was received, and was recognized as lord and king." Rodriguez Frayle noted that "from this ceremony came the name of El Dorado, which has cost so many lives."[4]

The legend of El Dorado was one of the great myths that lured conquistadors across the Andes and Amazonia, a flickering tale that ensnared explorers from the Orinoco Basin to Tierra del Fuego. Though great treasures were found, many secrets eluded the invaders and looters. One such region was the Sierra Nevada de Santa Marta and the site of Ciudad Perdida. That is where I went.

The Sierra de Santa Marta is the home of the Kogi, an indigenous society that has fiercely preserved its culture. While writing another book in 2001, I read about the Kogi in the writings of the great anthropologist Gerardo Reichel-Dolmatoff (1912–94), an Austrian-Czech who sought refuge in Colombia in 1939 as World War II erupted. An energetic and sensitive scholar, Reichel-Dolmatoff was the father of Colombian anthropology, and we know about the Kogi and the Sierra Nevada de Santa Marta because of his ground-breaking research. After becoming a Colombian citizen in 1942, Reichel-Dolmatoff and his wife, Alice Dusan, made numerous expeditions into the Sierra Nevada, producing classic ethnographic accounts of Kogi society and culture, particularly of their complex cosmology and religious life.[5]

"The Kogi," Reichel-Dolmatoff wrote, "are a deeply religious people and they are guided in their faith by a highly formalized priesthood." These native priests, called *mámas*, "are sun-priests who, high up in the mountains behind the villages, officiate in ceremonial centers where people gather at certain times of the year." The mámas "are not simple curers or shamanistic practitioners, but fulfill priestly functions, taught during years of training and exercised in solemn rituals."[6]

The rigors and complexity of Kogi religious knowledge stunned me. The Mother-Goddess created the universe at the beginning of time, forming a cosmos of nine layered worlds. We humans live on the fifth and middle world. The cosmos is referenced by seven points: North, South, East, West, Zenith, Nadir, and Center. The four cardinal directions are linked to totemic pairings of animals in which the males feed on the females: jaguar/peccary (East), puma/deer (South), eagle/snake (West), and marsupial/armadillo (North). Based on such principles, the Kogi spun a complex set of associations and oppositions encoded in a canon of esoteric knowledge known as "the Law of the Mother." A fundamental notion of the Law of the Mother is this: the cosmos is shaped like an egg.

These sophisticated and nuanced ideas deeply moved me, and I resolved to visit the land of the Kogi and the site of Ciudad Perdida. Much in the way the legend of El Dorado had led conquistadors to explore this continent, the subtle Kogi concepts surrounding the cosmic egg drew me to the Sierra Nevada de Santa Marta.

¶

I traveled with my good friend Doug, whom I have known for thirty years. Like me, Doug was trained as an archaeologist but became a professional photographer with broad experience in Latin America. For months we planned our trip via emails: we would meet in Santa Marta and travel to the Ciudad Perdida with a trekking tour operator, as only organized groups are allowed to visit the site. We would trek for six days, a leisurely pace to cover the 56-km round-trip. A few days of acclimating before the trek—in other words, drinking beers by the Caribbean—and a few days of recuperating afterward—in other words, drinking beers by the Caribbean—would bracket our trek.

A rebuilt and rattling Toyota Land Cruiser picked us up at our hotel a little before 9 a.m. Doug and I were joined by one of our guides, Yorman, and three other trekkers: two vacationing economists from Chile and a man from New York who spoke little Spanish and was principally interested in dope. We headed east from Santa Marta on the coastal highway. We drove through small villages with roadside stands whose gleaming chrome blenders whirred juices from mangoes, pineapple, and passion fruit. Drying laundry hung like Tibetan prayer flags. We stopped for fuel at a small gas station. The owner had decorated the storefront with newspaper images of bathing beauties and hanging mobiles of dead and dried animals. A dusty goshawk twisted in the slight midday breeze. A desiccated macaw hung crucified from the wall.

We turned onto a dirt road and headed south into the mountains. The Land Cruiser jolted and shook as we climbed. After thirty years of archaeological expeditions in Peru and Mexico, it felt good to be riding on dirt roads in a shuddering truck. This was my first trip to Colombia, and I was very excited to be on my way to the Ciudad Perdida.

In the early afternoon, we jostled into the village of Machete Pelado (literally "Skinned" or "Naked" Machete) and were met by our principal guide, Juan Carlos, and the mules. Juan Carlos was a taut, muscled man in his late thirties who sported the remnants of a military buzz cut the Colombian Army gives all its recruits. He wore a tight T-shirt and

knee-length shorts and carried a short machete at his side, like most *campesino* men. Juan Carlos strutted like a platoon sergeant, barking orders at the muleteers and swaggering for the gringas. "Come! Eat!" he commanded, and we sat at long plank tables in a large restaurant without walls frequented by several trekking operators.

A group of British and Dutch girls had just returned from Ciudad Perdida and were waiting for transport back to Santa Marta. They were listless and sun-burned, little interested in their meals of whole fried fish as they compared blisters and insect bites. We newcomers were served cheese and white-bread sandwiches. "Eat," Juan Carlos barked. "This is your last meal for a long time."

The mules were white and gray and brown. The muleteer, Don Ricardo, packed the mules, leaving us to carry only very light loads. Doug and I had a large plastic soda bottle filled with good rum, and we handed that and most of our gear to Don Ricardo. We only carried raingear, cameras, and water bottles in our packs. Doug's pack still weighed thirty pounds, as he had several cameras and lenses in protective cases. My pack was much lighter, although Juan Carlos looked at me, shook his head, and said, "Too much."

We left Machete Pelado, hiking along a dirt road that crossed several small farms and followed a river. It was very hot and humid, but the road was flat. Small patches of secondary forest hung with philodendrons. Heliotrope flowers sprouted bright flames. We had walked about a kilometer when we came to a stream-crossing. We knew that the trail to Ciudad Perdida involved numerous fords of streams and rivers; this was the first. It was a simple matter of boulder hopping, and the stream was less than knee-deep. The young guide, Yorman, and the other three members of our party quickly crossed and kept going. I was a bit more tentative—I had an arthritic knee, and I hiked with a brace on my left leg—but I crossed the stepping stones across the ford, steadying myself with trekking poles.

As Juan Carlos and I watched, Doug began fording the stream. Two-thirds of the way across he slipped, soaking his boots and legs but not falling. Doug thrashed to the stream bank, took another five steps, sat down on the edge of the road and said, "That's it for me."

The Kogi survived despite brutal onslaughts of Spanish colonialism and Colombian nationalism. For more than five centuries, there were campaigns to enslave the Kogi and other indigenous peoples and annihilate their culture and religion. A sense of Spanish hatred of the native peoples comes from the 1627 work of Friar Pedro Simon—whose book *Noticias Historicas de las Conquistas de Tierra Firme en las Indias Occidentales* also contains the story of the traitorous tyrant Lope de Aguirre, depicted in Werner Herzog's *Aguirre: The Wrath of God.* Father Pedro Simon repeats the 1525 description of the Indians of Colombia made by a Dominican priest:

> They are a people who eat human flesh . . . lacking laws among themselves; and they walk about naked and without shame; they are like asses—stupid, wild, and foolish—and they care not if they kill or are

killed . . . they prize drunkenness and wines from various fruits, roots, and grains; they stupefy themselves with smokes and certain herbs from which they extract a juice. They are bestial in their vices; without obedience or courtesy between young and old, children and parents, as they lack the capacity for doctrine or punishment. They are traitors, cruel and vengeful, unforgiveable enemies of religion. They are lazy good-for-nothings, thieves, liars, they are two-faced and lack judgment; they are without faith, order, or loyalty between husbands and wives or wives and husbands. They are sorcerers, and workers of black magic. They are as cowardly as hares and as dirty as pigs; they eat lice, spiders, and raw worms and anything else there is. They have no arts or crafts.[7]

Given such assessments, it is not surprising that the Spaniards waged war against the Indians of Colombia, especially in the vicinity of Santa Marta. Hot waves of epidemics swept through native villages. As the Spaniards controlled the coastal plain and the great rivers, native trade networks and political systems were disrupted. Cut off from the coast, the Sierra Nevada de Santa Marta became a sanctuary, a mountainous asylum for different native groups. Although spared the most direct attacks, the people of the sierra were reduced by disease and proselytized by Catholic priests. Yet as the Colombian anthropologist Augusto Oyuela-Caycedo has written, "The process of domination was never complete."[8]

In these mountains—the mountains where I self-consciously rode my mule—the Kogi mámas pursue a profoundly serious task: the search for cosmic balance. Oyuela-Caycedo wrote that the Sierra Nevada de Santa Marta "is the place where the center of learning and transmission of the 'Mother Laws' occurs, for in the uplands near the snow and the sacred lakes is where the ancestors and masters live. In addition, the uplands are where the most prestigious Mámas live." These native priests were charged with a heroic task: "to preserve the equilibrium between the different forces of the universe through offerings and rituals associated with each of the masters of the forest, streams and rains, animals, and others. The Máma has to resolve the conflicts between individuals and discover the cause of disease, putting chaos in order."[9]

The mámas' task is endless, their knowledge profound. And they live in the mountains surrounding the Lost City.

⌂

For today the farce has ended.

WERNER HERZOG, *Conquest of the Useless*

I urged Doug to change his mind. He didn't. I offered to go back with him. He insisted that I continue; I wanted this trip more than he did. We decided that if he was going to turn back, this was a good place to do it. Juan Carlos accompanied him back to Machete Pelado, where Doug could catch a ride back to Santa Marta.

I went on. The road narrowed to a track as it climbed upslope. The afternoon broiled in the low 90s. The younger trekkers hiked quickly and were soon out of sight. My first water bottle was empty, and the second bottle had only a few mouthfuls. As the slope rose, my pace slackened; a few steps, a pause, a few steps.

Returning from Machete Pelado, Juan Carlos caught up with me and asked a passing campesino on a horse to let me ride the saddled mule he led. I do not swing into the saddle like John Wayne once did. My bad left knee makes it hard to get into the saddle, and we had to maneuver the mule next to a stump or boulder. We found a place where I could clamber into the saddle. The mule's name was Cinnamon. An hour's ride and we reached the summit. An enterprising campesina had a stand selling soft drinks, water, and slices of melon. I drank three bottles of Gatorade and ate two slices of watermelon. I began to feel normal again, an elusive sensation over the next five days.

We traveled on the ridge crests, so narrow that they are literally called "knife blades" (*cuchillos*). We halted to rest at a small store owned by Don Ricardo and his wife. This entire region of the Sierra Nevada was served only by pack trains and porters, lacking roads for any wheeled vehicles. Don Ricardo's mules were the major form of transport. As he rode along, people would shout or whistle, run up to Don Ricardo, and

entrust him with goods—a bag of pineapples, a stalk of bananas—or
messages—"Tell Roberto that I will pay him tomorrow"—to convey
along his route. His ridge-top store was a major center, one of the few
places where phones could get a cell signal to Santa Marta. He and his
wife had several phones—one each for the different phone services
in Colombia—dangling from loops of fishing line under the eaves of
their open-walled store, protected from the rain but available to receive

incoming calls or used by locals for a small fee. Juan Carlos negotiated for Don Ricardo to send a mule for me the next day. We rested for fifteen minutes and then hiked on.

The trail first followed the ridge but then dipped into a river valley. Even going downhill, I walked slowly on slick clay and stones. The sun fell behind the ridge as we crossed a stream, hiked around a hill, and arrived at Alfredo's camp.

Alfredo's camp consisted of open-walled, corrugated roofed sheds built from posts and rafters. Dozens of hammocks hung in banks, each cocooned in mosquito netting. The camp's kitchen held a dozen firewood-efficient cooking hearths, half-domes covered with mud and concrete. Water piped from an upslope stream fed the showers, and the gray water flowed into forest-green plastic treatment tanks. Alfredo's camp was one of the trekking camps funded by the United States Agency for International Development (USAID) and the Global Heritage Fund. Alfredo's camp was also part of a long-term strategy to pry the Sierra Nevada de Santa Marta from the control of leftist guerrillas, *narcotraficantes*, and paramilitaries by creating a program of sustainable economic development focused on cultural tourism as an economic alternative. The region had been cleared of guerrillas—no tourists had been taken hostage during the last nine years—and the campesinos raised cocoa and coffee instead of coca and marijuana. The string of camps was carefully designed and environmentally sensitive. They formed development corridors where small businesses could thrive along the trail to Ciudad Perdida. The woman who sold us Gatorade and watermelon and Don Ricardo's store with its dangling cell phones were evidence of success.

But for me on the evening of the first day, Campo Alfredo was simply one of the most welcome sights of my life. I respond to physical misery with conceptual myopia. I pulled off my sweat-streaked shirt and mud-caked boots and washed in cold spring water. I changed into dry clothes and sandals and limped to the long, rough-plank dinner table with a first rum and water in hand. I began to resume human form. I was transformed.

Ⅱ

The Kogi build temples that replicate this egg-shaped, multi-level cosmos. Kogi temples are circular buildings with walls of densely placed upright posts capped by a densely thatched cone that hangs down to form eaves. Reichel-Dolmatoff wrote, "The first temple was created in the depths of the primeval sea, and was a model of the cosmos . . . and it is believed that downward and upward a sequence of invisible, inverted and upright temples" emanate from the Kogi temple, which is thus an axis mundi. In these temples, by the flickering lights of hearths or torches, Kogi boys are trained to be priests.[10]

Initiates into the Kogi priesthood undergo an extensive apprenticeship. Boys are chosen as future mámas when they are only two or three years old, and their apprenticeship lasts around eighteen years. This forms two nine-year periods that flank puberty. During this time, the initiates are kept indoors, hidden from the sun, and only allowed to eat foods that are white: manioc, white beans, potatoes, land snails, freshwater shrimp, and mushrooms. Their food is boiled in a breast-shaped clay pot. The initiates are forbidden to eat salt, chilies, or the meat of game. They are deprived of food, sleep, sunlight, and sex.

Over the years of their apprenticeship, the initiates are taught the Law of the Mother—a complex body of esoteric knowledge that ranges over the fields of geography and astronomy, botany and cosmology, zoology and myth. This canon of ritual knowledge involves learning special ceremonial languages, distinct vocabularies, and modes of rhetoric. The Law of the Mother provides instruction in ethical teachings, ritual dances, and the skill of divination. Kogi mámas-in-training learn curing spells, the mythical origins of social groups, and the art of interpreting symbols, portents, and dreams.

"The manifest intention of the priestly teachers," Reichel-Dolmatoff wrote, "is to deflect the child-novices from their accustomed circadian activity rhythms, and to ungear or 'declutch' their time perception."[11] Repeatedly using an automotive metaphor—essentially a neutral state in which a person is neither in "forward" nor "reverse"—

Reichel-Dolmatoff discerned that stepping out of time was central to the mámas' ritual practice.

Importantly, all other Kogi were deeply enmeshed in time, vast but nested cycles of time that governed all levels of the cosmic egg, from the cycles of planting maize to the movements of the stars. The average Kogi was expected to live quietly and contentedly within these cycles and to seek equilibrium in all of his or her actions. Prizing cooperation and avoiding ostentation, the average Kogi man and woman knew his or her respective place in the cycles of time, and "the life of man, as an individual and social being, must be completely geared to the cosmic clockwork of orbits and cycles."

This was not true of the mámas.

Reichel-Dolmatoff repeats a Kogi legend about a máma who predicted the moment of his death and invited his fellow priests to be there to witness the moment. Although the máma accurately predicted his death to the minute, the priestly invitees failed to attend: some of the priests arrived before the death, some arrived afterward, and others simply forgot about the moment. Rather than reflecting a group of absentminded invitees, the Kogi told this legend, according to Reichel-Dolmatoff: "This tale makes an important point in Kogi teachings: one must be able to forget time."[12] The ability "to step outside of time" meant that Kogi priests could escape "the cogwheels of biology and environment," and in this atemporal space the mámas sought transformation.[13] This transformation was achieved through various means and was motivated by divergent reasons. Mámas achieved this metamorphosis either through hallucinogens or sensory deprivations, but it was predicated on intense preparation. Enlightenment did not come to the untrained mind.

The search for transformation was motivated by a range of reasons, a continuum between two moral poles. At one extreme, a máma sought to escape time because he had achieved "spiritual enlightenment and moral perfection," his decades of learning and contemplation leading him to a rarefied state whose next step was a benign transformation. In contrast, transformation could be sought in pursuit of horrific acts, as being out of time rendered normal moral codes of behavior irrelevant.

"A person might want to step outside of time," Reichel-Dolmatoff wrote, "because of his manifest evil intentions."[14] When shamans were transformed into jaguars—similar to the images sculpted in the stones of San Agustin—this reflected their "determination to act against all cultural norms" or to conduct "certain rituals that contradict all established rules."[15]

In his ethnographic work among the Kogi mámas and with shamans elsewhere in Colombia, Reichel-Dolmatoff returns to the issue of transformation. From one perspective, it is somewhat unremarkable that Reichel-Dolmatoff would give "transformation" such prominence in his writings on indigenous religion; after all, variations on this theme are not only part of shamanic practice around the world but occur in a broad array of religious practice, from vodun to Pentecostalism. And yet, one cannot help but wonder if "transformation" and its associated state of "stepping out of time" did not have a particular relevance for Reichel-Dolmatoff, as he himself had been transformed.

Before he became the father of Colombian anthropology and founded the Department of Anthropology at the University of the Andes;

Before he received honorary memberships in international scientific organizations and visiting professorships at universities around the globe, from UCLA to Cambridge;

Before being lauded as the "heir to a long and honorable list of Americanists of European intellectual heritage or education whose major concern has been the ideological universe of the indigenous peoples of the New World";[16]

Before leaving Europe in 1939 when World War II was declared;

Before his work with the Free French in Colombia, for which he received the French Order de Merit from Charles de Gaulle;

Before the cogwheels of time had clicked into unity:

Gerardo Reichel-Dolmatoff had been an SS assassin.

I left the next morning on a mule led by Cristobal, one of Don Ricardo's sons, who also rode a mule. I traveled without illusions. I knew that no Kogi priest would kindly usher me into a beehive temple and instruct me by torchlight in the Laws of the Mother. I simply wanted to know this part of the world with my own eyes, to visit the Sierra Nevada de Santa Marta and to see the plazas and staircases of Ciudad Perdida.

The trail led up steep slopes and down long grades as it climbed ridges and slid into river valleys. The route was very difficult, and it took us five hours to cover two miles. We forded the Río Buritaca, the iron shoes of the mules clattering across cobbles as we rode through fast, clear water.

Cristobal was young but a competent muleteer, an *arriero* who knew the route. I was anything but competent. My left stirrup was too small, and my boot slipped out hundreds of times that day. This would usually happen as we descended a steep part of the trail or splashed across boulder-strewn river crossings or just as my mule had edged to the brink of a switchback. I lurched and grabbed and fretted.

The trail passed through thick forest, the trees crowned with bromeliads. Sunlight shafted the trail. Butterflies flickered in the light, their wings electric blue and suede. The butterflies clustered on piles of mule shit, their wings pulsing as they probed the dung.

We rode past a Kogi village. There were about twenty houses, round single-room buildings 5–7 m in diameter, each capped with domes of thatching. Smaller buildings were storerooms, and a much larger structure sat on the edge of the village, although I couldn't tell if it was a temple. The houses were arrayed in two or three loose rows. A couple of Kogi children ran after a milk cow. I heard a few voices, but the village seemed largely empty. Or we were being avoided. The Kogi sustain indifference to the outside world, partly as a strategy for cultural survival but essentially because of their sense of superiority.

Further along the trail, we passed a Kogi family. The father and older sons had shoulder-length hair and wore immaculate knee-long white cotton tunics cinched at the waist, loose cotton pants, and black rubber

boots purchased in Machete Pelado. The father carried a single-shot, percussion-cap shotgun. The mother and younger children followed, the woman with a tumpline load of pineapples and a nursing infant at her breast. One of the younger children followed with a piglet on a leash.

Like most Kogi men, the father had two woven bags, cross-strapped from his shoulders like a bandolier. The bags are pendulous sacks like the hanging nests woven by tropical orioles. One bag was from agave fiber, a loose weave of coarse twine. The other bag was from cotton, a well-woven bag of tight thread. Reichel-Dolmatoff had recorded that the coarse agave bag held everyday items—matches, a pocket knife, shotgun shells—while the fine cotton bag contained more sacred items, including a packet of coca leaves and a pear-shaped gourd of powdered lime.

Coca leaves are chewed throughout South America, and the alkaloids in the leaves are broken down by adding calcium carbonate or another alkaline to the wad of leaves. The lime frees the organic acids in the coca leaves. The Kogi make their lime by burning carefully chosen seashells, grinding them into a powder carried in a small gourd bottle. A slender spindle about the size of a drumstick is inserted into the gourd, swiveled about in the lime powder, and then added to the coca leaves before the mass is chewed.

We turned our pack animals off the trail so the Kogi could pass, and they did so in silence.

More than twenty-five years ago, the Kogi spoke. In the late 1980s a BBC documentary filmmaker, Alan Ereira, climbed into the Sierra Nevada de Santa Marta, finally winning permission from the Kogi to pass into their homeland.[17] As Ereira documented in his 1990 film *The Heart of the World: The Elder Brother's Warning*, the Kogi mámas issued a warning to people in the outside world, whom they called "the Younger Brothers."

It is a remarkable scene. The mámas and other Kogi men sit on the floor of a large and darkened temple, constantly rubbing their lime sticks on the coca gourds. An elder máma sits on a swinging hammock and looks into the camera: "I am here, we all are here, to give a warning. I am speaking on behalf of us all, to send out a message to all the Younger Brothers, and I am going to have to say it in a way they can understand." He turns to the camera and with a flourish of his right hand casts his words to us: "I want the whole world to listen to the warning that we speak to you."

The máma reminds us that the Kogi have followed the Law of the Mother, that they have done so from the beginning of time, and through their efforts the Earth has continued to exist. "The Great Mother taught," he says, "and she taught and taught . . . and her teaching has not been forgotten, right up to this day." But we, the Younger Brothers, have so violated the Great Mother, the máma continues, that "you are bringing the world to an end." As we, the Younger Brothers, have dug into the Earth, we have taken out her heart, cut into her liver, and blinded her: "The Mother is being cut to pieces and stripped of everything. The Mother too is sad and she will end and the world will end if they do not stop digging and digging."

From off-camera another irate máma shouts, "Stop digging into the Earth and stealing the gold. If you go on, the world will end! You are bringing the world to an end!"

The Kogi máma have been working to maintain the world, to keep the cosmos in order by following the Law of the Mother. Yet their efforts enacted over centuries are imperiled by the thoughtless defilements of the Younger Brother.

And in the late 1980s, when few people in the outside world had heard the phrase *global warming*, the Kogi máma warned of the melting glaciers in the Sierra Nevada de Santa Marta, the desiccation of the high-elevation grasslands of the paramo, and the end of the world.

More than twenty-five years ago, the Kogi spoke to the Younger Brothers. Few of us have ever listened.

Cristobal, Cinnamon, and I rode into Campo Tezhumake at mid-afternoon. The camp was a cluster of long roofed sheds with bunkbeds draped in mosquito netting, an open kitchen, and a bathhouse on the south bank of the Río Buritaca. The buildings flanked the trail, and a steady stream of trekkers, guides, and Kogi passed through the camp. Stands of angel's trumpet grew along the riverbank, the white flowers drifting a sweet narcotic smell. I was glad to get off the mule.

That night Juan Carlos called a meeting, and we sat around a rough-plank table by candlelight. Juan Carlos laid out tomorrow's plan. Our small party would divide. The younger and faster trekkers would have an easy day, waking up late and walking a few miles to Campo Romulo, where they would rest that afternoon and spend the next night. The following morning they would get up early and climb to Ciuidad Perdida, see the ruins, and then descend and hike back to Campo Tezhumake, where we were at the moment.

As for me, I would leave the next morning at dawn with Yorman, hike to Campo Romulo for lunch, and then climb to Ciudad Perdida, where I would be allowed to sleep at the park headquarters. Usually, people were not allowed to sleep at the park headquarters, but I was privileged because I was "a famous gringo archaeologist" as Juan Carlos said with obvious exaggeration. (Months later I learned that people were not allowed to sleep at the ruins because guerrillas had kidnapped tourists sleeping there in 2003.) Yorman and I would explore the site in the morning and then descend and return to Campo Romulo, rendezvousing with the other people in my group. There were only two problems.

First, it was essential that we wade through the last ford on the Río Buritaca before it rained in the afternoon and the river rose. Second, Juan Carlos said the trail was too difficult for the mules. I would be on foot.

Later that evening Juan Carlos talked about the bad old days in the sierra, when two leftist guerrilla groups battled against paramilitaries across the mountains. He told how the tourists had been captured in 2003 and how the Colombian military had sprayed the area with herbicides to eradicate coca. There were reports from these years of how Kogi and people from other indigenous groups were held hostage by the guerrillas or enslaved by the paramilitary. To the mámas, it must have seemed like the world had, in fact, ended.

But as Juan Carlos talked, I barely listened. All I could think of was his statement "the trail was too difficult for the mules." I went to bed wondering if, after all this, I would actually see the Lost City.

The world is spotty and hard to decipher.

WERNER HERZOG, *Conquest of the Useless*

I learned that Gerardo Reichel-Dolmatoff had been a Nazi when I was in a supermarket in Santa Marta. I had just stepped into the Exito Hypermarket (the Colombian equivalent of a Wal-Mart) when I heard someone shout "Jerry! Jerry!" and I turned to see my colleague, Augusto Oyuela-Caycedo. Augusto was born in Colombia and has conducted extensive research there, including excavations at Ciudad Perdida. Now a professor at the University of Florida, Augusto was visiting Santa Marta for a few days, meeting with local scientists before leaving for the Amazon.

We went to the small coffee shop in one corner of the Exito Hypermarket and chatted over espressos. I told him about my trek to Ciudad Perdida. He told me about his work in the Amazon, mentioning that after a few weeks of fieldwork he would be going on to Vienna for a conference. The conference was an international gathering of anthropologists, archaeologists, and other scholars who work in the Americas. Augusto said he would be participating in a session in honor of Reichel-Dolmatoff. I asked Augusto if he was going to present the results of his research in the Amazon, an area where Reichel-Dolmatoff had also worked.

"No." A deep sadness crossed his face and he looked at his coffee. "No, Jerry—and this is confidential for right now—I am giving a talk on Reichel-Dolmatoff, and I am documenting that he was a Nazi."

"Is that a surprise?" I asked. "Many people got caught up in the war."

"No, Jerry, it wasn't like that at all." Augusto's face darkened in sorrow. "He was an early member of the SS, and he killed a dozen people."

This was a shocking revelation and a burdensome discovery for Augusto. Among anthropologists in Colombia and elsewhere, Reichel-Dolmatoff's status was nearly divine. He had established the Department of Anthropology at the University of the Andes in Bogotá and literally established the intellectual contours of ethnography and archaeology in Colombia. A man of refinement and liberal outlook, Reichel-Dolmatoff's work showed no hints of a Nazi past or sense of racial superiority. Rather, his ethnographic research led to a nuanced and pluralistic vision of Colombia's indigenous peoples, treating the different worldviews as sophisticated philosophies deserving of respect and reflection. Ironically, Reichel-Dolmatoff's ethnographic embrace of diversity contradicted racist notions of ethnic superiority widely held in Colombia when he arrived in 1939. Augusto had been to Reichel-Dolmatoff's home for tea, and after Reichel-Dolmatoff died in May 1994, Augusto wrote his obituary for the journal of the Society for American Archaeology, noting that his former professor "always thought of research holistically" and repeatedly "expressed the view that if humanity wanted to survive and stop its destruction of nature, we had to start learning the lessons of the past and incorporating them into our understanding."[18]

A video was made of Augusto's presentation in Vienna in July 2012; you can watch it on YouTube.[19] In it, Augusto lays out the evidence. Gerardo Reichel-Dolmatoff's given name was Erasmus Reichel. He had joined the Hitler Youth at age fourteen and was a member of the Nazi Party as a nineteen-year-old. In 1933, at age twenty-one, Reichel was a member of the Leibstandarte SS, a force with different roles within the Nazi Party. Although some members of the Leibstandarte SS were Hitler's bodyguards, it seems as if Reichel was in a unit sent from Munich to Berlin to guard buildings and facilities important to the Third Reich. As the German historians Holger Stoecker and Sören Flachowsky, who worked with Augusto on this research, clarified in an August 25, 2012, interview with the Colombian newspaper *El Tiempo*, it is not known if Reichel actually knew Hitler, although he was clearly an acolyte.[20]

And he seems to have been a murderer.

Reichel killed rival Nazis in the June 1934 purge known as the Night of the Long Knives, killings he documented in a lengthy, although obscurely published, article, "Confessions of a Gestapo Assassin."

If you watch the twenty-five-minute video of his seminar, you will see Augusto become increasingly upset as he details the evidence of Reichel-Dolmatoff's Nazi past. He hits the wrong buttons on his computer, derailing his Power Point presentation. He fumbles with his briefcase and finds a typed translation of Reichel's account. Augusto's voice trembles and catches, and then he reads Reichel's account: "I rang

the bell. An old man came out, scowling, and saw me and said 'Oh, that'
and gestured, and I shot him twice. The man fell and tried to sit up on
the staircase but I jumped up and shot him again in the front, from very
close distance; my assistant ran down the staircase and I followed when
I heard a woman scream and two children ran out the door screaming
'Assassin! Assassin!'"

In the video, Oyuela-Caycedo loses his voice, his shoulders slump,
he stifles a cry, and he says "it pains me to read this." He slightly regains
his composure, "I am sorry but this pains me because I knew Gerardo
Reichel, and this is difficult."

During 1934–35, Reichel was stationed at Dachau, the prototypical
concentration camp, which housed German political prisoners in these
early years. According to Stoecker and Flachowsky, Reichel's role was
to train Austrian recruits as guards. But then something happened.
Sometime in 1935 he requested permission to wed—Himmler gave per-
missions for SS members to marry—although no wedding occurred.
There are allusions to a mental breakdown. In January 17, 1936, Reichel
was expelled from the SS, classified as "inept," and no longer trusted. He
requested German citizenship but was denied. He began studying art in
1936, but his problems with the SS and the Gestapo continued. Stoecker
and Flachowsky note that in 1936–37 many of his former colleagues
died under "strange circumstances."[21] Reichel fled Munich, obtaining
a twenty-four-hour pass to leave Germany through his wealthy father's
intervention with Nazi leaders in Austria.

At this point, the trail becomes murky. Reichel may have gone to
Budapest, but he seems to have been in Paris in 1937. Some sources
allege that in Paris Reichel-Dolmatoff studied under the great French
social scientist Marcel Mauss, but this entire phase of his life is obscure,
including the moment at which he decided to change his name.
Germany annexed Austria in 1938, Czechoslovakia was handed to
Hitler in 1939, and the Nazis invaded Poland in 1939.

Gerardo Reichel-Dolmatoff transformed his life. In 1939 Reichel-
Dolmatoff arrived in Colombia, bearing letters of introduction from
the French anti-fascist Paul Rivet, an ethnographer who had worked in

the Ecuadorian Amazon and was the founding curator of the Musee de l'Homme. Rivet himself would seek exile in Colombia in 1942.

The revelations of Reichel-Dolmatoff's Nazi past set off shock waves in Colombia and beyond. As Augusto noted in his talk in Vienna, "The problem is that, basically, when we are speaking of Gerardo Reichel-Dolmatoff, we see him as a type of monument, a pillar, a founder of Colombian anthropology, and this is the image that we have always had."[22]

Based on these documents, Reichel-Dolmatoff's case was not one of a youth "caught up" in the war. Erasmus Reichel had embraced Hitler's murderous ideology. There was another problem. Despite his expulsion from the SS and the vague allusions to his "mental crisis," there is no clear evidence of renunciation. Flachowsky states that Reichel-Dolmatoff "did not leave [Europe] as a dissident; he sunk out of view to hide and to save his life. Being a dissident implies breaking with an ideology and passing to resistance. He did neither in Germany. Neither in the archival documents [n]or in his diary is there a single phrase or word criticizing or rejecting the National Socialist ideology."[23]

And yet the evidence of transformation is there in the hundreds of pages of articles and books Reichel-Dolmatoff wrote. The Colombian anthropologist Gerardo Ardila, in an interview in October 2012 on Bogotá's public television program *Hagamos Memoria*, responded to Stoecker and Flachowsky's charge, demanding of them in absentia "there is no evidence that he [Reichel-Dolmatoff] had changed his way of thinking—have they read his works? Have they read his works?"[24]

Reichel-Dolmatoff's writings about the Kogi and other indigenous societies *are* the evidence of transformation. There is nothing in the later life of Gerardo Reichel-Domatoff that connects him to the earlier actions of Erasmus Reichel, except for the fact that they seem to be the same person.

It is as if two separate lives were joined by little more than fragments of a name and obscurity.

Ⅱ

At night the rivers have fevers.

WERNER HERZOG, *Conquest of the Useless*

It was still dark when Yorman called my name. I fumbled through the mosquito netting, put on yesterday's still-damp clothes, and shoved my feet into my boots. I stumbled to the kitchen hearth, and Yorman gave me a cup of coffee. All the other beds were still. After a quick breakfast, we hiked out of Campo Tezhumake at 6 a.m.

We left early and we traveled light. Yorman carried a single pack with our food and bedding. I carried a day-sack with water bottle, a first aid kit, and my camera and notebook in a dry bag.

The sky lightened to slate, and the forest erupted with bird song. Parakeets flew in chaotic squawking. Cacique birds blasted "ee-choo-kee-ong." As first sunlight beamed through the forest and the temperature rose, the electric buzz of insects blanketed the forest. We crossed a recently built suspension bridge and at this point entered the Kogi territory.

The trail edged through dense forest to a ridge crest between the Buritaca and Nulicuandecue Rivers. White fungus that looked like splats of shaving cream sprouted from downed logs in the forest shade. As we gained the crest, the trail cut through the rock walls of ancient terraces. A few potsherds fell from the walls, undecorated fragments of clay cooking pots and griddles. A deep trough grinding slab made from stone tumbled from the ruins.

The ridge trail was clear and the sun was bright. We passed large agave plants with sword-like leaves as tall as a man. Yorman said the Kogi planted agaves near their settlements, providing raw fibers for bags and nets. We soon came upon an abandoned Kogi homestead, a single house with a trapiche, a traditional sugarcane press. A thick screw press carved from dense hardwood and joined with pegs and sockets, the trapiche would be turned by a mule or ox, squeezing the cane until its sweet juice ran into a wooden bucket.

The trail continued to climb. At about 8:30 a.m. we gained the summit and a gate that marked our entry into territory controlled by a Kogi máma, Raymuldo. An entrepreneur, Raymuldo had established a small stand that sold cold drinks and snacks to trekkers, and an Afro-Colombian man worked the stand for Raymuldo.

I was hiking very slowly, and the other folks from my group, led by Juan Carlos, overtook us. Yorman was sent on with the others, and I continued with Juan Carlos. The trail passed through an open pasture with traces of terraces, another Tairona site. We hiked through banana stands and moved into the forest. The path descended toward the Buritaca.

We forded the river that ran clean and fast over cobbles. The route climbed again and followed the riverbank, a slick and narrow trail across moss-covered bedrock, and then we waded across the Buritaca again. Each time we crossed, we stopped and removed our boots and socks to keep them dry and then forded the river. As Juan Carlos and I sat on the far side of the river and put our boots back on again, two Kogi boys came running down the trail and literally ran across the river in their black rubber boots, jumping from boulder to boulder without pause or hesitation, seeming to fly across the riffles where water contoured stone.

My knee throbbed despite a full brace on my left leg, and when we reached Campo Romulo just after noon, I was done out. I collapsed into a hammock and instantly fell asleep. I slept for fifteen minutes when Yorman called for me to eat a lunch of spaghetti and cheese, and then I fell asleep again for a few minutes after which Yorman shook me awake again.

"We have to go, Jerry. This next part is urgent. It is only twenty minutes to the crossing, but we have to cross before the river rises."

I stumbled out of the hammock, grabbed my trekking poles and camera bag, and followed Yorman to the trail. As soon as we left Campo Romulo, it began to rain.

The path hugged the west bank of the Río Buritaca. In one section, the hillside had collapsed and demolished the trail, and a rough gangway of logs bridged the slide with a rickety railing of saplings incongruously ribboned with bright-yellow crime scene tape labeled "¡Peligro!"

Dark, heavy clouds settled into the headwaters of the drainage. Thunder exploded from the crest. The forest streamed.

We got to the ford of the Buritaca. The water ran knee-deep and fast. Since we were already soaked, Yorman and I decided to splash across without removing our boots. That small decision saved our lives.

We moved across the river carefully but quickly, the river about 30 m wide at this point. We gained the opposite bank, found the first stone steps leading to Ciudad Perdida, and had climbed up about ten steps when we heard an enormous roar and looked behind us.

A flash flood pulsed down the Buritaca, an angry wall of brown and white water and maddened snag wood and debris. If we had stopped and taken off our boots, we would have been in the middle of the river and been swept away.

Juan Carlos ran up from Campo Romulo and shouted from the opposite side of the bank. Yorman whistled and waved that we were still alive. With that we turned and began to climb the 1,200 stone steps to the Lost City.

The steps streamed with rainwater and were green-black with leaves and moss. We climbed to the first cleared terraces in the late afternoon, just as it finally stopped raining. The terraces were faced with fieldstone retaining walls up to 4 m tall. Circular stone foundations marked ancient houses and temples. The Tairona had leveled a long ridge top, creating a series of plazas along a principal axis. A bank of circular foundations overlooked a long U-shaped plaza. At the uphill end of the plaza, a stone slab projected from a vertical retaining wall; it is called "the Shaman's chair." A chain of large circular plazas crested the ridge.

The view was spectacular: the mountains were green folds to the south, and warm gray clouds sat above the Caribbean to the north. But for me, it was even more important to try to see the invisible, to see the traces of ancient lives. Ciudad Perdida was a thriving community six centuries ago, and more than 200 circular structures dot this web of

ridges. This site was just one of dozens of Tairona communities sprin-
kled across the Sierra Nevada de Santa Marta, villages and towns linked
by cobblestone paths. A large stone slab at the site has been etched with
a complex pattern of lines and starbursts, apparently a petroglyph that
is an ancient map of the region, showing Ciudad Perdida and other
communities and the rivers that flow northward from the mountains
into the sea. The dense forest covers the physical traces of ancient lives,

and I was deeply privileged to stand there and felt subtly changed by this journey.

A few years before his death, Gerardo Reichel-Dolmatoff had written, "The entire Sierra Nevada is a sacred mountain, composed of innumerable smaller sacred mountains that, in another image, constitute a pantheon or a Kogi family. A Kogi, when looking at the far-flung panorama of the Sierra Nevada, will see in it a range of snow-capped mountains, a village with a temple in its center, an assembly of divine Mothers, a group of people, a spindle, a world axis, all fading into each other, all of them sending their mute messages far over the land."[25]

I realize that I did not see what the Kogi saw. I did not discern what Reichel-Dolmatoff had discovered. But I tried to see what I could see as I walked to the Lost City, knowing that—as in all things—much remained hidden.

NOTES

1. For information on the archaeological site of Ciudad Perdida, see Santiago Giraldo, "Lords of the Snowy Ranges: Politics, Place, and Landscape Transformation in Two Tairona Towns in the Sierra Nevada de Santa Marta,

Colombia" (PhD dissertation, University of Chicago, 2010); Augusto Oyuela-Caycedo, "Ideology, Temples, and Priests: Change and Continuity in House Societies in the Sierra Nevada de Santa Marta," in *Recent Advances in the Archaeology of the Northern Andes: In Memory of Gerardo Reichel-Dolmatoff*, edited by Augusto Oyuela-Caycedo and J. Scott Raymond, Institute of Archaeology Monograph 39, 39–53 (Los Angeles: University of California, 1998); Augusto Oyuela-Caycedo, "Late Pre-Hispanic Chiefdoms of Northern Colombia and the Formation of Anthropogenic Landscapes," in *Handbook of South American Archaeology*, edited by Helaine Silverman and William Isbell, 450–28 (New York: Springer, 2008).

2. For overviews of the archaeology of Colombian chiefdoms and related matters, see Robert Drennan, "Chiefdoms in Northern South America," *Journal of World Prehistory* 9, no. 3 (1995): 301–40; Robert Drennan, "Chiefdoms of Southwestern Colombia," in *Handbook of South American Archaeology*, edited by Helaine Silverman and William Isbell, 381–403 (New York: Springer, 2008). Also see A. Boada Rivas, *The Evolution of Social Hierarchy in a Muisca Chiefdom of the Northern Andes of Colombia*, Memoirs in Latin American Archaeology 17 (Pittsburgh: University of Pittsburgh, 2007); Carl Langebaek, "The Political Economy of Pre-Colombian Goldwork: Four Examples from Northern South America," in *Gold and Power in Ancient Costa Rica, Panama, and Colombia*, edited by Jeffrey Quilter and John Hoopes, 245–78 (Washington, DC: Dumbarton Oaks Research Library and Collection, 2003), 248–49; and the individual case studies in Carl Langebaek, *Recent Advances in the Archaeology of the Northern Andes: In Memory of Gerardo Reichel-Dolmatoff*, edited by Augusto Oyuelo-Caycedo and J. Scott Raymond, Institute of Archaeology, Monograph 39 (Los Angeles: University of California, 1998).

3. Gerardo Reichel-Dolmatoff, *Goldwork and Shamanism. An Iconographic Study of the Gold Museum* (Medellín, Colombia: Editorial Colina, 1988), 25.

4. Juan Rodriguez Frayle, *Conquista i descubrimiento del nuevo reino de Granada: De las del Dorado de las Indias Occidentales del mar océana, i fundación de la cuidad de Santa Fé de Bogotá . . . Cuéntase en ella su descubrimiento, algunas guerras civiles que habia entre sus naturales; sus costumbres i jente, i de qué procedió este nombre tan celebrado del Dorado . . .* (Bogatá: Pizano i Pérez, 1859 [1636]), 14, my translation, accessed October 17, 2016, https://catalog.hathitrust.org/Record /011604895.

5. For biographical information on Reichel-Dolmatoff, see Augusto Oyuela-Caycedo and J. Scott Raymond, "Preface," in *Recent Advances in the Archaeology of the Northern Andes: In Memory of Gerardo Reichel-Dolmatoff*, edited by Augusto Oyuela-Caycedo and J. Scott Raymond, vii–viii, Institute of Archaeology, Monograph 39 (Los Angeles: University of California, 1998); Augusto Oyuela-Caycedo, "Obituary: Gerardo Reichel-Dolmatoff 1912–1994," *American Antiquity* 61, no. 1 (1996): 52–56; see Jon Landaburu, "Gerardo Reichel-Dolmatoff, " *Journal de*

la Société des Américanistes 80 (1994): 276–79; Alicia Dussan de Reichel, "Biblioteca Virtual: Gerardo Reichel-Dolmatoff Ficha Biografica," accessed September 15, 2015, http://www.banrepcultural.org/blaavirtual/biografias/reicgera.htm.

6. Gerardo Reichel-Dolmatoff, "Training for the Priesthood among the Kogi of Colombia," in *Enculturation in Latin America: An Anthology*, edited by Johanes Wilbert, 265–88 (Los Angeles: Latin American Center, University of California, 1976), 271.

7. Pedro Simon, *Noticias Historicas de las Conquistas de Tierra Firme en las Indias Occidentales* (Bogatá: Medaro Rivas, 1882 [1627]), capitulo 4, p. 7, accessed October 17, 2016, https://archive.org/details/tierrafirmeindias01simbrich.

8. Augusto Oyuela-Caycedo, "Ideology and Structure of Gender Spaces: The Case of the Kaggaba Indians," in *Archaeology of Gender*, edited by Dale Walde and Noreen D. Willows, 327–55 (Calgary, AB: Archaeology Association of the University of Calgary, 1991), 330.

9. Ibid.

10. Gerardo Reichel-Dolmatoff, *The Sacred Mountain of Colombia's Kogi Indians* (Leiden: E. J. Brill, 1990), 10. See also Gerardo Reichel-Dolmatoff, "Funerary Customs and Religious Symbolism among the Kogi," in *Native South Americans: Ethnology of the Least Known Continent*, edited by Patricia J. Lyons, 289–301 (Boston: Little, Brown, 1974); Gerardo Reichel-Dolmatoff, "Training for the Priesthood among the Kogi of Colombia," *UCLA Latin American Studies Series* 37 (1976): 265–88; Gerardo Reichel-Dolmatoff, "The Loom of Life: A Kogi Principle of Integration," *Journal of Latin American Lore* 4, no. 1 (1978): 5–27; Gerardo Reichel-Dolmatoff, *Los Kogi: una tribu de la Sierra Nevada de Santa Marta, Colombia*, 2nd ed. (Bogotá: Imprenta Procultura, 1985).

11. Reichel-Dolmatoff, *Sacred Mountain*, 7.

12. Ibid.

13. Ibid., 9.

14. Ibid.

15. Ibid.

16. Peter Furst and Jill Furst, "Seeing a Culture without Seams: The Ethnography of Gerardo Reichel Dolmatoff," *Latin American Research Review* 16, no. 1 (1981): 258–63, 262.

17. Accessed March 20, 2016, https://www.youtube.com/watch?v=fvckocaVPNA.

18. Oyuela-Caycedo, "Obituary," 52.

19. Accessed October 17, 2016, http://www.youtube.com/watch?v=Y1kDazfCjnU. A transcript in Spanish and German is available at http://www.academia.edu/1815012 /El_pasado_Nazi_y_en_la_SS_de_Gerardo_Reichel-Dolmatoff_o_Erasmus_Reichel_ ponencia_presentad_con_la_colaboracion_de_Manuela_Fischer_y_Holdger_ Stoecker (same access date). I have translated the Spanish into English.

20. Patricia Salazar Figueroa, "La historia del pasado nazi del padre de la antropología colombiana," *El Tiempo*, August 25, 2012, Bogotá, accessed September 14, 2015, http://www.eltiempo.com/archivo/documento/CMS-12163993.

21. Ibid.

22. See note 19; my translation.

23. Quoted in Salazar Figueroa, "La Historia."

24. "En Hagamos Memoria, Gerardo Reichel Dolmatoff," *Canal Capital*, Bogotá, November 1, 2012, accessed March 20, 2016, https://www.youtube.com/watch?v=PoL8by1TtMQ.

25. Reichel-Dolmatoff, *Sacred Mountain*, 14.

CHAPTER SEVEN

Avenue of the Volcanoes

In June 2010 commercial flights into Guayaquil were canceled because eruptions from Volcán Tungurahua coated Ecuador with ash. The airport and the volcano are 137 km apart. Tungurahua is the most active volcano in Ecuador, and its caldera was formed in several major events when the mountain erupted and collapsed upon itself. With its ice-capped peak at 5,023 m above sea level, Tungurahua tends to explosive eruptions with major periods of activity followed by decades of quiescence. Tungurahua repeatedly erupted in the 1640s and again between 1773 and 1781. Silent for a century, the volcano was consistently active from 1885 to 1888 and again from 1916 to 1920. Eighty years of calm gave way to fairly constant activity from 2000 until late 2014. The mountain is known as the "Black Giant."[1]

Tungurahua's recent eruptions are classified as stromboli, named after the volcanic island off the coast of Sicily. Stromboli eruptions generally lack lava flows but have nearly continuous eruptions, when ash, volcanic bombs, and blocks of stone are launched from the summit.

These contrast with Plinian eruptions, which are massive explosions that shoot large volumes of gases and ashes into the stratosphere, accompanied by the spread of toxic fumes; they are named for Pliny the Elder (AD 23–79), the Roman military commander and naturalist who died during the eruption of Mount Vesuvius. Volcanic eruptions vary in their intensity and are commonly described by a Volcanic Explosivity Index (VEI), a scale ranging from 1 ("Effusive") to 8 ("Apocalyptic").[2] Stromboli eruptions have VEI values ranging from 2 to 3 ("Gentle" to "Explosive"). Plinian eruptions have VEI values from 4 to 6 ("Cataclysmic" to "Colossal"), and there are rare examples of Ultra-Plinian eruptions (VEI = 7) classified as "Mega-Colossal." There have not been any VEI 8 eruptions on Earth for the last 10,000 years.

On the northern base of Tungurahua, the town of Baños de Agua Santa is in a narrow valley on the Río Pastaza. Famous for its thermal baths (thus its name), Baños is serenaded by water. The Río Pastaza roars past town, mud-brown and wicked in the rainy season. Waterfalls splatter from surrounding cliffs, cascades of metallic dashings. Eaves drip.

Baños was founded in the 1570s in the transitional zone between the sierra and the selva as Dominican priests proselytized in the adjacent highlands of Ambato and made tentative inroads into the lowlands.[3] At first, only a humble chapel was built in Baños, but one night the chapel's sacristan saw a small statue of the Virgin Mary fly through the air before the Virgin's image fell into a spring that flowed from the mountain. Night after night, the sacristan witnessed this vision of revelation and inundation. The priests gathered the people together in the small chapel to pray to the Holy Virgin, beseeching her to clearly manifest her will. That night the Virgin appeared, asking that a chapel be built near the spring where lepers could heal their sores with thermal waters and faith. The chapel was constructed according to the Virgin's wishes, but the night before her statue was to be moved to the new chapel, the Virgin's image disappeared once again.

The next afternoon a lone mule loaded with a crate wandered into the town plaza. No one recognized the mule—an odd thing in a small

town—so the animal was unloaded and fed while the owner was sought. The crate was placed in the church for safe-keeping. For the next two months the mule's owner was sought, to no avail. Finally, the priests decided to open the crate, searching for evidence of its owner, and the parishioners were invited as witnesses. The crate was pried open. The statue of the Virgin of the Baños was inside.

The Basilica de la Virgen de Agua Santa sits in the center of Baños. The current basilica was finished in 1929. Two towers flank the gabled facade, and at the end of the long nave the Virgin of Holy Waters stands above the altar. She holds the presidential staff of authority, which a former president gave her in 1959, recognizing her as a holy protector of Ecuador. Inside the basilica is a fountain of sacred water, combining features of a holy font with a drinking fountain. Four spigots on each side of the fountain spurt clear water, and people line up with jugs to carry home this *agua pura*.

The basilica walls hold large votive paintings extolling the Virgin's miraculous protections. There is a painting depicting the horrific destructions of massive earthquakes that leveled all the towns—except for Baños. The people of Baños have survived as a result of divine interventions, flanked by the dangers of water and fire. They live in the Avenue of the Volcanoes.

Begin at the beginning and go on until the end. Then stop.

Alice in Wonderland, LEWIS CARROLL

The Avenue of the Volcanoes is a broad corridor of highland valleys in Ecuador trending north-south between extremely tall, snow-capped volcanoes and a score of subsidiary cinder cones and vents. "The whole of the mountainous part of the kingdom of Quito," the Prussian polymath Alexander von Humboldt wrote in 1807, "may be considered as an immense volcano, occupying more than seven hundred square leagues of surface, and throwing out flames by different cones."[4] The two parallel chains of volcanoes run for about 300 km between Otavalo and Riobamba, bordering a 15–20-km-wide swathe of relatively flat and extremely fertile land. Today, the Pan-American Highway runs through the Avenue of the Volcanoes, following the route of the earlier Inca road that linked Quito and Cusco.

I traveled to highland Ecuador in 2011. It was an easy journey, although confusing at points. At noon, I picked up a small rental car at the Guayaquil airport. Although I had a map of Ecuador, I asked for directions for leaving the airport and finding Highway 25 North that would take me toward Quito. A big mistake.

I have driven in Latin America for nearly forty years, but I am still perplexed by the directions I get from local folks, always earnest and helpful. I was once driving in a rural valley on the coast of Peru, and I saw a track leading off into the desert. A *campesino* walked by and I asked, "Is there a road over there?" He looked at me, looked at the route, and answered "Almost." I once asked a man in Baños how to get to Riobamba. He answered, "Go to the *terminal terrestre* and take a bus."

I realize that asking people who do not drive for directions is like asking folks without children for parenting advice, but one might think that the folks at Hertz Rental Car at the Guayaquil airport would be accustomed to giving directions. They were not. The agent, sincerely trying to be helpful, said: "From the parking lot, turn right, then left,

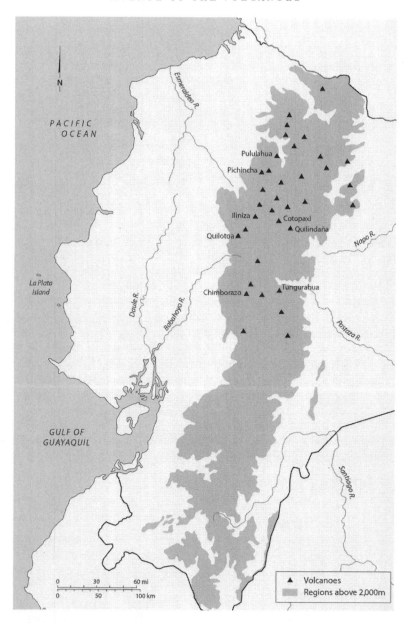

right again, and then go straight past three stoplights. The first one isn't working. Keep going straight past a large shopping center on your left. Don't stop there. Keep going straight until you reach the roundabout, but don't go south, go the other way." In fact, all he needed to say was "follow the signs to Duran, and then follow the signs to Babahoyo."

I finally found Highway 25N, which headed north through the vast floodplains of the Río Guayas and its tributaries, a broad, hot region of banana plantations and rice paddies. At Babahoyo the route turned northeast into the western slopes of the Andes. As the road climbed, bananas and rice gave way to sorghum and maize and then to orchards of cacao. Moisture from the Pacific Ocean thickened in the cool air of higher elevations, and the trip was shrouded in fog. The road was generally good, except in small towns and construction zones. At about 3,500 m I broke through the mist and gained the paramo. It was beautiful, stark grassland, with drifts of volcanic ash anchored by tussocks of bunchgrass. The road curved around the western flanks of Chimborazo, snow-capped and silent. A small herd of vicuña grazed on a short-grass moor watered by a silver chain of ponds and streams.

But as the road descended into the city of Ambato, the madness began. Highway 25 passes through the west side of Ambato to intersect with the Pan-American Highway. Traffic crawled and honked, stopped every block at signal lights. I finally found the Pan-American Highway but quickly lost it again, as this was road construction season and traffic was diverted onto city streets.[5] I repeatedly lost the route, asking passersby for directions as I was stopped at a red light and getting answers like "just follow that bus" while the bus drove away, turned a corner, and disappeared. At one point, I ended up in a suburban cul-de-sac with a small park, but I could see the Pan-American Highway on the far side of the park. Easing my tiny rental car up and over the curb, I drove through the park—passing the jungle gym and rather terrifying garbage cans shaped like Disney characters (Minnie Mouse was particularly grim)—and with a bump and a scrape, I regained the Pan-American Highway.

At nightfall, I was nearing the town of Latacunga when I noticed that the northbound lanes were partially closed, traffic diverted to the left with lines of white painted stones. After a few minutes something odd happened: cars rushed up behind me, the drivers flashing their high

beams and then swerving around my right, yelling at me. I was looking in my rear-view mirror when I glanced forward and saw the head-
lights of oncoming traffic. Without warning, the highway had become
a four-lane route again, and I swerved right and just avoided a head-on
collision. I got to the crossroads at Lasso at 7 p.m. and stopped at a
gas station mini-mart for final directions and a six-pack of beer. The
directions were good: I found the turnoff, then drove across the railroad tracks and down a eucalyptus-lined lane to the brilliantly lighted
stone facade of the Hacienda La Ciénaga.

Ⅱ

I had explored the mysterious sources of the Amazon, and then I
sought to ascend the pinnacle of the Universe. I strove bravely forward
in the footsteps of La Condamine and Humboldt, and nothing could
hold me back.

SIMON BOLIVAR, *Mi delirio sobre el Chimborazo*

The Hacienda La Ciénaga is set among beautiful gardens, although
on a parcel much reduced from its once-vast holdings, but it is still an
impressive expanse of orchards and flowerbeds with buzzing sentinels
of hummingbirds. A graveled drive flowed around a large central fountain before ending at a stone-pillared portico. The entranceway leads to
long sitting rooms with large plate-glass windows overlooking formal
gardens flanked by a beautiful chapel.

The great volcanic peak Cotopaxi is 24 km northeast of the Hacienda
La Ciénaga. Built up from hardened layers of lava, pumice, and ash,
Cotopaxi is a stratovolcano similar to Mounts Pinatubo, Krakatoa, and
Vesuvius. In 1802 von Humboldt prepared a detailed profile of Cotopaxi
while staying at the Hacienda La Ciénaga, the guest of the aristocrat
Juan José Matheu Arias-Dávila y Herrera (1783–1850), the Count of
Puñonrostro and the tenth Marquis of Maenza. From the hacienda,
Humboldt wrote, "one can observe all at once, and in frightening prox-
imity, the colossal volcano of Cotopaxi, the slender peaks of Iliniza, and

the Nevado de Quilindaña. It is one of the most majestic and impressive sites that I have seen in either hemisphere."[6]

Von Humboldt carefully sighted on the slopes and topographic features using his Ramsden sextant, one of the most precise scientific instruments of his day. He had two fundamental scientific objectives in his study of mountains: the demonstration of similarity and the documentation of variation. On the first objective he wrote, "A comparison of the mountains of both continents [Europe and South America] reveals a similarity in shape that would be unimaginable if one reflected upon the combination of forces that, in the primal world, had a tumultous effect on the soft surface of our planet . . . Each region of the globe has its specific physiognomy; but even when one is surrounded by characteristic features that give the natural realm such a rich and varied appearance, one is struck by a resemblance in shape that is based both on similar causes and local circumstances."[7] Alternatively, such studies could document change over time: if precise drawings using scientific instruments were "repeated century after century, we would eventually come to understand the random changes that the surface of the globe undergoes."[8] Despite his commitment to precision, Humboldt confessed to a slight artistic license to signal that Cotopaxi was still an active volcano: "I took the liberty of including a thin plume of smoke above the crater of Cotopaxi, although I did not see any smoke emitted when I made this sketch."[9]

In June 2011, Cotopaxi stood clear against a bright blue sky east of the hacienda, and I decided to drive into the *parque nacional*. I paid the two dollar admission along with throngs of tourists from Quito, families who had come to drive up the mountain—there is a parking lot at 4,343 m—so their kids could play in the snow. The crowds were more than I could take and the road a bit rougher than my car could manage, so I avoided the peak and went to Laguna Limpiopungo on the northwest shoulder of the volcano. At 3,900 m a stroll around the lake was an easy walk, although the clouds built up toward noon. The sky darkened and hailed, the marbles of ice bouncing off the ground. I got my little car turned around and headed back down the mountain, resolving to return earlier tomorrow—hoping to get to the high parking lot before the crowds. It was not to be. The rain and hail continued throughout the night, the roads were carved with newly eroded gullies, and though I made it to the snowline, climbing further was out of the question. Cotopaxi's high elevation and uncertain weather thwarted my plans, as it had the plans of many previous travelers.

In June 1742, the members of the French-Spanish Geodesic Survey, led by the French savant Charles Marie de La Condamine, were descending Volcán Pichincha, fortunately quiescent at the time, when they saw a plume of smoke rising from Cotopaxi, 50 km to the southeast. They hurried on to the Hacienda La Ciénaga, where La

Condamine had a good view of the chaos. Cotopaxi's initial eruptions built in fury, he wrote, until "cataracts of fire pried open new routes down the mountainside, where avalanches of half-melted snow barreled down the mountain into the plains below. In just a few minutes, a sea of boiling water covered the land for several leagues around, with fiery blocks of lava, blocks of ice and fragments of rocks tumbling pell-mell into the mass."[10]

Sixty years later Alexander von Humboldt observed, "The shape of Cotopaxi is the most beautiful and the most regular of all the colossal peaks in the upper Andes. It is a perfect cone that, cloaked in an enormous layer of snow, shines dazzlingly at sunset and stands out delightfully against the azure sky."[11] He reported that "Cotopaxi is also the most feared of all the volcanoes in the kingdom of Quito, the one with the most frequent and most devastating explosions."[12] The amount of volcanic scoria and rocks surrounding Cotopaxi covered several square leagues—a mass that, if heaped together, would form an enormous peak itself. The power of its explosions was fearsome. In January 1803, when Humboldt was in Guayaquil and 225 km south of Cotopaxi, he "heard the volcano roaring night and day like the repeated discharge" of artillery.[13] Even earlier, von Humboldt noted, "On April 4, 1768, the quantity of ash spewed from the mouth of Cotopaxi was so great that in the cities of Ambato and Latacunga it was still night time at three o'clock in the afternoon, forcing the inhabitants to carry lanterns with them in the streets."[14] Similar stories of darkness, explosions of flames, and the falling sky are known from across South America, legends told in many voices.

Given their dominating presence and danger, it is not surprising that volcanoes were subjects of local legends and myths. South of Cotopaxi, Chimborazo and Tungurahua rise on opposite sides of the Avenue of the Volcanoes. The volcanoes were not only animate, locals believed, they were also sexual: "The Indians say that Chimborazo is the male and Tungurahua is the female, and they have intercourse [when] Chimborazo goes to see his woman and the woman her husband and they have their sexual unions."[15]

In 1577 the priest Fray Juan de Paz Maldonado reported on the indigenous pueblo of San Andres de Xunxi, located at the base of Chimborazo 2 leagues from Riobamba.[16] Paz Maldonado wrote that "today there are some fallen edifices, where those [from] the land surrounding would gather to make offerings whenever something was desired, and they made spells and in some of these placed offerings and today there are some [objects] that the Inca had left as offerings."[17] Chimborazo "was held in great veneration and adoration in the past and today, although this is not obvious, because they say they were born from him. They used to sacrifice virgin maidens to this mountain, daughters of the Lords, and llamas [*ovejas de tierra*], and others, thrown in alive; and today they keep many [llamas] at the snowline, which the Indians do not kill or go to do evil to them, because the said volcano will hurl ice and hail on their planted fields, and so they do this as a form of augury." Outraged by this pagan tradition, a Spanish judge (*visitador*) ordered that Chimborazo's sacred herds of llamas be slaughtered, "and many Indians went and protested and cried out and wept, saying that their fields would be covered with hail if the Spaniards slaughtered the llamas offered to said volcano. Knowing this the *visitador* sent his men [to kill the sacred herds], and upon their return they found the maize stalks covered with ice because it hailed during those days, confirming the augury and occurring because the Spaniards had killed the llamas . . . And because these llamas had been an offering, [the Indians] did not eat the meat of the llamas, although the meat was good."[18]

Such offerings were intended to placate the volcanoes, although sometimes they were not effective. Cieza de Leon reports on a volcano that had a formidable eruption in pre-Columbian times. He writes, "There is, on the right hand of this village of Mulahalo, a volcano or mouth of fire which the Indians say broke out anciently and threw up such a great quantity of stones and ashes that as far as the cataclysm extended it destroyed a great portion of the villages."[19] Mulahalo has been identified with the later Inca *tampu* at Callo, just 2 km from Hacienda La Ciénaga.[20]

Accounts of cataclysmic volcanic eruptions and other celestial disasters are widespread among traditional South American societies. The ethnographers Johannes Wilbert and Karin Simoneau made an extensive study of South American catastrophe myths, writing: "Accounts of universal or local catastrophes are told by all our sample societies . . . Many tribes describe a number of disasters, some ordered by a supernatural being as punishment for perceived offenses, others simply regarded as spontaneous events which the myths attempt to rationalize. Whatever their source, such cataclysms play a major role in shaping the world as we know it today. The Flood motif and the Great Fire are the most common, but the Long Drought, the Wave of Cold, the Fall of a Meteor, the Great Darkness, and the Collapse of the Sky also appear."[21]

Legends of catastrophe do not *necessarily* represent historical disasters, as myths inevitably express complex cultural beliefs. In his review of native South American religion, Lawrence Sullivan writes, "The cosmic conflagration demonstrates the absolute spirituality of matter in the primordial world and shows that being in all its forms is susceptible to total spiritualization. No cozy blaze, the cosmic sea of flames, like all mythic realities[,] is a full manifestation of a primordial mode of being."[22]

Fire transforms—indigestible roots become food, clay becomes pottery, the dead become ashes—and a cosmic conflagration portends the possibility of universal transformations. In 1938 the anthropologist Bernard Mishkin recorded this myth in the Quechua village of Kauri, located seventy miles east of Cusco:

> The story is told by many of my informants that in the earliest times, these lands were owned by the mountain divinities (*aukis*) who lived in darkness, having only the moon for light. Among the ancient inhabitants there were prophets who announced that their end was approaching and that soon a flaming comet would rise from the east. Those who wanted to survive the cataclysm were cautioned to construct houses on the peaks of the highest mountains so that they could be cooled by

the winds. Some people observed the caution but the largest majority including the bravest marched off in the direction indicated, armed with bows and arrows to do battle with the Sun. But Inti Huayna Ccapac, the Sun, rose behind the back of the multitude and burned them to a crisp while those who remained hidden in their houses were likewise burned to death.[23]

Myths of cosmic fires and associated disasters—floods that inundate the world, darkness that blocks all light, cataclysmic stars that fall from the sky—are found across South America. "Myths of catastrophe, the most dramatic and widespread myths in South America," Sullivan writes, "furnish South American cultures with imagery and language with which to critique the status of absolute being and meaning. The imagery of disaster proves essential to apprehending all instances of breakthrough. Only through the symbolism of disaster can one come to grips with a completely new mode of being."[24]

While Sullivan emphasizes the metaphorical uses of these myths of cosmic catastrophe, some may reflect actual environmental events that became the stuff of legends. Not every myth is a folk history of a specific catastrophe, but some may be. Wilbert and Simoneau write, "Doubtless many such tales reflect the environmental hazards faced by the Indians, as long-gone natural disasters, dimly preserved in tribal memory, tie in with creation or other myths to explain the present natural order."[25] Using the Wilbert and Simoneau studies as a data set—4,259 myths recorded from twenty cultural groups east of the Andes—W. Bruce Masse and Michael Masse plotted the distribution of legends regarding the "Sky Fall" and "Great Darkness" myths across South America.[26] The results are intriguing.

The Sky Fall and Great Darkness myths are not uniformly distributed across South America but rather are clustered in the northern Amazon/Orinoco Basin, the Guiana highlands, the Brazilian highlands, the Gran Chaco, and Tierra del Fuego. Of these regions, only Tierra del Fuego contains active volcanoes, but—intriguingly—all of these areas are adjacent to the three major active volcanic zones in the Andes: the southernmost group along the Chilean/Argentine border; a central

GUAJIRO
(1 Darkness)

CUIVA
(4 Sky Fall)

NORTHWEST
VENEZUELA

GUYANA
SURINAME

FRENCH GUIANA

N

YANOMANI
(11 Sky Fall
2 Darkness)

COLUMBIA

ECUADOR

GUIANA
HIGHLANDS

BRAZIL

PERU

BRAZILIAN
HIGHLANDS

BOLIVIA

GE
(1 Darkness)

CHOROTE
(1 Sky Fall)

AYOREO
(1 Darkness)

NIVAKLE
(9 Sky Fall)

PARAGUAY
GRAN
CHACO

MATACO
(1 Darkness)

CHAMACOCO
(1 Sky Fall)

MAKKA
(1 Darkness)

CHILE

URUGUAY

TOBA
(12 Darkness)

ARGENTINA

PATAGONIA

YAMANA
(1 Darkness)

| 0 | 500 | 1000 mi |
| 0 | 500 1000 | 1500 km |

△ Holocene volcanoes
Location of 'Sky Fall' myth
Location of 'Great Darkness' myth

cluster in northern Chile, Bolivia, and southern Peru; and the north-
ernmost group in Ecuador and southern Colombia that includes the
Avenue of the Volcanoes.

Numerous factors complicate this simple correlation. First, wind patterns vary across South America; they do not uniformly carry volcanic ash eastward. As noted, the ash from eruptions in the Avenue of the Volcanoes often falls to the west and south of the Andes. Yet recent volcanoes have demonstrated the incredible power and vast impact of volcanic eruptions in South America. For example, after more than nine millennia of silence, the Volcán Chaiten in Chile erupted in May 2008 and was active for the next six months. The ash cloud stretched across Argentina for more than 500 km southeast to the Atlantic Coast. In June 2011 the eruption of Puyehue-Cordon-Caulle Volcanoes in Chile produced ash that was pushed to the northwest by winds, resulting in the closing of the international airport in Buenos Aires, 950 km away.

In a world where mountains explode, ash clouds billow, and the sky darkens at midday, it is not surprising that native traditions reflect those events in the catastrophic myths of the Sky Fall and Great Darkness. But in addition to those enduring myths, we know from archaeological evidence that such catastrophes impacted ancient lives in the Avenue of the Volcanoes.

The archaeologists James Zeidler and John Isaacson have sum-
marized the evidence for prehistoric volcanic eruptions in northern
Ecuador. "Since the late Pleistocene," they write, "20 or more of the
northern Ecuadorian volcanoes have had major eruptions,"[27] and some
of these active phases resulted in long periods of ash clouds, streams
of lava, and other volcanic events. The impacts of these eruptions were
most intense in the Avenue of the Volcanoes and the montaña and
coastal plains to the west, where their consequences were widespread
and varied. In this northern zone, entire regions were abandoned by
humans although subsequently resettled, resulting in a discontinuous archaeological record. In contrast, the southwest coast of Ecuador
was occupied continuously by humans beginning 13,000 to 11,000
years ago.[28] People settled into villages around 8,000–6,000 years ago.
Plant cultivation led to agriculture between 9,000 and 6,000 years ago.
Relatively complex societies emerged after 5,000 years ago, a series of
societies that created different pottery styles—Valdivia, Machalilla,
and Chorrera—and continued to occupy regions south of the volcanoes' major impact zones. To give just one example, the coastal site of
Salango was first settled around 5,000 years ago and was still occupied
when the Spaniards arrived in the 1500s.

Just a short distance to the north, the situation was much different.
Not only were highland zones abandoned when settlements and valleys were mantled with tephras, but even regions away from the eruptions were affected. For example, the Jama Valley is a medium-sized
drainage about 75 km long in the coastal northern Manabi Province,
80 km northwest of Manta.[29] The river valley runs east-west, beginning
in the low hills of the coastal ranges (rather than in the Andean cordillera). The prehistoric center of this valley was San Isidro, a 40-hectare
site with a 17-m-tall mound, 100 m in diameter. At about 1900 BC "a
massive volcanic eruption emanating from the Ecuadorian highlands
blanketed a large swath of the western lowlands with a tephras mantle
so thick that Early Formative lifeways were completely devastated and
resident populations of northern Manabi were forced to either migrate
or succumb to asphyxiation and/or famine."[30] The volcanic ash covered

San Isidro and the Jama Valley, turning farm fields into wastelands. The countryside was coated with loose black ash and gray lapilli, the small volcanic nuggets often used as decorative stone in gardens and outdoor landscaping in the United States. In the rainy season, the unconsolidated deposits flowed in dark slurries down the rivers and streams, choking once-productive estuaries with volcanic silt. It is amazing how unstable these deposits are, as I saw for myself as I journeyed to the Black Sheep Inn.

Π

The Black Sheep Inn is an award-winning eco-lodge in the small village of Chugchilán. I left Baños on an early bus one day in May 2008 and traveled north along the Pan-American Highway to the city of Latacunga, where I waited in the *terminal terrestre* for a connecting bus to Chugchilán. The day began clear and dry, but dark clouds thickened with moisture from the Pacific, and it started to drizzle as we headed into the mountains. The road was good as we were heading west, but when we turned at Zumbahua and headed north to Chugchilán, the pavement gave way to dirt, initially wide and graded but quickly deteriorating as the road became a track.[31] The rainclouds swathed the mountains. The soils were black ash.

The route follows the Quilotoa Circuit, named for an impressive crater lake named Laguna Quilotoa. At about 3,500 m above sea level, Laguna Quilotoa is 3.5 km² in area and 248 m deep.[32] The steep walls of the caldera loom 400 m above the lake. Laguna Quilotoa is a beautiful body of water and a popular hiking destination. It is also a very deadly place.

Around AD 1150 Quilotoa exploded in a massive Plinian eruption that propelled clouds of ash 35 km into the sky. The fine-grained crystalline ash coated a huge portion of Ecuador: a 10-cm-thick layer of ash was cast over 37,000 km², and more than 810,000 km² were covered with at least traces of Quilotoa's ash. Closer to the volcano, ash fell into massive layers more than 200 m thick.

The road to Chugchilán cut through those layers. Rainfall raked the slopes of Volcán Quilotoa. The route narrowed into an undependable track edged by steep drops. The road was undercut in places, and the driver slowed the bus to a crawl as two *ayudantes*—young men who assisted the driver—stood in the open door watching for the route to give way. The ayudantes were afraid we were going over; so was I. We passed within inches of the edge. As we descended into Chugchilán, the road made a tight hairpin curve. Thick ash and lava boulders flowed over the roadway in dark, slick rivers. At one point the bus had to stop as the ayudantes stepped out into the rain and cleared a new slide with broad-bladed hoes. I have ridden many Latin American buses, and I decided that this was the second-most-terrifying bus ride in my life.

But the eruption 800 years ago must have been beyond terror. Quilotoa had been quiet for 14,000 years—a silent, unthreatening peak when humans arrived and settled in northern South America. Like other volcanos in the Western Cordillera, Quilotoa was "characterized by having highly explosive, large-volume eruptions separated by long periods of inactivity."[33]

The AD 1150 eruption produced "a violent expulsion of a large volume of lake water, estimated at 250 million m³" that "flowed over the eastern caldera rim" and created a "sculpted landscape of gullies and ridges that have a veneer of sand, gravel, blocks, and boulders."[34] When the magma hit water, the steam accelerated the eruption, sending volcanic material into the stratosphere. The magma shattered, creating dacite—a lightweight, silica-rich lava that forms viscous flows. Given the extent of the volcanic ash and the volume of the caldera created in the AD 1150 explosion, it is estimated that Volcán Quilotoa's ash column was as high as the 1991 Pinatubo explosion in the Philippines, but Quilotoa's overall volume was greater. With an estimated Volcanic Explosivity Index of 6, Quilotoa's eruption is classified as "Ultra-Plinian."[35] It must have seemed that this was a time of the Sky Falling and of the Great Darkness.

The AD 1150 eruptions continued for at least three days. We do not know how many people were lost, how many lives were upended.[36] But even when the eruptions subsided, the devastation continued. The volcanologists Minard L. Hall and Patricia A. Mothes write, "The greatest impact upon human settlement was probably not the short-lived violent eruptive events, but rather the extended loss of hospitable, fertile

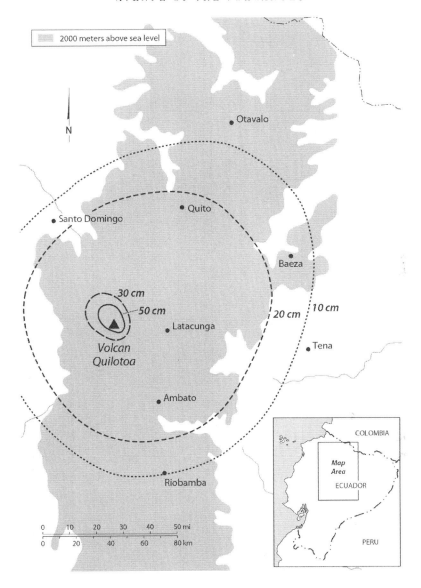

lands due to burial by eruption products . . . In such cases it might have been necessary to abandon the area for long periods of time, possibly hundreds to thousands of years."[37]

There is little archaeological evidence for prehistoric settlements near Laguna Quilotoa, but presumably the hillsides were covered with homesteads and cornfields as they are today. Further eruptions occurred between 1725 and 1797; since then, there have been no major eruptions at Quilotoa. That does not mean the lake is safe. Gases emitted from deep in the crater mix with upper water levels in the lake, emitting high concentrations of carbon dioxide. The liminoligist Günter Gunkel and colleagues have studied CO_2 concentrations in Laguna Quilotoa and report that "during periods of calm or no wind, toxic CO_2 gas clouds can form within the caldera and pose a high risk of asphyxiation."[38] They point out that "the emission of CO_2 in volcanically active zones is common, and many reports of its lethal impact on animals and humans are known . . . CO_2 is lethal at concentrations of 3% within one hour, and has a narcotic effect, so that people are not aware of, and unable to react to, its effects. A CO_2 gas cloud has a higher density than air, and will spread out at ground level; a high risk of CO_2 poisoning exists in caves, small valleys, and calderas."[39]

In some ways, I am glad I did not know all this in 2008 during that bus trip to the Black Sheep Inn.

Massive volcanic eruptions repeatedly disrupted the lives of ancient Ecuadorian societies. As Mothes and Hall have noted, the archaeological record of Ecuador seems to reflect "abrupt interruptions, rather than smooth transitions."[40] Unlike the Central Andes, where different prehistoric societies shared some cultural continuities, Ecuadorean prehistory has been characterized as a procession of distinctive cultural traditions only tenuously connected.

Ecuador is not the only region where ancient societies lived among volcanoes, nor were South American societies the only people who incorporated eruptions into their myths. Obviously the most famous—and still harrowing—case was the AD 79 explosion of Mount Vesuvius that covered Pompeii and Herculaneum with an incandescent cloud of ash and toxic gases that burned and suffocated residents before encasing their corpses in volcanic debris.[41] In Central America, the AD 590 eruption of volcanic ash near the village of Cerén, El Salvador, gave the inhabitants advanced warning as a flow of basaltic magma spread through a fissure into the nearby Río Sucio, creating a massive explosion of steam that caused all the inhabitants to flee before the ash-fall settled over their houses and fields.[42] Across the Pacific Ocean in Papua New Guinea, Vince Neall and colleagues have documented human responses over the last 40,000 years on New Britain, a 320-mile-long island formed from volcanoes that has experienced at least twenty-two major eruptive events, including eight major eruptions in the last thousand years. After major Plinian and lesser eruptions, "People abandoned the region for significant periods of time. In some cases, these cataclysmic events caused major cultural disasters characterized by local population extinction and loss of some significant types of cultural behavior. Despite the punctuated record of settlement and changes in material culture, over the long-term, human populations found effective ways to maintain themselves within an active volcanic environment."[43]

The apocalyptic impacts of volcanic eruptions may be overstated in both scholarly literature and the popular imagination.[44] Katherine Cashman and Guido Giordano give a sense of these varied cultural responses: "Volcanological events most likely to affect cultures are large eruptions, which can destroy proximal communities and affect populations living far from the volcano."[45] Further away, eruptions can disrupt food supplies, often leading to "site abandonment, local population extinction, migration, and changes in cultural behavior following large eruptions (plinian to subplinian)."[46] Between eruptions, humans may reoccupy the impacted regions, often using new subsistence strategies and experiencing actual increases in population. However, Cashman and Giordano observe, "Areas characterized by [a] high density of volcanoes, such as Ecuador, may be severely affected by the effects of volcanic eruptions when intense eruptive phases of several volcanoes overlap over restricted periods of time."[47]

The Avenue of the Volcanoes was wedged between two explosive chains of mountains, and when they erupted, the impacts were significant and terrifying. The volcanologists Hall and Mothes describe some of the impacts: "First, pyroclastic flows and especially ash flows, given their fatally high temperatures, great speed, and their widespread distribution, would have had the greatest impact, destroying everything in their paths and leaving thick deposits of pyroclastic material over the countryside." In ancient and recent events, "Large debris flows and lahars [i.e., mud flows] have frequently devastated the valley bottoms," as they "typically leave extensive deposits, 2–10 m thick, upon the floodplains of river valleys . . . composed of unconsolidated boulders, gravel, and sand, and as such may destroy or bury settlements and useable agricultural lands. It is important to recall that both pyroclastic flows and debris flows characteristically follow river channels of the valleys and can travel tens of kilometers downstream. Thus, both phenomena would have represented considerable danger to pre-existing cultures which chose to live along the floodplains of the Inter-Andean Valley, generally the lands most suitable for agriculture."[48] Such disruptions had a direct and recurrent impact on highland Ecuadorean societies, although these events were often separated by centuries or millennia when explosive events were translated into myths or simply faded from collective memories.

There are few places where this is as evident as at the Formative village of Cotocollao.[49] At about 3,000 m above sea level in an intermontane basin that today is a northern suburb of Quito covered with apartment buildings and malls, the site of Cotocollao was discovered accidentally when a new housing development began construction in the late 1970s. Trenches for roadways and waterlines cut into dense concentrations of ceramics, exposed human bones from buried cemeteries, and uncovered the traces of ancient dwellings—all under a meter or more of volcanic ash and alluvium. A salvage excavation directed by the archaeologist Marcello Villalba carefully exposed the hidden traces of ancient lives.

Formative Cotocollao was a modest settlement scattered over about 26 hectares. Households were clustered without a grid or formalized settlement plan, "although there was an intentional planning in reference to the cemetery, which seems to have served as a central point, not in an equidistant, spatial sense but through its ceremonial or ritual function."[50] At circa 1500–1100 BC, there were 27–37 houses in the village, but between 1100 and 500 BC the population grew to more than one hundred dwellings. At 6–7 people per house, early Cotocollao had approximately 150–250 residents, while the later community had more than 600 occupants.

The houses at Cotocollao were built on small terraces that climbed the gentle hillside. The houses were 4–5 m wide and 6–8 m long. The dwellings were rectangular; lines of postholes mark the traces of walls built from large, heavy timbers interwoven with a wattle of sticks covered with mud daub. The walls were probably 2–3 m tall. Based on the grass phytoliths recovered from the floors during archaeological excavations, the roofs were thickly thatched. In the center of each house was a hearth surrounded by sleeping platforms. Cotocollao was a village of farmers who grew maize, potatoes, beans, quinoa, oca, achira, and agave. They hunted deer and other game, skinning and butchering the animals with obsidian tools. They cooked and served food in a variety of ceramic jars, jugs, bottles, and bowls—some decorated with incised lines or punctations, a few slipped with red pigments, and many simple and plain. Some vessels were placed in graves as offerings. The burials included complete, primary internments flexed in a fetal position and secondary burials consisting of skulls and long bones. "These funerary practices," Villalba writes, "reproduced the social reality of the living and guaranteed communal rights, especially about land, that invoked and included the dead ancestors as active members and protectors of the community . . . [representing] a link of unity, identity, and connectedness. This concept of continuity between the living and the dead is a necessary condition, among others, for the function of the community."[51]

This continuity abruptly snapped around 400 BC when Volcán Pululahua, less than 10 km away, erupted and covered Cotocollao in ash. Unlike Pompeii, there are no ash-covered bodies at Cotocollao: there must have been some warning—tremors or ventings—and the inhabitants fled before the sky became dark and ash clouds settled. The effects of Pululahua's eruption were widespread. Villalba has discovered seventy Cotocollao sites in the Quito Valley and nearby areas. All were abandoned at this same time.[52]

But here is a curious fact. The well-preserved outlines of houses and burial pits at Cotocollao exist because they were excavated into a durable layer of *cangahua*, a dense layer of wind-blown, fine volcanic ash that water hardens into dense sediment. This evidence of earlier volcanic activity was overlooked or not understood, as generations at Cotocollao lived on this hillside for centuries, only to have their lives disrupted by a volcanic eruption: their houses abandoned, their fields covered with ash, the rivers turned into ugly sluices of boulders, stones, and sludge. Two thousand years later, the traces of ancient lives were exposed by bulldozers and backhoes carving roads and trenching pipelines for another community, another effort at establishing lives in this beautiful and uncertain landscape.

Near Baños, a series of geological exposures contains evidence for massive eruptions at Tungurahua, including one that occurred in approximately 1100 BC.[53] It was a Plinian eruption, similar in scale to the 1980 explosion of Mount St. Helens, and its blast deposit covered 600 km². This was accompanied by a vertical column of tephras and ash 20–25 km tall, "and a rain of lapilli showered the area with pumice and scoria fragments."[54] The ash blew west to the area between Quilotoa and Chimborazo and settled into sierra lakes in southern Ecuador. The 1100 BC event was the largest known volcanic eruption in the history of Tungurahua, two orders of magnitude greater than the 2006 eruption when lava poured down the western slopes of the volcano—destroying five villages, killing seven people, and devastating 200 km² of farmland.

The 1100 BC eruption destroyed ancient settlements. Traces of dwellings have not been found, but pottery shards indicate the presence of humans in the region when the ash and lapilli fell. These ceramics have some traits similar to the pottery from Cotocollao but are actually slightly older. It is possible—although far from proven—that this earlier pottery drew upon two other ceramic traditions: a coastal pottery style known as Machalilla and another pottery tradition recently discovered in the upper Pastaza region east of Baños. In this portion

of western Amazonia, archaeological knowledge is limited, but 2013 excavations at the site of Pambay have uncovered extremely tantalizing information about the movements of people from Amazonia into the Avenue of the Volcanoes.[55] Just south of the town of Puyo and approximately 50 km east of Tungurahua, the archaeologists Geoffroy de Saulieu and Stéphen Rostain and the volcanologist Jean-Luc Le Pennec uncovered the remains of a large, very early house dating to 1495–1317 BC. Located on a small hill between two streams, the Pambay dwelling was an elliptical structure, 16 m × 10 m in size, made from large upright timbers whose postholes were still preserved, as was a large section of timber amazingly well preserved in a layer of clay. A few poorly preserved pottery shards appear similar to the ceramics recovered from under the lapilli layers near Baños, which in turn appear similar to the ceramics at Cotocollao.

So here is an interesting possibility: it may be that people moved from western Amazonia into the highlands of Ecuador sometime between 1500 and 1100 BC, following the natural corridors formed by the Río Pastaza and other rivers. Some immigrants settled the flanks of Tunguragua, while other families continued northward, moving into rich valleys flanked by the snow-peaked volcanoes. The 1100 BC eruption at Tungurahua devastated the small villages on the upper Pastaza. Undoubtedly, highland communities—including the people of Cotocollao—knew about the eruption, even though it did not cause them to abandon the region. Only seven centuries later, when Puluahua erupted, were Cotocollao and other contemporary settlements abandoned in northern Ecuador, communities who—like their ancestors and their descendents in the Avenue of the Volcanoes—experienced the days of the Great Darkness and the Collapse of the Sky.

NOTES

1. Smithsonian Institution, Natural History Museum, Global Volcanism Program, accessed January 20, 2015, http://www.volcano.si.edu/volcano.cfm?vn= 352080.

2. Christopher G. Newhall and Stephen Self, "The Volcanic Explosivity Index (VEI): An Estimate of Explosive Magnitude for Historical Volcanism," *Journal of Geophysical Research* C2 (1982): 1231–38.

3. Information from http://archivoexvotos.revista-sanssoleil.com/2011/09/09 /basilica-de-la-virgen-del-rosario-de-agua-santa-banos/, accessed January 20, 2015.

4. Alexander von Humboldt, *Personal Narrative of Travels to the Equinoctial Regions of America, during the Years 1799–1804*, translated and edited by Thomasina Ross (London: Henry G. Bohn, 1852), vol. 1:113.

5. This was the condition of the Pan-American Highway in 2011. The road has since been extensively improved, in stretches a marvelous six- to eight-lane freeway, as I discovered in June 2015.

6. Alexander Von Humboldt, *Views of the Cordillera and Monuments of the Indigenous Peoples of the Americas: A Critical Edition*, edited by Vera Kutzinski and Ottmar Ette, translated by J. Ryan Poynter (Chicago: University of Chicago Press, 2012), 66.

7. Ibid., 62.

8. Ibid., 61–62.

9. Ibid., 66.

10. Quoted in Larrie Ferriero, *Measure of the Earth: The Enlightenment Expedition That Reshaped Our World* (New York: Basic Books, 2013), 217.

11. Humboldt, *Views of the Cordillera*, 64.

12. Ibid., 62.

13. Ibid., 65.

14. Ibid., 64.

15. Ibid., 322, my translation. Bandelier provided a bit more reserved translation, writing: "The Indians say the volcano of Chimborazo is the man, and the

one of Tunguragua the woman, and that they communicate [have intercourse with each other], Chimborazo going to see his wife and the wife her husband, and that they hold their meetings." Adolph F. Bandelier, "Traditions of Precolumbian Earthquakes and Volcanic Eruptions in Western South America," *American Anthropologist* 8, no. 1 (1906): 47–81, 53.

16. Fray Juan de Paz Maldonado, "Relación del Pueblo de San Andres de Xunxi, Provincia de Riobamba, para el muy Ilustre Señor Licenciado Francisco de Auncibay, del Consejo de Su Majestad y Su Oidor en la Real Audiencia de Quito," in *Relaciones Historico-Geográficas de la Audiencia de Quito, S. XVI–XIX*, edited by Pilar Ponce Leiva, 319–24 (Madrid: Consejo de Superior Investigaciones Cientíﬁcas, Centro de Estudios Históricos, Departmento de Historia de América, 1991 [1572]), 320–21, my translation.

17. Ibid.

18. Ibid.

19. Quoted in Bandelier, "Traditions of Precolumbian Earthquakes and Volcanic Eruptions," 53. Bandelier suggested that Cieza de Leon confused his right hand and left hand as he was traveling south, as the only nearby active volcano was Cotopaxi to the left and east. Bandelier assumed that the only active volcano to the west was the quiet Iliniza, which has no known Holocene eruptions; he did not know about the AD 1150 explosion of Volcan Quilotoa discussed below.

20. César W. Astuhuamán Gonzáles, "Incas, Jívaros y la obra de Humboldt *Vues des Cordillères*," *HiN—Alexander von Humboldt im Netz* 10 (2009): 19; accessed March 18, 2016, https://www.uni-potsdam.de/romanistik/hin/hin19/inh_astuhuaman.htm.

21. Johannes Wilbert and Karin Simoneau, eds., *Folk Literature of South American Indians: General Index* (Los Angeles: UCLA Latin American Center Publications, University of California, 1992), 27.

22. Lawrence Sullivan, *Icanchu's Drum: An Orientation to Meanings in South American Religions* (New York: Macmillan, 1988), 66.

23. Bernard Mishkin, "Cosmological Ideas among the Indians of the Southern Andes," *Journal of American Folklore* 53, no. 210 (October–December 1940): 225–41, 235.

24. Sullivan, *Icanchu's Drum*, 619.

25. Wilbert and Simoneau, *Folk Literature of South American Indians*, 27.

26. W. Bruce Masse and Michael J. Masse, "Myth and Catastrophic Reality: Using Cosmic Mythology to Identify Cosmic Impacts and Massive Plinian Eruptions in Holocene South America," Geological Society, London, Special Publications 273:277–202.

27. James Zeidler and John Isaacson, "Settlement Process and Historical Contingency in the Western Ecuadorian Formative," in *Archaeology of Formative Ecuador*, edited by J. Scott Raymond and Richard Burger, 69–123 (Washington, DC: Dumbarton Oaks Research Libraries and Collections, 2003), 73.

28. The following is based on James Zeidler, "The Ecuadorian Formative," in *Handbook of South American Archaeology*, edited by Helaine Silverman and William Isbell, 459–88 (New York: Springer, 2008).

29. The following is based on James Zeidler and Deborah Pearsall, *Regional Archaeology in Northern Manabí, Ecuador*, vol. 1: *Environment, Cultural Chronology, and Prehistoric Subsistence in the Jama River Valley*, Memoirs in Latin American Archaeology 8 (Pittsburgh: University of Pittsburgh, 1994); Zeidler, "Ecuadorian Formative."

30. Zeidler, "Ecuadorian Formative," 466.

31. The following describes the road on the west side of the Quilotoa Loop in 2008. Since then the road has been paved, a more extensive tourist industry has developed, and the Black Sheep Inn is under new ownership, as I discovered during a trip in June 2015.

32. Patricia A. Mothes and Minard L. Hall, "Quilotoa's 800Y BP Ash: A Valuable Stratigraphic Marker for the Integration Period," in *Actividad volcánica y pueblos precolombinos en el Ecuador*, edited by Patricia A. Mothes, 111–38 (Quito: Editorial Abya Yala, 1998).

33. Patricia A. Mothes and Minard L. Hall, "The Plinian Fallout Associated with Quilotoa's 800 yr BP Eruption, Ecuadorian Andes," *Journal of Volcanology and Geothermal Research* 176 (2008): 56–69, 57.

34. Minard L. Hall and Patricia A. Mothes, "Quilotoa Volcano—Ecuador: An Overview of Young Dacitic Volcanism in a Lake-Filled Caldera," *Journal of Volcanology and Geothermal Research* 176 (2008): 44–55, 51.

35. Ibid., 56.

36. Archaeological excavations in the province of Imbabura, directed in the late 1990s by Elizabeth Currie, found a layer of Quilotoa ash covering raised agricultural fields; farming was suspended, but the fields were quickly renovated—but this was nearly 150 km from the eruption. Elizabeth Currie, "Archaeological Investigations in the Northern Highlands of Ecuador at Hacienda Zuleta," *Antiquity* 74, no. 284 (2000): 273–74.

37. Minard L. Hall and Patricia A. Mothes, "Volcanic Impediments in the Progressive Development of Pre-Columbian Civilizations in the Ecuadorian Andes," *Journal of Volcanology and Geothermal Research* 176 (2008): 344–55, 354.

38. Günter Gunkel, Camilla Beulker, Bernd Grupe, and Francisco Viteri, "Hazards of Volcanic Lakes: Analysis of Lakes Quilotoa and Cuicocha, Ecuador," *Advances in Geosciences*, European Geosciences Union (EGU) 14 (2008): 29–33, 30.

39. Ibid.

40. Hall and Mothes, "Volcanic Impediments," 344.

41. For an overview, see Mary Beard, *The Fires of Vesuvius: Pompeii Lost and Found* (Cambridge, MA: Harvard University Press, 2008).

42. Payson Sheets, ed., *Before the Volcano Erupted: The Ancient Cerén Village in Central America* (Austin: University of Texas Press, 2002).

43. Vince E. Neall, R. Cleland Wallace, and Robin Torrence, "The Volcanic Environment for 40,000 Years of Human Occupation on the Willaumez Isthmus, West New Britain, Papua New Guinea," *Journal of Volcanology and Geothermal Research* 176 (2008): 330–43, 330.

44. John Grattan, "Aspects of Armageddon: An Exploration of the Role of Volcanic Eruptions in Human History and Civilization," *Quaternary International* 151 (2006): 10–18.

45. Katherine Cashman and Guido Giordano, "Volcanoes and Human History," *Journal of Volcanology and Geothermal Research* 176 (2008): 325–29, 326.

46. Ibid.

47. Ibid.

48. Hall and Mothes, "Volcanic Impediments," 346.

49. Marcello Villalba, *Cotocollao: Una Aldea Formativa de Valle de Quito*, Miscelánea Antropológica Ecuatoriana, Serie Monografica (Quito: Museos del Banco Central del Ecuador, 1988).

50. Ibid., 64, my translation.

51. Ibid., 108–9, my translation.

52. As reported by Zeidler, "Ecuadorian Formative," 472.

53. Jean-Luc Le Pennec, Geoffroy de Saulieu, Pablo Samaniego, Diego Jaya, and Lydie-Sarah Gailler, "A Devastating Plinian Eruption at Tungurahua Volcano Reveals Formative Occupation at ~1100 Cal BC in Central Ecuador," *Radiocarbon* 55, no. 2–3 (2013): 1199–1214.

54. Ibid., 1208.

55. Geoffroy de Saulieu, Stéphen Rostain, and Jean-Luc Le Pennec, "El Formativo del Alto Pastaza (Ecuador), entre arqueología y vulcanología," in *Antes de Orellana: Actas del 3er Encuentro Internacional de Arqueología Amazónica*, edited by Stephen Rostain, 199–205, 518–20 (Lima: Instituto Francés de Estudios Andinos, 2014); see also Stéphen Rostain and Geoffroy de Saulieu, "El sol se levanta por el Este: arqueología en la Amazonia ecuatoriana," *Revista del Patrimonio Cultural del Ecuador* 5 (2014): 42–55; Stéphen Rostain and Geoffroy de Saulieu, "'Au-dessous du volcán': Archéologie de la haute Amazonie, au pied des Andes," *Les nouvelles de l'archéologie* 139 (2015): 18–24, accessed March 18, 2016, http://nda.revues.org/2861.

CHAPTER EIGHT

Measuring the Cosmos

THE AVENUE OF THE VOLCANOES IN ECUADOR was the scene of one of the most fascinating expeditions in the annals of science: an expedition to determine the shape of the earth.[1] By the eighteenth century it was well-known that the Earth was spherical, but its precise form remained a matter of debate. Was the planet precisely round? Was it larger at the poles or wider at the Equator? Isaac Newton had predicted that the Earth would bulge near the Equator, an oblate form something like a very ripe tomato. A rival theory argued that the Earth protruded at the poles like a bi-conical egg. Which was longer, the polar or equatorial circumference of the planet?

In the 1730s the French Academy of Sciences received royal patronage to send two expeditions to measure the shape of the earth, sending one party northward and the other to the Equator to measure the length of a degree of latitude in two different places. One expedition left in 1736 for Lapland, led by the Swedish physicist Andrus Celsius (as in "degrees Celsius") and the French mathematician Pierre Louis Maupertius.

Another expedition left France in 1735 under the direction of three French astronomers—Charles Marie de La Condamine, Pierre Bouguer, and Louis Godin—and two Spanish royal appointees and naval officers, the metallurgist Antonio de Ulloa and the scientist Jorge Juan.

La Condamine was a *philosophe* and also adept at self-promotion. Born to wealth, in addition he devised a very clever way to win vast riches from a French government lottery. The lottery sold different priced tickets, each costing 1 percent of the amount of different cash prizes—for example, a $1 ticket could win $100, a $10 ticket could win $1,000—but each ticket, regardless of purchase price, had the same probability of being selected for a "grand prize." La Condamine realized that the mathematics behind the lottery were flawed: if he bought a large percentage of inexpensive lottery tickets, he had a very good chance of wining a "mega-lotto" prize worth 500,000 *livres*—about $4.5 million in 2010 US dollars.[2] Although a gambler, La Condamine was unwilling to risk only his wealth, so he invited other investors into the scheme, most prominently the author and playwright Voltaire. They made a killing. Between his winnings and his inheritance, La Condamine provided most of the finances for the expedition to Ecuador. The French-Spanish Geodesic Expedition traveled to the province of Quito and began measuring the Earth.

In 1736 the French-Spanish Geodesic Expedition arrived in the Avenue of the Volcanoes and began its survey. The strategy was elegant but laborious, as it required establishing a geodesic chain. Since the Renaissance, grids had been used to depict volumes and space in European art, for example, as explained and illustrated in Leon

Alberti Battista's *La Pintura* in which the angled lines of perspective are demonstrated, in Leonardo da Vinci's drawing inscribing man within a circle and a square, and in Albrecht Dürer's engraving showing the use of a druid grid and sighting rod in portraiture. It was a straightforward translation from using such tools to depict the feminine contours of breasts and belly to portraying the contours of landscape.

The application of grid to landscape had even older antecedents. The geographer Denis Cosgrove writes, "That graticule of latitude and longitude represents an abstract, intellectual inscription of measure across the globe. It is a measure determined by astronomical movements, the expression of spherical geometry . . . Thus, the ancients also acknowledged the Platonic aspects of geometry, as a pure product of mind with immutable and therefore divine properties. It is impossible to separate the history and uses of geometry from those of cosmography and cosmology, the practicalities of latitude and longitude from the poetics of mathematical measure."[3]

Revived in the Renaissance, this classical knowledge of proportion and measure was brought to the Americas. Cosgrove observes: "The cultural world that launched the Columbian encounter possessed a profound belief in the power of mathematical measure . . . Geometry united humanity and nature; it was the secret measure by which God's original creation had been ordered and sustained. It thus behooved God's highest creatures to employ that same measure in making their own, lesser worlds. Man would author the earth, and most especially, a new-found land to the West."[4] Maps and drawings of the New World incorporated Western notions of point of view and frame. William Fox writes, "Accepting such visual representations for what they are—both painting and cartography being framed strategies of a particular vantage point—is safer than taking maps too literally for what they pretend to be, an objective and disinterested analog of the world."[5] But if the Western measures of space and form were applied to the New World, they were not the only means employed in measuring the cosmos.

Approximately 1,600 km south of the Avenue of the Volcanoes, I am standing at the Center of the Universe. I am in Cusco. The Quechua word "*qosco*" is translated as "navel of the universe," and the Incas envisioned their capital city as an axis mundi. Specifically, the Incas believed the four quarters (*suyus*) of the cosmos converged in the Temple of the Sun, the Qoricancha. In 1615 the bilingual and bicultural author Guaman Poma de Ayala drew a map showing the Andes bounded to the east by the forested arch of Amazonia and four quadrants converging at Cusco, each suyu connected via a great road, four major systems of the Qhapaq Ñan that intersected in the main plaza in Cusco. Rather than equal quadrants, the four suyu—Chinchaysuyu, Antisuyu, Collasuyu, and Cuntisuyu (beginning to the northwest of Cusco and continuing clockwise)—were spatial divisions that defined fields of action, not static territory. The dynamism of these fields becomes evident when one considers the lines of the ceque system.

The ceque lines composed a system of alignments and pathways that radiated out from the Qoricancha. In 1653 the Jesuit father Bernabe Cobo wrote: "From the Temple of the Sun as from the center there went out certain lines which the Indians call ceques: they formed four parts corresponding to the four royal roads which went out from Cuzco. On each one of those ceques were arranged in order the guacas and shrines which there were in Cusco and its district, like stations of holy places, the veneration of which was common to all."[6] Based on Cobo's account, there were 42 ceque lines with 328 shrines and sacred places along their routes. Although some scholars have argued that the ceques were straight lines emanating from the Qoricancha, more recent research demonstrates that many of the ceques zigzagged across the Cusco Valley, linking shrines as the faithful followed sacred paths across the landscape. As a result of the research of many scholars—notably the scholarship of the archaeologist Brian Bauer, who has conducted extensive research in Cusco and the surrounding regions—some of the shrines along the ceque are known while others have been lost to time.[7]

I leave the Temple of the Sun and step outside into the piercing Andean sunlight, which scores the ancient walls with lines of shadow. It is late May 2015, and I decide to follow the first ceque in Chinchaysuyu, the very first ceque Cobo described. From the Temple of the Sun I walk northwest to the Plaza de Armas following Calle Loreto with its flanking walls of standing Inca stonework, including the famous Hatunrumiyoc, a large twelve-cornered stone block. An Inca re-enactor poses in front of the Hatunrumiyoc for tourists' pictures. Crossing the plaza, I wind uphill through the San Blas district, a dense neighborhood of narrow streets and folklore shops. The first shrine on this ceque was some-where in the San Blas district, although its exact location is unknown. Cobo reports that this shrine was very ancient, created when a brother of the first Inca, Manco Capac, was transformed into stone. This shrine, or *wak'a*, Cobo writes, received offerings of gold, fine textiles, seashells, and other rich offerings that "made for good rains."[8]

I continue through the streets and crowded buildings, hiking up the slopes that surround Cusco before crossing a busy road and climbing

onto a quiet hilltop fringed with eucalyptus groves and divided by a dry ravine. The city is below me. This is the probable location of the second shrine on the first ceque of Chinchaysuyu, a place, Cobo reports, where the founder of the Inca Empire, Pachacuti Inca Yupanqui, once lived and died. Today, this area is known as Q'enqo, including two extensive sets of elaborately carved limestone outcrops (Q'enqo Grande and Q'enqo Chico) and another limestone outcrop and ancient walls just to the north (also known as Qochapata or Q'enqo West)—a place where modern shamans leave offerings.[9]

"Q'enqo" means "zigzag," and some surfaces at Q'enqo Grande have been carved with sharply twisting grooves, creating narrow canals down which maize beer (*chicha*) was poured as offerings, as Cobo writes, "for the health and the prosperity of the Inca."[10] The outcrops were also carved with broad, flat benches or seats, either for onlookers or ancestral mummies who witnessed the ceremonies conducted among the boulders and stones. On the day I stood among these sculpted boulders, Q'enqo was quiet with a few other visitors murmuring among the stones, but this place was made in a clatter of pounding stones, the high-pitched gratings of rock on rock as these boulders were etched, ground, and transformed.

The third shrine on the first ceque of Chinchaysuyu was at Pillcopuquio, a small spring that flowed between Q'enqo Grande and Q'enqo Chico. It was a place where "ordinary sacrifice" was made, according to Cobo, and a thin trickle flowed as I walked to the next shrine.

I walk along the road for about 5 km, cutting cross-country on back lanes and walking through quiet meadows before arriving at the Inca fortress Puca Pucara. In the distance, I can see the white peaks surrounding Mount Ausangate, nearly 100 km to the east and just south of the glaciers of Qoyllur Rit'i. I know I have lost the ceque route by this point, but I cross the highway and enter the protected area around the famous Inca fountain complex at Tambomachay. Tambomachay is an elegant Inca site, consisting of niched walls, aqueducts, and fountains. There are small crowds of tourists admiring the site, but I smell smoke and hear muffled laughter from the other side of a hedgerow. The early wheat crop is being harvested by Quechua women who have paused for lunch, roasting potatoes in a pit oven. The soft flow of their words erupts with giggles.

Like many other examples of Inca constructions, the terrace walls at Tambomachay incorporate natural boulders into the building, a fusion of the built and the natural also seen at Q'enqo Grande and Q'enqo Chico (as well as at numerous famous Inca sites such as

Machu Picchu). The art historian Carolyn Dean writes that "the Inka practice of grafting structures onto rock outcrops served to inter-weave the built environment and the natural environment, creating a stunning amalgamation of nature and architecture."[11] Rather than describe such constructions as "buildings," Dean suggests the term *grafting* may be more appropriate, a notion also found in the Quechua term *qhariwarmi*, which essentially means the union created between a man and a woman but which also applies to the union of comple-ments. Qhariwarmi reflects "Andean notions of complementarity [that] involve pairs that are flexible and relative rather than fixed and permanent."[12]

Tambomachay means "way-station cave," and a small cave sits on the hillside above the Inca buildings. The cave may be the fourth shrine on the first ceque of Chinchaysuyu, a cave called Cirocaya.[13] This cave, Cobo records, was a cavern "from which they believed the hail issued. Hence, at the season when they were afraid of it, all went to sacrifice in the cave so that hail should not come out and destroy their crops."[14] Following a path past the cave, I climb a short distance to the top of the ridge and look northwest to the top of Cerro Catunque, which Bauer suggests was the fifth and final shrine. Cobo called this place Sonconancay, a "hill where it was a very ancient custom to offer sacrifices for the health of the Inca."[15] Even today the hill is considered a major *apu*, a mountain deity.

Some scholars have suggested that the forty-two lines of the ceque system were like azimuth bearings, similar to a compass but calibrated to the Temple of the Sun rather than oriented to "true" north. Yet as I walked this first ceque of Chinchaysuyu, I understood that this "line" was really not geometric. This first ceque was a path, a progression. Along its route, the faithful gave offerings to encourage rain and prevent hail, to honor dead Incas and venerate mountain gods. The pilgrim paused at specific places, fusions of nature and culture, *tampu* of history and faith, and interacted with a cosmos that was vital, dynamic, and lived. Rather than straight vectors, the ceque lines were actually paths that wove together sets of sacred features on the landscape, bound together by the movements of priests and faithful who walked the lines. Following their steps, I realized the ceque lines were not Andean azimuths but rather routes of worship. In general, the Incas' thinking about measuring the cosmos reflected a profound recognition of its lack of fixity and the need to keep the cosmos on its proper course.

Ⅱ

Used for surveys throughout Europe, the geodesic chain involved basic Euclidian geometry: if the length of one side and two angles of a triangle are known, then the length of the other two sides and the remaining angle can be calculated. If a baseline of sufficient length can be precisely measured and the angles are correctly determined, then this initial triangle can become the foundation for a chain of triangles. For each subsequent triangle, the baseline does not require another measurement, as the lengths of all sides of the subsequent triangles can be calculated from the angles—assuming the initial baseline measurement is extremely accurate. At the end of the chain, a final baseline was measured to check the precision of the overall calculations.

Establishing a geodesic chain encountered two principal challenges. First, the baseline had to be straight and accurately measured, which

meant the terrain should be as level and open as possible. Second, the corners of the triangle had to be visible and permanent. These two requirements and eighteenth-century global politics were the fundamental reasons the French-Spanish Geodesic Expedition went to Ecuador.

In 1731 a twenty-five-year alliance between France and Great Britain ended, a pact initially designed to check Spain's political aspirations in Europe. France nimbly established an alliance with Spain, a compact made somewhat easier by the shared Bourbon origins of Spain's Felipe V and his nephew, Louis XV of France. It also made the viceroyalty of Peru—which included the Audiencia of Quito—an ideal place to measure the Earth near the Equator. Within Ecuador, the Avenue of the Volcanoes was the perfect field site. The region was relatively flat, the volcanic peaks were obvious landmarks for triangulations, and there were towns and settlements—Quito, Riobamba, Ambato, and Cuenca—where provisions and laborers could be obtained.

After a year's travels and delays, the measurement of the baseline began in October 1736. The baseline was about 11.27 km long and 46 cm wide, the ends marked by large millstones. Trees were felled, field walls breached, and ravines filled in to create a straight, reasonably level surface. Once cleared, the measurements began. The scientists divided into two groups, one team measuring the baseline from the north and the other team starting at the south, independent efforts to gauge precisely the baseline's length. Three wooden poles were used as large rulers 6 m long, their ends tipped with damage-resistant copper. Each measuring pole was painted a different color so the sequence of their placements would be obvious and consistent. The first pole was laid and leveled with wooden planks and shims, and then the second pole was carefully set, the copper tips touching. The third pole was similarly placed, the distance was recorded, and the first pole would then be moved to the head of the line. This process was repeated more than 660 times. It took a month to measure the baseline, but when it was completed, the two teams had measured more than 11.2 km and their results varied by only 7.6 cm. Averaging the two sums, the baseline measured 12,239 m With this information in hand, the triangulation of the geodesic chain could begin.

But it did not. A year was lost to political intrigues between the French and local authorities and among the scientists themselves. For months, the Andes were shrouded with thick clouds. The survey stations on the high peaks were frigid, wind-blasted camps where the surveyors and local porters shivered in huts covered with hides and rushes, cold so bitter that they kept their dinner plates on ember-filled chafing dishes to prevent their food from freezing as they ate. The surveyors suffered from altitude sickness—with headaches, bleeding gums, and lapses into unconsciousness—as they waited for the clouds to clear so a triangulating shot could be made. Not until late January 1738 was the first triangle completed. The measure of the geodesic chain required nearly two years' work.

After weeks of calculations and calibrations—independently determined for accuracy by La Condamine and Bouguer—the two men shared the results: Bouguer measured 162,965 *toises* (about 317.39 km), and La Condamine arrived at 162,995 *toises* (317.46 km), a difference of about 32 m. The results were remarkably close given the tools, the terrain, and the numerous opportunities for error and miscalculation. With this information in hand, the expedition only needed to wait to measure the stars.

The long chain of simple and easy reasoning by which geometers are accustomed to reach the conclusions of their most difficult demonstrations, led me to imagine that all things, to the knowledge of which man is competent, are mutually connected in some way, and there is nothing so far removed from us or beyond our reach or so hidden that we cannot discover it.

RENÉ DESCARTES, *Discourse on Method*

During their survey, La Condamine and Bouguer visited the site of Ingapirca and on May 29, 1737, made the first scientific map of an archaeological site in Ecuador. With the precision one might expect from someone who was measuring the Earth, La Condamine wrote, "The Fortress consists in its present state of a Terreplein (AB) made by hand, raised level to the height of 14, 15, and 17 ft above an unequal Ground. In the middle of the Terreplein there is a square lodgement, which very likely served for the Guard. The Terreplein as well as the Platform which ends it is eight *toises* [15.5 m] across and twenty *toises* [38.8 m] long; the two extremities (A B) are rounded so that the shape is of a very long oval, little or not at all enlarged at the middle."[16]

The oval platform at Ingapirca was built from

a sort of granite, well quarried, perfectly joined, without the least appearance of cement, and of which not a single one has given way to the present day. All the courses of Stones are exactly parallel, and of the same height; [t]he joints of the stones would be imperceptible if their exterior surface were flat, but this is worked in relief . . . To give this regular and uniform convexity to all these Stones, and even to polish so perfectly the interior faces where they touch, what labor and industry would be required with even our instruments, among peoples who did not have any use of iron, and who could not work Stones harder than marble except with axes of Flint, nor smooth them save by rubbing them together?[17]

Ingapirca covers about 2 km², and much of it remains unexcavated. Apparently, it was originally built by the Cañaris between AD 1020 and 1220, but it was extensively rebuilt when the Incas conquered Ecuador in the 1400s.[18] The Incas constructed extensive storerooms and other buildings and extended a well-made section of the Qhapaq Ñan directly to the rock outcrop and elliptical platform.[19]

The elliptical platform is intriguing because of its placement and possible form. The archaeologist Antonio Fresco writes, "The religious sector [of Ingapirca] is dominated by two temples: the great ellipse or 'Castillo' (Temple of the Sun) in the northwest and Pilaloma to the southeast. The first monument may have had a religious function before the Inca arrival . . . although the indications of this are few and indirect; the second monument has a clear pre-Inca, Cañari occupation that continued during the period of Inca occupation. The intervening buildings between both temples apparently were a service area (workshops, dwellings, and storerooms) directly linked to the cult."[20] The stone outcrop may have been a sacred place of origin for the Cañaris, what the cusqueños would have called a *pacarina,* which the Inca conquerors enclosed and expropriated within curving walls of extraordinary stonework.

Not only did the Incas expropriate this sacred landscape, they also constructed a two-room building on top of the elliptical platform. The doorways were evidently positioned to frame the rising and setting sun on the June and December solstices. Essentially, the movement of the sun was marked by the jambs of the doorways, illuminating with sunlight an interior wall made from fine Inca stone. On the west-facing interior, four niches apparently aligned with the solstices and equinoxes.

Ironically, the Inca building at Ingapirca may have been used as an observatory, an architectural construction that measured the course of time, something like the survey huts La Condamine and Bouguer erected as they were measuring the Earth. Despite their superficial similarity, the French geometers' huts and the solar observatory at Ingapirca were motivated by very different cultural expectations. The French built their huts to measure positions they assumed were fixed. The Incas constructed an observatory to calibrate a cosmos that constantly changed and posed the possibility of chaos.

╓╖

Looking up at the night sky, we imagine the stars to be invisibly connected by ghostly lines to form constellations. Only by doing so can we tell stories about them. Survey lines, such as those linking triangulation points, are of an equally ghostly nature, as are geodesic lines such as the grid of latitude and longitude, and the lines of the equator, the tropics and the polar circles.

TIM INGOLD, *Lines: A Brief History,* 49

Various Andean peoples measured the cosmos, but they did so in pursuit of other domains of knowledge than did European scientists.[21] If La Condamine and his colleagues attempted to establish the fixity of the Earth, Andean peoples seem more concerned with its variations. As far as is known, Andean measurements of length and area were extrapolated from the human body: the distance between thumb and finger (*yuku*), the length between finger and elbow (*khococ*), and the length of a human body (*rikra*). Distances along the road systems were calculated by the pace (*thatkiy*) and the *tupu*, which may have been approximately 6,000 paces, or 7.2 km. Somewhat confusingly, *tupu* was also applied to measurements of area, specifically of land, its length unrelated to walking distances. Bernabe Cobo stated that a tupu of farmland was 50 fathoms by 25 fathoms in size, while the term may have meant a *sufficient* quantity of land to support a family. As John Rowe observed, "Inca skill in engineering works almost required a system of measurement at least as exact as that in use in sixteenth-century Europe," but there was a certain pragmatic lack of precision involved in the measurements of landscape.[22]

But the Andean sky was quite different. An amazingly detailed body of knowledge was deployed to mark the passage of the stars, the waning of the moon, and the appearance of the sun. Some of these celestial preoccupations are known from Colonial documents. For example, the eloquent drawings by Felipe Guaman Poma de Ayala include both ritual and agricultural calendars. Guaman Poma observed the "months and years and Sundays that the Incas of this realm counted, that the philosophers and astrologers counted the week had ten days and thirty days each month. And . . . they knew from the stars the passage of the year, and they knew quite well that the Sun was greater than the Moon and was put above her . . . Even today they make and follow the planting of food in such and such month and day and hour and know where the Sun is in its movement."[23] Guaman Poma illustrates the celebration of Capac Inti Raymi in December (the austral summer solstice), noting that it was the "the great and solemn passage of the Sun."[24]

Although such observations were made at different places in the Andes, some of the most important occurred in Cusco and especially in the central plaza, the Haucaypata. As David Dearborn and colleagues have discussed, the solar cult was particularly well-developed in Cusco and was written, with various degrees of accuracy, by a number of early Spanish chroniclers.[25] One of the earliest accounts, by Juan de Betanzos in 1557, describes two sets of pillars on opposite hilltops framing Cusco, one set for sunrises and the other for sunsets. Other accounts vary in detail. Garsilaso de la Vega recorded a total of sixteen pillars, four sets of four each, on opposite sides of the valley of Cusco. Father Bernabe Cobo recorded that to the west of Cusco were three pairs of pillars that respectively marked the winter solstice in June, the time for planting maize, and the summer solstice in December, the Capac Inti Raymi. An anonymous manuscript written around 1570, *Discurso de la sucesion y gobierno de los yngas*, states that four stone pillars arrayed along 200 paces on a hill west of Cusco, Cerro Picchu, were used to calibrate the spring planting season in August, when groups of people gathered in the Haucaypata at a specific sacred stone—the *ushnu*—and watched the sun set between the inner pillars. Drawing on similar sources, the ethnohistorian R. Thomas Zuidema wrote that "a series of observations were made . . . by means of a group of four pillars erected on the gentle slope of Picchu, a mountain 2 km west of the central plaza of Cuzco, from which they were observed."[26]

It is June 2, 2015, around noon, and I am in the Plaza de Armas in Cusco—one portion of the Haucaypata. Among the hundreds of tourists armed with digital cameras, smart phones, Go-Pros, and sel-fie-sticks, I suspect I am the only one with an azimuth compass. Using the bearings reported by Dearborn and colleagues and Zuidema, I turn toward the west to find Cerro Picchu. It is impossible to miss: in place of the solar pillars, Cerro Picchu is spiked by two dozen communication towers and a large white dish antennae transmitting FM radio, high-definition television, and cell phone communications.[27]

The solar pillars are long gone, and yet, as Dearborn and colleagues point out, the important conclusion from the Spanish descriptions is not just that the Inca had developed ways to mark the sun's transit but rather that these solar variations were viewed by a group of people in the Haucaypata: "The horizons surrounding the imperial capital held a series of large solar markers, visible to everyone, that were used as part of enormous public rituals held in the central square of the city . . . [The widely spaced solar pillars] permitted hundreds, if not thousands,

of people gathered in the central plaza to witness simultaneously a marked sunset. If this was the case, then the pillars were used in large ritual gatherings during which group participation was considered more important than precise date determination."[28]

The measurement of the sky by Andean societies had multiple contexts and purposes. In his classic studies of Andean archaeoastronomy, Gary Urton showed how the night sky in the southern Andes exhibited a progression of astronomical features, not only individual stars and stellar constellations as in Western astronomy but also "dark cloud" constellations—the masses in the Milky Way empty of stellar light.[29] The Milky Way is the Mayu, a celestial river that flows around the earth, empties westward into the cosmic sea (Mamacocha), flows underground, and rises in the east to bring water as rain—a continuous hydraulic cycle that bathes the universe. Spread across the Mayu, the dark cloud constellations are animate and animals: a serpent, toad, tinamou, llama, baby llama (or llama's umbilicus), fox, and tinamou. The entire procession of dark cloud animals is not visible every night of the year, and appearance in the night sky varies—most visible on the autumnal equinox, most hidden on the vernal equinox. This stellar progression varies with the rainy and dry seasons: the Serpent is visible during the rainy season (October–April) but slithers underground during the dry season (May–July). In turn, this march of celestial animals provided information about times for planting and harvestings.

In addition to observing seasonal variations, Andean societies developed precise tools for naked-eye astronomy. The Torreon at Machu Picchu was constructed as "a precise instrument for observing the June solstice" as well as for watching constellations.[30] A constructed cave at Machu Picchu, the Intimachay, admitted sunlight only just before and immediately after the December solstice.[31] On the Island of the Sun in Lake Titicaca, Brian Bauer and Charles Stanish identified two solar pillars that marked the December solstice. Not only did these solar pillars calibrate an astronomical event, but access to the vantage points delineated sacred space and social space. Stanish writes, "The Island of the Sun hosted a solstice ceremony that was substantially more complex than suggested in historical documents. The Inca did not just arrive to count the solstice days. The entire landscape was altered to create a monument where time, sacred space, and social space were defined and negotiated in ways that we are just beginning to understand."[32]

The concerns with measuring and understanding a changing cosmos were not limited to the Incas or peoples of the Southern Andes. Writing of the Desana and other Tukanoan groups in Colombia, the ethnographer Gerardo Reichel-Dolmatoff observed, "The sky is seen as an enormous blueprint of everything that did, does, or will happen on the earth; an enormous map replete with information on every aspect of biological and cultural behavior, time, space, evolution, and psychological phenomena; in sum, an encyclopedic body of what one might call 'survival information,' the knowledge of which alone can give Man a measure of security."[33] This knowledge takes two broad forms: one we might term *pragmatic*—the occurrence of rainy and dry seasons, the availability of game animals ranging from tapirs to edible grubs, and the appropriate times to travel or build a house—and another more *conceptual*, based on "cyclic phenomena of the heavens and of nature, [onto which] the Indians project cycles of specific cultural relevance, such as the menstruation cycle, the cycle of embryonic development, the human life cycle, psychological developments, plant growth, and any number of other recurring events, but assessed by the predictable appearance."[34] This predictability is writ in the skies, as the stability of heavenly bodies and the orderly progression of celestial phenomena are evidence of universal order. "These fixed spaces and fixed orbits are very important," for the Desana and other Tukanoan peoples, "who see in them a set of principles of order, of organization."[35] In contrast, "Any dissonance in this heavenly harmony is thought to be harmful. Eclipses, comets, meteorites, shooting stars, tektites, and planetary conjunctions are greatly feared, because they are thought to mirror calamitous conditions that exist somewhere on this earth. Dissonances do not predict coming events; instead, they point to malfunctionings that are actually taking place in human society or in nature. The observation of these celestial dysfunctions is thus a diagnostic procedure, not a prognostic one."[36]

Traditional societies around the world have complex ideas about the sequences and meanings of celestial events, but not all societies construct features on the landscape to gauge the passage of the heavens. On the coast of Peru, this was done at different places and times. For example, on the south coast of Peru in the Chincha Valley, people of the Late Paracas Culture (400–100 BC) constructed long lines of stones extending from ceremonial platforms and residential mounds, linear geoglyphs that marked the winter sunset in June. Beyond this astronomical function, the Chincha linear geoglyphs were associated with specific mounds. As Stanish and colleagues write, "These particular geoglyphs (and associated mounds) were used to mark time and attract participants to attend a recurring set of social events. They also mark special places on the landscape for those events, some sacred, some secular . . . important to late Paracas people. Alongside nondomestic mounds and stone platforms, the linear geoglyphs formed a coherent ritualized landscape that structured those events. The lines integrated domestic and ceremonial areas within a larger desert landscape."[37]

At the same time the people of Chincha were marking the winter solstice, 520 km to the north a monumental complex combining a fortified temple and solar towers was built at the site of Chankillo in the Casma Valley, Peru. Chankillo dates to between 400 BC and AD 100, and the site consists of several remarkable constructions that stretch over 4 km². Chankillo is a well-known site—the nineteenth-century traveler Ephraim George Squier produced a map of the site in his 1865 *Incidents of Travel and Exploration in the Land of the Incas*—but more recent investigations directed by the archaeologist Ivan Ghezzi have clarified the dating and function of the site.

In addition to large plazas, storerooms, and residences, two areas at Chankillo are particularly intriguing: the fortified temple and the Thirteen Towers. The fortified temple is a striking construction of concentric walls with offset, baffled doorways, and its defendable position overlooking the valley has led many scholars to interpret it as a fortress. More than simply a defensive refuge, Ghezzi and the archaeoastronomer Clive Ruggles argue that Chankillo was built by an elite class of warrior-kings whose authority was bolstered by force of arms, feasts, and astronomical knowledge. The Thirteen Towers are a series of flat-topped cubes 2–6 m tall built along a ridge top a kilometer east of the fortified temple, evenly spaced between 4.7 m and 5.1 m apart and forming "an artificial toothed horizon with narrow gaps at regular intervals."[38] These towers mark the passage of the sun between the solstices and the solar zeniths, anticipating the Incas' solar preoccupations by nearly 2,000 years. Ghezzi and Ruggles write: "Thus, at Chankillo, the individuals with access to sacred spaces, and in control of astronomical

knowledge and the calendar, would have been the instigators and great benefactors of public banquets scheduled by the movement of the sun. These leaders would have possessed the ability to manipulate time, ideology, calendrical rituals and the solar cult amidst an impressive scenario that integrated society while the same time accentuating its growing inequality."[39] More than simply a device for tracking the movement of the sun, Ghezzi and Ruggles argue, Chankillo was "not solely the expression of advanced astronomical knowledge, nor simply an empirical instrument for solar observations, but a place where the ceremonial calendar was regulated and re-created, and where the established social hierarchies were reproduced."[40]

Several points emerge from these examples. First, the indigenous observations of the Andean cosmos were always rooted in social concerns: agricultural cycles, the occurrence of feasts, and the advancement of elites. Second, Andean sky-watchers were concerned with a cosmos that was usually predictable but always entailed the potential for catastrophic change. In repeated places and on various occasions, the skies were scanned for portents of fundamental change and disorder, and the order of the cosmos was only reconfirmed—but never insured—at those moments when stars and stones aligned.

⊓

In that Empire, the Art of Cartography attained such Perfection that the
map of a single Province occupied the entirety of a City, and the map of
the Empire, the entirety of a Province. In time, those Unconscionable
Maps no longer satisfied, and the Cartographers Guilds struck a Map
of the Empire whose size was that of the Empire, and which coincided
point for point with it. The following Generations, who were not so
fond of the Study of Cartography as their Forebears had been, saw that
that vast Map was Useless, and not without some Pitilessness was it,
that they delivered it up to the Inclemencies of Sun and Winters. In the
Deserts of the West, still today, there are Tattered Ruins of that Map,
inhabited by Animals and Beggars; in all the Land there is no other
Relic of the Disciplines of Geography.

> SUAREZ MIRANDA, *Viajes de varones prudentes*, Libro IV, Cap. XLV, Lerida, 1658
> On Exactitude in Science
> Jorge Luis Borges, *Collected Fictions*, translated by Andrew Hurley

In *Measuring the New World*, Neal Safier provides a scathing indictment of La Condamine and colleagues' disparagement of traditional
Andean people and their cosmological knowledge. La Condamine envisioned the expedition as bringing the "sacred fire" of scientific knowledge from Europe to South America. As they measured the cosmos, La
Condamine and his colleagues established temporary survey markers,
using tall wooden crosses or in some cases scavenging cut stones and
boulders from prehispanic sites. At one point, La Condamine described
placing a tall wooden cross on such a scavenged pile, "a way of sym-
bolizing the emergence of European science from the literal rubble of
ancient Amerindian civilization."[41] In another misguided act of physical
expropriation, La Condamine and his colleagues built elaborate pyra-
midal monuments to mark the ends of the baseline—supposedly permanent markers impervious to time. They were not.

More than makeshift monuments, La Condamine's pyramids were
objects of careful planning and attention. Prior to his expedition to
South America, he had visited Alexandria and was inspired by ancient

Egyptian obelisks, durable pyramids of stone covered with hiero-glyphic inscriptions. La Condamine designed pyramid markers for the French-Spanish Geodesic Survey, describing these monuments with a creator's passion and writing a book on them after his return to Paris, the *Histoire des Pyramides de Quito*. The monuments were to be tetrahedral pyramids erected on a square plinth 1.5–1.8 m tall, built from local stone and covered with fired brick.[42] An inscription carved in marble was attached to one side of the pyramid. "The monuments that we had left," La Condamine wrote, "were to serve to perpetuate the memory of a labor useful for all Nations, initiated by the Academy, executed by order of the King, with the agreement and the protection of His Catholic Majesty; and that it was especially destined to fix the measure that we had made that was the foundation of all our geographical and astronomical operations."[43]

The pyramids and inscriptions were erected in 1740–41 while the expedition's two Spanish naval officers, Jorge Juan and Antonio de Ulloa, were away in Lima and Chile to assist in the defense of Spanish naval positions under attack from a British fleet. Upon their return to Quito, Juan and Ulloa were offended by the pyramids as disrespectful to the King of Spain and dismissive of their own scientific contributions.

Written in flowery Latin, the inscriptions stated that the expedition had been conducted under the auspices of the Spanish king, "sovereign of the most extensive monarchy of the globe," but Spain's priority was undermined when La Condamine topped the monument with a carved stone *fleur-de-lis*—a symbol associated with the House of Bourbon and thus the Spanish king Felipe VI but an icon more solidly linked to France.

In 1742 Juan and Ulloa filed suit against La Condamine in the Audiencia of Quito. Among various grievances, La Condamine was accused of dishonoring Spain in the inscription, of neglecting to mention Juan and Ulloa's participation in the measurement of the arc of latitude, and of placing the French *fleur-de-lis* on top of the pyramids rather that a clearer symbol of the Spanish crown. The suit droned on for nearly two years, but La Condamine finally won and a court order preserving the pyramids was issued. In May 1743 La Condamine left Quito, traveled down the Río Pastaza to the Marañon and Amazon, and returned to France in February 1745.[44]

This matter was not over. Ulloa continued to petition for the pyramids' destruction, and a demolition decree was issued in 1746. In 1751 La Condamine published his *Histoire des Pyramides de Quito*, a curious tract designed to shape the remembrance of things past, lamenting, "I positively had no way to know that a small time later the Pyramids would be demolished and the inscriptions broken."[45] In 1802 Alexander von Humboldt traveled north of Quito to visit the ruins of La Condamine's pyramids. He paused among the "trampled fragments of broken marble tablets, shards of a broken *fleur-de-lis* made of ash-green porphyry stone, illegible inscriptions formed with Latin characters, and discarded cube-shaped stone pedestals"—the archaeological ruins of European science.[46] Humboldt wrote, "We might imagine ourselves among Turks, when we find the most important monuments to the progress of the human spirit ransacked before us."[47] Neal Safier has written, "To Humboldt, the state into which this ruined pyramid had fallen reflected a mysterious and unpredictable encounter between the aspirations of human culture, the destructive power of nature, and the fleeting character of human memory."[48]

In fact, the pyramids erected were not demolished by the Audiencia of Quito, although La Condamine did not know this when he wrote *Histoire des Pyramides de Quito*. The demolition order was rescinded and replaced by a royal edict commanding that the offending inscriptions be chiseled out and the disrespectful *fleur-de-lis* removed. The ruins Humboldt visited in 1802 were not the results of an iconoclastic destruction but rather of the processes that commonly afflict monuments: time, decay, and human thoughtlessness.[49] The bricks were scavenged and the inscription blocks salvaged. One large stone was taken to a nearby hacienda, where it served as a mounting block for saddling horses and mules. At another hacienda an inscription plaque was used as a support for the posts of a balustrade. Another block, its inscription illegible, was used as a laundry stone for washing clothes. Small bits of brick and plaster surrounded the base of the pyramids. The Colombian naturalist and political leader Francisco José de Caldas, who would later accompany Humboldt and Aimé Bonpland, wrote, "In 1801 I approached Quito. I could not see without emotion the plateau Yaruqui. The Pyramids no longer exist; they perished, victims of a mad vanity, fanaticism and barbarism. The crowning *fleur-de-lis* are scattered in the countryside; their irritating inscriptions are transformed into bridges and door sills. Indians from Yaruqui and Puembo trample underfoot the projects of a learned academy. Posterity is just; it will avenge insults against Sciences."[50] In 1802 even Humboldt engaged in the pyramids' destruction, pocketing a porphyry fragment of a *fleur-de-lis*.

With Ecuador's independence, the pyramids were viewed as historical monuments of national importance. Although Humboldt and Bolivar had thought they should be rebuilt, they were not until the second president of Ecuador, Vincente Rocafuerte, had them reconstructed in 1836. This rebuilding was supported by Ecuador's ally, France, and the French government detailed a naval engineer to complete the task. The pyramids were reconstructed, although without re-measuring La Condamine's baseline—historical monuments but no longer the precisely placed benchmarks used to measure the size of the Earth.

NOTES

1. A variety of sources describe the French-Spanish Geodesic Survey. Recent popular sources include Larrie Ferreiro, *Measure of the Earth: The Enlightenment Expedition That Reshaped the World* (New York: Basic Books, 2011); Joyce Appleby, *Shores of Knowledge: New World Discoveries and the Scientific Imagination* (New York: W. W. Norton, 2013). Neil Safier, *Measuring the World: Enlightenment Science and South America* (Chicago: University of Chicago Press, 2008), is a particularly insightful, critical discussion.

2. US dollars in 2010, based on Ferreiro, *Measure of the Earth*, 295–96.

3. Denis Cosgrove, "The Measures of America," in *Taking Measures across the American Landscape*, edited by James Corner and Alex MacLean, 3–13 (New Haven, CT: Yale University Press, 1996), 5.

4. Ibid..

5. William L. Fox, *The Void, the Grid, and the Sign: Traversing the Great Basin* (Salt Lake City: University of Utah Press, 2000), 116.

6. Bernabe de Cobo, *Inca Religion and Customs*, translated and edited by Roland Hamilton (Austin: University of Texas Press, 1990 [1653]), 51.

7. Brian Bauer, "Ritual Pathways of the Inca: An Analysis of the Collasuyu Ceques in Cuzco," *Latin American Antiquity* 3, no. 3 (1992): 183–205; Brian Bauer, *Sacred Landscape of the Inca: The Cusco Ceque System* (Austin: University of Texas Press, 1998); Brian Bauer, *Ancient Cuzco: Heartland of the Inca* (Austin: University of Texas Press, 2010).

8. Cobo, *Inca Religion and Customs*, 51.

9. Jessica Christie, "A New Look at Q'enqo as a Model of Inka Visual Representation," *Ethnohistory* 59, no. 3 (2012): 597–630, 600–601.

10. Cobo, *Inca Religion and Customs*, 51. See also Carolyn Dean, *A Culture of Stone: Inka Perspectives on Rock* (Durham, NC: Duke University Press, 2010).

11. Carolyn Dean, "The Inka Married the Earth: Integrated Outcrops and the Making of Place," *Art Bulletin* 89, no. 3 (2007): 502–18, 502.

12. Ibid., 506.

13. Bauer, *Sacred Landscape of the Inca*, 51.

14. Cobo, *Inca Religion and Customs*, 54.

15. Ibid.

16. Translated by Monica Barnes and David Fleming, "Charles Marie de La Condamine's Report on Ingapirca and the Development of Scientific Fieldwork in the Andes, 1735–1744," *Andean Past* 2, no. 2 (1989): 175–235, 202–3.

17. Ibid., 203.

18. Dates based on José Alcina Franch, "Ingapirca: Arquitectura y areas de ásentamiento," *Revista española de antropología americana* 8 (1978): 127–46.

19. Personal observation, June 13, 2015.

20. Antonio Fresco, "Excavaciones en Ingapirca: 1978–1982," *Revista Española de Antropología Americana* 14 (1984): 85–101, 100, my translation.

21. Gary Urton, "Recording Measure(ment)s in the Inka Khipu," in *The Archaeology of Measurement: Comprehending Heaven, Earth and Time in Ancient Societies*, edited by Iain Morley and Colin Renfrew, 54–68 (Cambridge: Cambridge University Press, 2010), 54.

22. John Rowe, "Inca Culture at the Time of the Spanish Conquest," in *Handbook of South American Indians*, edited by Julian Steward, vol. 2:183–330 (Washington, DC: Smithsonian Institution, 1948), 323. For scholars who argue that tupu referred to a sufficiency of land rather than a specific measurement of area, see Cecilia Sanhueza Tohá, "Medir, Amojonar, Repartir: Territorialidades y Prácticas Demarcatorias en el Camino Incaico de Atacama (II Región, Chile)," *Chungara, Revista de Antropología Chilena* 36, no. 2 (2004): 483–94; Nathan Wachtel, *Vision of the Vanquished: The Spanish Conquest of Peru through Indian Eyes*, translated by Ben Reynolds and Sian Reynolds (New York: Harvester, 1977), 65–69.

23. Felipe Guaman Poma de Ayala, *Nueva Crónica y Buen Gobierno*, edited by Franklin Pease, translated by Jan Szemínski, 3 vols. (Mexico City: Fondo de Cultura Economica, 1993 [1615]), 177, my translation.

24. Ibid., 192, my translation.

25. The following discussion is from David S. Dearborn, Matthew T. Seddon, and Brian Bauer, "The Sanctuary of Titicaca: Where the Sun Returns to Earth," *Latin American Antiquity* 9, no. 3 (1998): 240–58.

26. R. Thomas Zuidema, "Catachillay: The Role of the Pleiades and of the Southern Cross and α and β Centauri in the Calendar of the Incas," *Ethnoastronomy and Archaeoastronomy in the American Tropics, New York Academy of Sciences Annals* 385 (1982): 203–29, 204.

27. A study of the radiation emitted by these towers and other locations in Peru indicates that the people living near Cerro Picchu are exposed to significant levels of non-iodizing radiation; see Victor Cruz Ornetta, "Diagnostico nacional de las radiaciones no ionizantes producidas por los servicios de telecomunicaciones en el Perú," accessed June 2, 2015, https://www.osiptel.gob.pe/Archivos/Transparencia /Info_adicional/125431Anexo1.pdf.

28. Dearborn, Seddon, and Bauer, "Sanctuary of Titicaca," 243–44.

29. Gary Urton, "Animals and Astronomy in the Quechua Universe," *Proceedings of the American Philosophical Society* 125, no. 2 (1981): 110–27; Gary Urton, *At the Crossroads of the Earth and the Sky: An Andean Cosmology* (Austin: University of Texas Press, 1981).

30. David S. Dearborn and Raymond E. White, "Archaeoastronomy at Machu Picchu," *Annals of the New York Academy of Sciences* 385, no. 1 (1982): 249–59, 253.

31. David S. Dearborn, Katharina J. Schreiber, and Raymond E. White, "Intimachay: A December Solstice Observatory at Machu Picchu, Peru," *American Antiquity* 52, no. 2 (1987): 346–52.

32. Charles Stanish, "Measuring Time, Sacred Space, and Social Place in the Inca Empire," in *The Archaeology of Measurement: Comprehending Heaven, Earth and Time in Ancient Societies*, edited by Ian Morley and Colin Renfrew, 216–28 (Cambridge: Cambridge University Press, 2010), 227.

33. Gerardo Reichel-Dolmatoff, "Astronomical Models of Social Behavior among Some Indians of Colombia," *Annals of the New York Academy of Sciences* 385 (1982): 165–81, 165–66.

34. Ibid.

35. Ibid.

36. Ibid., 166.

37. Charles Stanish, Henry Tantaleán, Benjamin T. Nigra, and Laura Griffin, "A 2,300-Year-Old Architectural and Astronomical Complex in the Chincha Valley, Peru," *Proceedings of the National Academy of Sciences* 111, no. 20 (2014): 7218–23, 7222.

38. Ivan Ghezzi and Clive L.N. Ruggles, "Chankillo: A 2300-Year-Old Solar Observatory in Coastal Peru," *Science*, New Series 315, no. 5816 (March 2, 2007): 1239–43, 1240.

39. Ivan Ghezzi and Clive L.N. Ruggles, "The Social and Ritual Context of Horizon Astronomical Observations at Chankillo," in *Oxford IX International Symposium on Archaeoastronomy Proceedings IAU Symposium no. 278*, edited by Clive L.N. Ruggles, 144–53 (Cambridge: Cambridge University Press, 2011), 152.

40. Ibid., 153.

41. Neal Safier, *Measuring the New World: Enlightenment Science and South America* (Chicago: University of Chicago Press, 2008), 37.

42. Ibid., 25.

43. Charles-Marie de La Condamine, *Histoire des pyramides de Quito, élevées par les académiciens envoyés sous l'equateur par ordre du roi* (Paris: s.n., 1751), accessed November 11, 2016, https://archive.org/details/histoiredespyram00laco, 4, my translation.

44. Ibid., 41.

45. Ibid., 4.

46. Quoted in Safier, *Measuring the New World*, 24.

47. Ibid.

48. Ibid.

49. The following is based on Ferreiro, *Measure of the Earth*, 283–85; Georges Perrier, "Histoire des pyramides de Quito: Documents Inédit," *Journal de la Société des Américanistes* 35 (1943): 91–122.

50. Quoted in Perrier, "Histoire des pyramides de Quito," 98, my translation.

CHAPTER NINE

Following Pizarro

A path is a prior interpretation of the best way to traverse a landscape, and to follow a route is to accept an interpretation, or to stalk
your predecessor on it as scholars and trackers and pilgrims do.
REBECCA SOLNIT[1]

TUMBES IS A NORTHWEST DEPARTMENT OF PERU THAT SITS ON THE
border with Ecuador. Peru and Ecuador fought over the frontier until
the 1940s, when the international limits were reconfirmed. The border at Tumbes was in conflict again in 1995 when fighting between
Ecuador and Peru broke out in the Amazonian border along the Río
Cenapa, a tributary of the Río Marañon. The region was militarized all
along the Río Zarumilla, a meandering stream that forms the border.
I drove into town a year later to conduct an archaeological survey in
Tumbes, a region generally ignored by archaeologists. Landmines were
placed extensively during the conflict, and an unknown number were
still there when my Peruvian colleagues and I conducted our research
in 1996. We carefully stayed on trails scuffed with cattle hoofprints,

hoping that the livestock would have tripped any anti-personnel devices. Some of the most interesting archaeological profiles we saw were in slit trenches from recent machine gun emplacements that cut into prehistoric sites.

Tumbes's history is threaded with conflict. In late prehistory, the local chiefdom, the Tumpis, continually battled with their archrivals, the people of Puná, who lived on an island in the Gulf of Guayaquil. The Tumpis and the Punaes constantly raided each other, sailing their balsa rafts across the Gulf of Guayaquil, sliding into the quiet canals of the mangrove swamps, and attacking villages to plunder and burn. In the 1470s the Incas conquered Tumbes, extending their empire of Tawantinsuyu northward and building a massive temple and fortress complex on the west bank of the Río Tumbes at a site now known as Cabeza de Vaca. And in 1532 Francisco Pizarro and 160 horsemen and foot soldiers marched south from Tumbes to conquer a land they knew as Cusco.

In June 2005, I followed Pizarro. I traveled with three Peruvian archaeologists: Carolina Vílchez, Bernardino Olaya, and Paul Garcia. Bernardino and I had worked together on the first 1996 field season. Carolina and I had co-directed a small excavation project in 2003. Paul was a new acquaintance. All are solid field archaeologists. We rented a red Nissan 4×4 pickup from Bernardino's brother-in-law. We scoured the marketplace in Tumbes for provisions and gear, as there would be no supplies in the interior. We bought five kilos of rice, a pound of salt, a liter of cooking oil, noodles, cans of tuna, instant coffee, canned milk, a kettle, and a cooking pot. The next morning we loaded packs, tents, water jugs, boxes of food, and gear into the pickup and left the city of Tumbes, driving south along the Pacific Coast on the Pan-American Highway before turning into the interior at Bocapan. The dirt track followed the dry bed of a quebrada and headed into the Cerros de Amotape.

The Cerros de Amotape are a chain of low hills rising to 1,000 m, a geological prelude to the taller peaks of the Andes further east. The hills are covered with a now-rare type of forest, a tropical dry forest with tall *ceibo* trees with buttressed trunks and branches dangling kapok pods.

The tropical dry forest is a tangle of bougainvillea vines, algarrobo trees and other acacias, and skeins of morning glory vines whose hallucinogenic leaves intoxicate livestock; the plant is thus known locally as "La Borrachera" or "the Drunk." The Cerros de Amotape are home to rare animal species—such as the spectacled bear and the miniature brocket deer—and a tremendous variety of birds. It is a strange habitat, different from Peru's coastal desert or highland puna, a world where the odd is commonplace. The naturalist Thaddäus Xaverius Peregrinus Haenke (1761–1816), a member of Spain's royal Malaspina Expedition, wrote that in these mountains "is found the *danta* or *antey*, commonly called 'the great beast.' This animal has the shape of a cow, but in size is smaller than a year-old calf; it has in front a solid and very strong bone, with which it opens a path in the thickets of the monte."[2] Having mistaken a prehensile snout for something like a unicorn's horn, Haenke was describing a tapir.

I drove the red pickup into the hills. The dirt road became rutted and loose as we climbed a hogback ridge, and I focused on my driving. Many archaeologists have the bad habit of not watching the road, instead looking at landscapes and sites as we drive. In one of my favorite documentary films from the 1960s, the archaeologist Richard "Scotty" MacNeish (1918–2001) is shown driving through the countryside of Oaxaca, Mexico, lecturing to the interviewer about his then-recent discoveries about the origins of maize—barely keeping a hand on the steering wheel as he gestures and jabs for emphasis, his eyes darting as he looks at the interviewer and scans the countryside, rarely glancing at the road.[3] An irrepressible archaeologist, MacNeish spent his life doing fieldwork in the Yukon, Mexico, Peru, Belize, and China. Many of his colleagues were deeply saddened when MacNeish died after he rolled his rental car on a loose gravel curve while visiting Mayan archaeological sites in Belize. British paratroopers passing by pulled MacNeish and a companion from the vehicle and drove them to hospital. The British driver was an archaeologist, and he and MacNeish talked archaeology on the way to the hospital, where MacNeish died a few hours later on the operating table.[4] He was eighty-two.

I kept both hands on the wheel, but I couldn't help glancing about as we drove through the scrub forest, and a line of cobblestones caught my eye. I stopped in the middle of the road—there was no other traffic out here—and we went to investigate. It was a section of the Qhapaq Ñan, "the beautiful road," a span of the Inca road system. This remnant ran between two fieldstone walls and was about 4.15 m wide. The section ran for about 100 m before the walls ended and the road dissolved into a web of livestock trails and footpaths. This was a modest segment of one the most impressive achievements in human history.

During their relatively brief empire, the Incas expanded rapidly over western South America, incorporating a vast territory stretching from northern Ecuador to central Chile.[5] The Qhapaq Ñan was the empire's principal artery. The Incas built new roads, improved existing trails, wove hanging bridges over deep canyons, and constructed bridges of stone and logs across rushing streams. Along the roads, the Incas established outposts of an empire: cities, fortresses, storerooms (qolcas), and roadside installations (tampu). Designed for foot travel, in some places the roads were stone staircases that led straight up mountain slopes or simply broad routes across deserts swept of stones. Two roughly parallel road networks—one in the highlands, the other on the coast—were joined by dozens of intersecting roads. The Inca road network was principally an instrument of war and rule, including religious processions and pilgrimages. Porters carried foodstuffs, textiles, and other manufactured goods to vast storerooms at provincial centers as well as to Cusco. Postal runners (chaski) carried messages from distant provinces to the Inca king. Armies marched quickly to suppress uprisings.

I have seen segments of the Inca road at various places across western South America. In 1986, while directing excavations in the Casma Valley on the north-central coast of Peru, I went for a jog and followed a distinct line of stones up a nearby hill before finally reaching the crest and seeing the Qhapac Ñan slice northward across a dry pampa. Twenty-three years later and 1,800 km to the south, Bill Fox and I walked another segment of the road that runs on the eastern edge of the Salar de Atacama, at the small tampu of Camar south of San Pedro

de Atacama, Chile.[6] And on various occasions I have stood in the Haucaypata, the plaza where the four great roads connecting the four quarters of the Inca Empire intersect in the heart of Cusco.

Whenever I have walked these and other segments of Inca roads, I have been impressed by the ways the routes created and defined Andean landscapes. In a fundamental way, they are different from modern routes and nodes of transport and communications, what the

anthropologist Marc Augé has referred to as "non-places" that con-
nect and characterize super-modernity: "all the air, rail, and motorway
routes . . . the airports and railway stations, hotel chains, leisure parks,
large retail outlets, and finally the complex skein of cable and wireless
networks . . . for the purposes of a communication so peculiar that it
often puts the individual in contact with another image of himself."[7] On
the contrary, when I walk these roads I understand that the routes were
deeply embedded in the prehistories of the Andes and in the life and
death that flowed along these roads.

The Qhapaq Ñan extended over 30,000 km.[8] Between 2001 and
2009, the ministries of culture of six Andean republics—Colombia,
Ecuador, Peru, Bolivia, Chile, and Argentina—conducted a coordinated study of the Qhapaq Ñan. In Peru alone, more than 11,757 km of
roads were documented, as were more than 1,900 archaeological sites
directly associated with the routes. More than 1,000 Peruvian communities live along and use sections of the Qhapaq Ñan—walking to mar-
kets or driving caravans of llamas along the road. In 2014 the United
Nations Educational, Scientific, and Cultural Organization (UNESCO)
included the Qhapaq Ñan on the World Heritage List, describing it as
part of humanity's shared cultural patrimony.

But here in the Cerros de Amotape we were looking at just a small
section of abandoned road that once linked Tumbes to the rest of
Tawantinsuyu. We photographed the road, determined its location
with a handheld GPS, and made some quick notes. We climbed into
the truck and headed on until the dirt road ended at the small community of Capitan Hoyle, where we found the house of the *teniente
gobernador*, the settlement's official. In addition to his political roles
and farming his own land, he was also a muleteer, and Carolina had
arranged to rent his two donkeys and for him to accompany us as a
guide. We unloaded the truck and packed our gear into large black
costales usually used for sacks of rice. The teniente gobernador tied
the enormous bags onto the small donkeys, lashing the sacks to homemade pack frames of wooden cross-ties padded with blanket scraps
and mattress ticking. Balancing the loads carefully, the donkeys were

burdened but patient. The teniente gobernador smacked his lips three times, said "Burro! Burro! Burro!" and whacked each animal on the rump with the flat of his machete. The donkeys trotted down the trail, and the five of us followed behind. The trail led into a dry stream bed called Quebrada Cusco.

Ⲛ

It is the paradox that the more closely and scrupulously you follow
someone's footsteps through the past the more conscious do you become
that they never existed wholly in any one place along the recorded path.
You cannot freeze them, you cannot pinpoint them, at any particular
turn in the road, bend in the river, view from the window. They are
always in motion, carrying their past lives with them into the future.

RICHARD HOLMES[9]

When Francisco Pizarro and his men traveled through the Quebrada
Cusco in 1532, he had been trying to conquer South America for more
than eight years. Pizarro had come to the Americas in 1502 as a young
man in his early twenties. Pizarro's birth date is uncertain; he was born
illegitimate in a society where genealogy and inheritance determined
social standing. Although his father recognized Francisco as his son,
he was excluded from his father's will. "More than most famous men,"
historian James Lockhart wrote, "Pizarro is hidden by his taciturnity
and illiteracy; his pattern of behavior is complex, not shaped totally by
any one ideal or force."[10]

Pizarro was at the forefront of Spain's advance in the Americas.
By 1509 he was a lieutenant general in the expedition led by Alonso
de Ojeda that established the first Spanish settlement on mainland
South America. Nuestra Señora Maria la Antigua del Darién was a
chaotic, dangerous outpost, located in the hot, unhealthy swamps on
the Caribbean coast of northwest Colombia, where over a hundred
Spaniards died from diseases and in battles with local natives equipped
with poisoned arrows.

In 1513 Pizarro was with Vasquez Nuñez de Balboa when the
Spaniards fought and slogged their way across the Isthmus of Panama,
climbed a hill, and first saw the Pacific Ocean in the distance. Four
days later the expedition stepped into the foam of the South Sea and
claimed it for the King of Spain, a fact duly legalized by a notary. Balboa
returned from Panama with a fortune in pearls, gold, and slaves; just

four years earlier, Balboa had escaped his creditors in Hispaniola by stowing away in a barrel on a ship bound for the coast of Urubá. From hounded debtor to wealthy hidalgo, the conquest created topsy-turvy changes in a man's life—a fact not lost on Francisco Pizarro. Over the next years, Pizarro was an increasingly major player in the conquest. "He was a good man, possessed of great courage and a strong body," a contemporary observed, "but without any knowledge or skill in governing."[11] Pizarro had prospered, gaining land and the control of native laborers during the conquests and becoming one of the wealthiest men in Panama. He became a favorite of the governor of Panama, Pedro de Avila, just as Panama became the springboard for the invasion of South America, a conquest fueled by rumors of gold.

Spanish conquests were "authorized" by a complex web of legal authority and royal practices rooted in the earlier *reconquista* of the Iberian Peninsula, the centuries of war that led to the unification of the Spanish kingdoms of Castille and Leon and the expulsion of the Moors in 1492. Initially, the Spanish advances in the New World were not state-funded enterprises but instead private enterprises authorized by royal decree. Conquests were entrusted to adventurers who swore loyalty to the Crown. The authorization to conquer was conferred by the king in a formal document, the *capitulación*, and the king's right to receive 20 percent of all loot—*el quinto real*—was unquestioned. Despite this, the opportunities for wealth were enormous if the wherewithal for conquests could be raised in a form of adventure capitalism. Conquered territories and peoples were ruled by royal authorities who literally embodied the king, forms of imperial transubstantiation. Killing a viceroy was an act of regicide. Subjects were obliged to follow the decrees of royal authorities; to disobey was an act of treason against the king. And yet, there was a complicating, countervailing principle: every subject—specifically every conquistador—had vowed loyalty to the king, but if the local royal authority *did not* obey the king's commands or intent, then a loyal subject was *obliged* to revolt and resist local officials to follow the greater authority of the king. On South America's frontier—where communication was slow and power loosely held—this

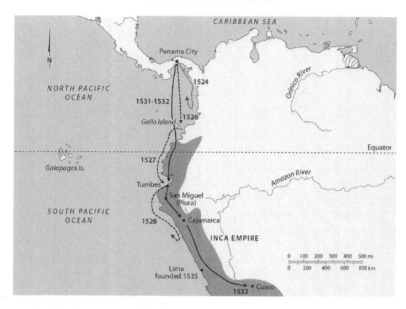

web of conflicted authority and contradictory principles encouraged intrigue, litigation, and revolt.[12]

Pizarro's expeditions in South America began in 1524 when he mounted a brief sortie from Panama that explored the coast of Colombia. Pizarro formed a contract to conquer with two other prominent Spaniards, the soldier Diego de Almagro and the priest Father Hernando de Luque, adding the Governor of Panama as a fourth partner to obtain the latter's authorization for the conquest (even allowing him to pay his 25 percent investment from any future treasure, a no-risk proposition for the governor). Pizarro was authorized to explore and subjugate "the Levant" and "to do battle with all the armies of the Grand Turk."[13] Such geographical uncertainty was only the beginning of their problems.

At some point, Pizarro and other conquistadors heard of the existence of a place called Peru. The soldier-chronicler (and Francisco Pizarro's cousin) Pedro Pizarro wrote, "Just then the people of *tierra firme* had news of a province which is called Peru, some two hundred leagues from *tierra firme* . . . So these three companions agreed to set forth to conquer this said province."[14]

The Spanish conquest of the Inca Empire is sometimes portrayed as the inevitable outcome of the clash between Europe and "the Other." For example, in the provocative 1997 book *Guns, Germs, and Steel*, Jared Diamond presents Pizarro's capture of the Inca ruler Atahualpa as paradigmatic, listing the "set of proximate factors that resulted in Europeans colonizing the New World instead of Native Americans colonizing Europe. Immediate reasons for Pizarro's success included military technology based on guns, steel weapons, and horses; infectious diseases endemic in Eurasia [but previously unknown in the Americas]; the centralized political organization of European states; and writing."[15] Perhaps such factors ensured the ultimate conquest of the New World by the Old, but nothing was inevitable when the Spaniards first set out to conquer South America.

Pizarro's first attempt at South American conquest was a miserable affair. In November 1524 he and sixty other men landed on the swampy Pacific Coast of Colombia. The landscape was a snarl of mangroves, the rainy season was fierce, and fevers flamed. Quickly running through their provisions and not finding native villages they could raid for food, the starving Spaniards named the place Puerto de Hambre. The expedition stumbled upon a native village seemingly abandoned at the Spaniards' advance. Once inside the village, the Spaniards were trapped as the natives attacked from all sides and torched their village. This village was named Punta Quemada. Pizarro and his men escaped to their boats and retreated to Panama.

Pizarro's second attempt was slightly more successful. In August 1526 he, Almagro, and Luque sailed from Panama with 160 men on two ships and three canoes. On the Pacific Coast of Colombia, Pizarro and a small troop landed among the mud banks and meanders at the mouth of the Río San Juan. It was terrible terrain for an army, a morass of swamps and rivers edged by tangles of mangrove roots trees where alligators hid. There was little food: small crabs, shellfish, and salty mangrove fruits. As Pizarro and his men rowed south against contrary currents, natives lined the riverbanks and taunted the Spaniards: "You must be idle vagabonds since you stay nowhere to work and sow the earth . . .

Why do you wander the world?"[16] The Spaniards pressed on—raiding a small village, capturing gold ornaments, and taking prisoners who told of even richer kingdoms further inland.

Retreating to his ships, Pizarro divided his force. Pizarro led a party inland to find the treasures of Colombia. Almagro was sent to Panama to recruit more men and gather supplies, taking the captured gold as evidence of future success. The second ship, captained by Bartolome de Ruiz, sailed south along the west coast of South America, holding offshore. On the open sea the men boarded a native vessel, a sailing balsa from Tumbes with a crew of twenty. The balsa was a trading vessel, and the Spaniards recorded that it held

> many objects of silver and gold for personal ornament to barter with those with whom they were going to trade, among which were crowns and diadems and belts and bracelets and armor for the legs and breastplates and tweezers and bells and strings and masses of beads and mirrors adorned with the said silver and cups and other drinking vessels; they [also] brought many textiles of wool and cloth and shirts and tunics and capes and many other garments all of them finely woven with rich detail, and of colors such as red and crimson and blue and yellow and with all the other colors and varied craftwork and figures of birds and animals and fish and trees.[17]

Despite the priceless cargo of shell beads and fine garments, it was the gold that attracted Ruiz and his crew. Ruiz traded for a few examples and persuaded or kidnapped (the sources are a bit unclear) two native men to board his ship, learn Spanish and serve as translators, and—most important—witness the richness of the lands to the south. Crossing the Equator and sailing further south without landing, Ruiz surveyed the coast of Peru before rejoining Pizarro's troop waiting on the coast of Colombia, having failed to find gold.

Reunited, Pizarro and his expedition attempted to invade the Atacames, a fiercely independent coastal kingdom on the north coast of Ecuador. The Atacamaes resisted. The Spaniards were weak. Pizarro and his men retreated to Isla del Gallo off the southern coast of Colombia

in 1527. There, they were met by a rescue ship sent by the new governor of Panama, Pedro de los Rios, who offered to retrieve any Spaniard
who wished to leave. In a famous historical moment, Pizarro drew a
line in the sand that he and a dozen other men crossed, deciding to
remain—a group later known as El Trece de Fama. Pizarro moved to
the better-provisioned Isla Gorgona, while Ruiz sailed back to Panama
for more supplies and men.

For six months Pizarro and his men lived on Isla Gorgona, a place
Pedro Cieza de Leon called "neither land nor an island, but the apparition of hell."[18] They survived on shellfish, capybaras, and a meager
store of maize. Six miles long and two miles wide, the tropical island
was a snake-infested jungle—which is why it was named for the gor-
gons, female sea monsters whose manes were viperous coils of snakes.
Subsequently, Isla Gorgona would be a pirate's lair and later a penal
colony, but in 1527 this was Pizarro's only refuge. Meanwhile, the
Tumbesinos learned Spanish, as Pizarro intended to use them as inter-
preters. Ruiz returned to Isla Gorgona with more supplies but no additional men. Leaving behind three Spaniards too ill to travel and some
native servants, the Spaniards voyaged south to explore the Peruvian
coast, taking the Tumbesinos with them.[19]

After a twenty-day voyage, the Tumbesinos recognized a pilgrimage
site on a small island near Isla Puná. The Spaniards and Tumbesinos
landed and sacked the shrine of its silver and gold offerings before continuing south. The next day they encountered five balsas from Tumbes
returning from a raid on Puná. The Spaniards escorted the warriors to
Tumbes, where twelve balsas filled with food and drink were sent to the
Spanish vessel, a gift from the Lord of Tumbes.

After months of near starvation, slogging through swamps, and desperate voyages, Tumbes was a marvel. The valley held broad farmland
edged by and watered from canals. Alonso de Molina and an unnamed
"black" were the first foreigners to visit Tumbes. After observing the
irrigated fields and herds of llamas, Molina visited the fortress of
Tumbes—undoubtedly the site of Huaca Cabeza de Vaca—passing
through three guarded gates before encountering the Lord of Tumbes.

The conquistador Don Alonso Enriquez de Guzman observed: "The great city of Tumbes is inhabited entirely by Indians. It is on the seashore; and in it there is a great house, belonging to the lord of the country, with walls built of adobes, like bricks, very beautifully painted with many colors and varnished [sic] so that I never saw anything more beautiful. The roof is of straw, also painted, so that it looks like gold, very strong and handsome."[20]

Around AD 1470, Huayna Capac had ordered the construction of a palace, fortress, and Temple of the Sun on a terrace on the west side of the valley overlooking farm fields and marshlands. The sprawling complex covered 100 hectares (1 million m²). Cieza de Leon comments:

> And in the port of Tumbes there had been made a royal fortress [of
> Huayna Capac], although some Indians state it that the building is
> older. Huayna Capac arrived, who commanded a Temple of the Sun
> to be built next to the fortress of Tumbes and gathered together more
> than two hundred virgins, the most beautiful to be found in the regions,
> daughters of the *principales* of the pueblos. And in this fortress (that
> then was not ruined and, they say, was a thing marvelous to see)
> Huayna Capac established his captain or deputy with a great number of
> mitimaes and many storerooms filled with precious things . . . And in
> this fortress of Tumbes there were a great number of silversmiths who
> made vessels of gold and silver and many other types of jewels for the
> service and decoration of the temple, which they held sacrosanct, as
> well as for their service of said Inka and to cover with this metal the
> walls of the temples and palaces. And the women were dedicated to the
> service of the temple and did nothing more than to spin and weave the
> finest woolen cloth which they did with great delicacy.[21]

In 1996, when Bernardino first took me to Cabeza de Vaca and told me it was a site, I thought he was joking; it looked like a large hill. Since then, excavations at Cabeza de Vaca—particularly research directed by Carolina since 2007—have documented that the elaborate Inca provincial capital described by the chroniclers, in fact, once existed here.[22] A fortress sat behind tall walls. There were workshops where ceramics were fired, silver was worked, and elegant figurines and tiny beads were made from the scarlet shells of the thorny oyster. One portion of the site held a Temple of the Sun, maintained by *mamacona*, or "chosen women," who maintained the religious objects, wove fine textiles, and brewed *chicha* in the vast quantities required for ceremonies and displays.

Molina was served chicha in gold and silver keros, conversed with the mamacona, and was offered one of the mamacona as a wife. Molina returned to the ship and reported what he had seen. After years of disappointments, the conquistadors remained skeptical. Pizarro sent the Greek artilleryman and soldier Pedro de Candia to verify the glories of Tumbes. Candia confirmed Molina's report, having seen the mamaconas and the walls in the Temple of the Sun hung with gold and silver sheets.[23] This was the Spaniards' first glimpse of the glories of the Inca Empire, and the Tumbesinos had a first encounter with firearms.

The accounts say that Candia was at the Inca fortress when the natives let loose a puma and a jaguar. It is unclear why. At this point the Tumbesinos had no hostile intentions, and they may have been simply curious about what would happen. Candia was armed with a harquebus, a muzzle-loading matchlock firearm, and he sparked the powder. The harquebus belched fire and smoke. The animals cowered. The Tumbesinos fell to the ground, terrified, and the puma and the jaguar—the story has it—peacefully and obediently laid down at Pedro de Candia's feet.

And then a profoundly Andean gesture was made. The Lord of Tumbes walked toward Candia with a tankard of chicha and poured the maize beer down the barrel of the weapon. Cieza de Leon records that the Lord of Tumbes "asked Candia for the harquebus and poured many cups of their maize wine down into the barrel, saying 'Take it, drink, since one makes such great noise with you that you are similar to the thunder of the heavens.'"[24] An obviously vital object, capable of producing thunder, lightning, and smoke, the harquebus deserved the honor of a blessing with chicha according to Andean beliefs.[25]

Surprisingly, Pizarro apparently did not disembark to see Tumbes for himself. Rather, in 1528 the Spaniards sailed south along the coast, reaching the Santa Valley before returning briefly to Tumbes and sailing back to Isla Gorgona, retrieving the two Spaniards who had survived. They then voyaged on to Panama.

Crossing the isthmus, Pizarro took passage to Spain to obtain royal authorization to conquer. The royal contract authorized Pizarro to continue the conquest of "the said province of Peru" for a distance of 200 leagues to the south, an ambiguous measurement of an unknown landscape that would contribute to later conflicts between Almagro and Pizarro.[26] The Queen of Spain proclaimed Pizarro governor and captain general of Peru for life, empowering him to establish forts, create cities, distribute lands, and make grants of Indian labor (*encomiendas*). Associated documents made Luque the bishop of Tumbes and Diego de Almagro commander of the fortress of Tumbes. Candia was to be the mayor (*alcalde*) of Tumbes. The royal documents established the salaries to be paid to each of the principals—the amounts to be paid from the "profits of the land," not the royal treasury—and the distribution of profits to the Crown. In addition, the queen elevated a handful of Pizarro's supporters to *hidalgo* status, including the navigator Bartolome Ruiz, Pedro de Candia, and others. Above all, the capitulación recognized Pizarro's right to lead the conquest of Peru. It was everything a conquistador could ask.

The Spaniards returned to Tumbes in February or March 1532. The once-rich city was in ruins. Attacked by their archrivals from the Isla de Puná, the Tumbesinos had fled into the Cerros de Amotape, abandoning the smoldering wreckage of their houses. The local lord had retreated inland in a futile attempt to maintain the independence of his now-reduced city. He was captured by Spanish horsemen and returned to Tumbes. For Pizarro and his men, the ruined city was of little interest: Tumbes had little gold, and the conquistadors had not suffered so much merely to become farmers or fishermen. They sought treasure, and treasure was reported in the land called Cusco. Leaving behind a few ill men to recuperate in Tumbes, on May 16, 1532, Pizarro and his men headed south, following the trail where we now walked.

In its lower reaches the Quebrada Cusco is a wide, sandy wash with large boulders that rolled during flash floods of rainy seasons. The stable banks of the quebrada are lined with algarrobo trees, whose splayed,

thorn-covered branches make the terrain look like a South African veldt. The teniente gobernador drove the burros ahead of us, dashing ahead of the animals as they turned into the brush to browse. He would pause, letting the animals forage for a few minutes before turning them up the trail again. We said little as we walked quickly up the quebrada, searching the trail and choosing our steps. It was late afternoon, and we wanted to get to our campsite before the abrupt tropical nightfall.

We saw the walls of the Inca tampu just an hour before dusk. There were long courses of well-laid fieldstones fronting a stepped terrace. We glanced at the site but hurried on to set up camp. We pitched our tents in a large flat downstream from several large spring-fed pools. The stream cut through stepped layers of resistant bedded shales. The spring's flow tumbled in two brief cascades and filled a narrow pool about 25 m long. It was pleasant to hear falling water in this hot scrub forest, but we camped away from the spring to avoid livestock and other animals that come to drink at night.

We unpacked our loads, and the tenienete gobernador hobbled his burros at the edge of the clearing. We pitched our tents. Our daypacks and cameras dangled from tree limbs. Large costales and cardboard boxes held our supplies. We arranged a kitchen area under the shady limbs of a broad algarrobo tree, building a cooking hearth between two lines of stones. Bernardino kindled a fire between the lines of stones and put water to boil. The flames licked the dead wood, and he fed branches and sticks to the fire. It was warm work, as the temperature was in the low 80s even at night—despite June being the South American "winter."

As we set up camp, the teniente gobernador went to the edge of the clearing and began cutting firewood for a separate fire. Although we had only spoken a few times that afternoon and our exchanges were polite, I sensed that he was either a reserved man or that my status as "*el doctor*" proved a social barrier. So I did not think it odd that he made his own camp a short distance from our tents. In fact, he was the only person in his pueblo willing to spend the night at Guineal, as most of his neighbors thought it was haunted.

I poured a rum and water as our cooking pots heated. As daylight fled westward, I turned on my headlamp and began to read *Nostromo*: "In the time of Spanish rule, and for many years afterwards, the town of . . . Sulaco had found an inviolable sanctuary from the temptations of a trading world in the solemn hush of the deep Golfo Placido as if within an enormous semi-circular and unroofed temple open to the ocean, with its walls of lofty mountains hung with the mourning draperies of cloud."[27]

The persistent thwack of the teniente gobernador's machete pulled me back from Conrad. This very energetic man had gathered a ten-foot-tall pile of brushwood and kindling, and he was in the process of gathering a second pile of equal size 30 ft away from the first. The burros were tethered between the piles. The teniente gobernador threw the last cuttings on top of the pile and wiped his machete and then his hands with a rag.

I looked at the huge piles of fuel and asked Bernardino, "Why does he need so much firewood?"

"*Es por los leones*," Bernardino answered. It's for the lions.

Of course, it made sense: the water attracted animals and the animals attracted predators. The splashing water in this hot scrub forest was a life-giving blessing, the reason for the wildlife, a reason for the Inca road passing nearby and the construction of a tambo, and one reason that Pizarro and his men had rested here for three days in March 1532. And indirectly, it was the reason we were here, as this beautiful spring in the Cerros de Amotape had attracted so many different lives over the centuries.

I asked the teniente gobernador if there were pumas nearby. He answered wryly, "*Muy pocos.*"

Ⅱ

Pizarro and 200 men left Tumbes and followed the Qhapaq Ñan up the east bank of the Río Tumbes to the Inca tambo at Ricaplaya, where the Qhapaq Ñan leaves the river, trending southward into the Cerro de Amatope. It took the Spaniards three days to reach the tambo at Guineal. The eyewitness chronicler of the journey, Francisco de Xerez, reports that they followed "a road completely hand-made, wide, and well-made [so] that in some bad passes it was paved with stone."[28] A few years later, the chronicler Cieza de Leon would write: "From the valley of Tumbes one goes in two days toward the Sullana Valley that anciently was very populated and in buildings and storerooms. The royal road of the Incas passed through these valleys between forests and other very pleasant refreshing places." After leaving the river, Xerez wrote "in the three following days, [Pizarro] arrived at a town between some mountains; the principal lord [*cacique*] of that town was named Juan."[29] There is no hint at irony that the native lord would have had the most common Spanish name.

A 1543 list of all the tambos along the major roads of Peru mentions the existence of a tambo at Solana to the south but none in the Cerros de Amotape, noting that all the Indians had been relocated north to Tumbes where they served a Spanish encomendero, Sebastian de Gama.[30] Apparently, the pueblo of Cacique Juan was abandoned, left to be overgrown by algarrobo trees and stalked by pumas.

Pizarro and his men traveled south to establish the first Spanish settlement in Peru, at San Miguel de Tangara in the Piura Valley. As he journeyed toward Chira, Pizarro learned of a plot among thirteen local caciques. According to Pedro Pizarro, Francisco Pizarro "assembled the caciques, he told them that he had certain information to the effect that they had wished to kill the Spaniards and had assembled to do so, and that, if they had not been detected, they would have done so, for which he condemned to death thirteen caciques, and, after giving them the garrote, they [the Spaniards] burned them."[31] Among the strangled and burned corpses was the cacique of Amotape for whom these hills are named.

▥

I slid out of my tent at first light. Bernardino was already up and starting a fire to heat water for coffee. I walked over to the pond to wash my face and look at birds. In this hot forest, the cool air over the ponds and cascades was delightful. Small fish schooled in the water, popping up silver to snag insects. Two hummingbirds hovered over the pond as upright as chess pieces. Further upstream I saw a female green kingfisher dive and spike the water and return to an overhanging branch where her mate was perched. The male kingfisher clicked his tail and plunged in turn.

I walked back to the campfire where the kettle boiled. I made a cup of instant coffee and sat down on a log.

"How did you sleep?" I asked Bernardino.

"Well," he replied, "better than the last time I was here."

"What happened then?"

He glanced at the ground and then looked up at me. "It was in the middle of the night, Jerry, and I was in a tent pitched over there." With his usual precision, Bernardino turned and pointed at the spot. "All of a sudden I woke with someone heavy sitting on my chest. He had my arms pinned down and I struggled with all my strength, but I couldn't move him. I tried to scream, but I couldn't. I fought and fought until in an instant he was gone, and I fell back into my sleeping bag, wet with sweat."

"Was it a *león*?"

"No, there were no rips in the tent or claw cuts on me. It was *un espanto*."

He used the word with subtle shades of horror. Un espanto is an apparition, a specter, an intense fear, a terrifying phantasm.

I have heard such stories throughout my decades of archaeology in Latin America. When I first came to Peru in the early 1980s, I thought of them as simple folk explanations of natural phenomena or as the everyday origins of magical realism. I have heard tales of mountains that scream at night and of potsherds that contain the souls of dead Indians and thus shine brilliantly on the night of Good Friday, hoping to be found and reclaimed by Christians. There are trees whose sap runs strong at the full moon, making their timbers particularly strong. And there are many, many stories about un espanto. Given all the death and destruction that followed in Pizarro's wake, the presence of angry spirits in these mountains should surprise no one. I have given up doubting the accuracy of such tales. I no longer attempt to explain them by reference to natural phenomena, tricks of perception, or the impairments of drunkenness. I just listen.

The ruins of the pueblo de Cacique Juan extend over 20 hectares on both sides of the Quebrada Cusco. Covered with thick vegetation, the actual plan of the site is somewhat obscured. On one side of the quebrada is a large plaza bordered by a line of large rooms, each about 7 m×6 m in area. Another half-dozen rooms edge the plaza. On the other side of the quebrada is a stepped mound built from boulders 100 m long and 6 m tall, topped by two rooms built in a classic Inca technique of double-faced fieldstone walls with an inner rubble core. A stairway down the front of the mound connects to a wide corridor that runs around the base of the mound. Across the wash are three stone buildings, and on a nearby hilltop is a small rectangular building, a vista point commanding the surrounding countryside, a lookout post for sentinels guarding the pueblo.

Thick layers of vegetation obscure the surface of the site, but a few pieces of pottery had eroded from the stream banks. We washed the muddy potsherds in the pool; they were bits of coarse utilitarian wares, the cooking pots and storage vessels of commoners.[32] We did not see any of the fine Inca polychrome ceramics or fragments of Colonial pottery—although, of course, they could be present but hidden.

We left at 8:30 a.m. to hike up the Quebrada Cusco to record the nearby archaeological sites of Modroño and Platanal. There was abundant water all along the route, pooled in the catch basins of long green pools. The trail followed the wash, and our steps clattered across pebbles and cobblestones. Whenever we paused and our footsteps no longer drummed, we heard an amazing choir of birds. There were high-pitched chirps from short-tailed loros, the four-note shriek-chirps of horneros whose pairs call in duets, the guttural "gwao" of antis, a long piercing whistle like that of a red-tailed hawk, and other shrills and peeps that I cannot describe. We crossed shingled beds of black shale and climbed up and over side ridges, and after a five-minute walk we saw a rock formation that looks like a dead puma; thus, the side wash is called Quebrada del Leon Muerto. At this very moment, in the light-gray sand of the trail, we spotted the fresh tracks of a puma.

The teniente gobernador's precautions were warranted: there were leones in the Cerro de Amotape and perhaps more than *muy pocos*. Bernardino told us that when he was surveying this northern section of the Qhapaq Ñan, there was a section to the south of us between Tumbes and the Chira Valley that his archaeological team could not visit; no locals would guide them into the forest because of the numerous pumas. One day while Bernardino and his team were following the Qhapaq Ñan, they came to a grove of trees and, looking up, saw puma carcasses dangling from the branches. Local people had shot the pumas and used machetes to break out their fangs before hanging the dead animals from tree limbs, an effort to keep the cats away from livestock. According to Bernardino, the campesinos were particularly incensed that the pumas had killed their goats and calves but only taken a few bites. It was as if the pumas were at war.

There is no hint of such concerns in the accounts of Pizarro's expedition. Perhaps subtle paw prints were overlooked or the clang of horses and swearing soldiers warned the leones to flee. But it is more likely that the Cerro de Amotape was more inhabited in the 1500s than it is today, its scant modern human population another part of Pizarro's legacy.

Throughout the Americas, native populations were decimated by introduced diseases. In South America, smallpox arrived in the Andes before the Spaniards did. The first known outbreak of hemorrhagic smallpox—also known as "bloody pox," as it causes blood to leak into mucous membranes and raises measles-like rashes on the skin—occurred in 1524–26. It was probably transmitted by native merchants who traded between the Caribbean and the Andes and inadvertently brought the virus back along with exotic goods. Hemorrhagic smallpox has a fatality rate of 100 percent, and the 1524–26 epidemic caused extremely high mortality—some scholars estimate as much as a 50 percent decline among certain populations from this epidemic alone. It also killed the Inka ruler Huayna Capac, leaving the succession a matter of dispute and triggering the civil war between Atahualpa and Huascar. Another smallpox epidemic in 1530–31 was followed by an outbreak of measles in 1531–32, with the combined mortality as high as 60 percent. Accompanied by other infectious diseases previously unknown in the Americas—typhus, plague, and influenza—the cumulative effect of disease during the period 1520–1620 produced an estimated average decline in population of more than 40 percent in the Andean highlands and 65 percent along the Peruvian coast, ultimately spreading into the deepest regions of South America. These diseases continued to decimate indigenous South Americans well into the early twentieth century, leaving a continent occupied by only a few survivors and ghosts. None of this was known in 1532 when Pizarro and his men camped at Guineal.[33]

In 1954 the explorer and author Victor Wolfgang von Hagen led a two-year expedition that followed the Inca road system. In Tumbes, von Hagen and his team followed the road from Cabeza de Vaca to Ricaplaya but apparently lost the traces of the route somewhere soon after. The party traveled in a Dodge Power Wagon and a jeep, and they did not follow the route on foot into the Cerro de Amotape but instead rejoined the Qhapaq Ñan on the banks of the Chira River. Yet von Hagen made an observation about the Inca road Pizarro followed from Tumbes south to Tawantinsuyu: "Although at that time the Spaniards did not realize it, the road that they found outside of Tumbes . . . was the very road that would lead them to their goal. Never had a people so carefully made arrangements for their own downfall as did the Incas. Just as the Persians paved the way for their conquest by the forces of Alexander the Great, so did the magnificent roads of the Incas betray them to the Spaniards."[34]

But all of that was yet to come.

NOTES

1. Rebecca Solnit, *Wanderlust: A History of Walking* (New York: Penguin, 2000), 68.

2. Thaddäus Haenke, *Descripción del Perú* (Lima: El Lucero, 1901), 238.

3. The film *Corn and the Origins of Settled Life in Meso-America* (Watertown, MA: Educational Services, Inc., 1964).

4. This information is from MacNeish's obituary: Robert Zeitlin, "Richard Stockton MacNeish (1918–2001)," *Journal de la société des américanistes* 87 (2001): 393–95; see also Kent Flannery and Joyce Marcus, "Richard Stockton MacNeish, 1918–2001," in National Academy of Sciences, *Biographical Memoirs* 80:220–25 (Washington, DC: National Academies Press, 2001).

5. For overviews of the Incas and their empire, see R. Alan Covey, "The Inca Empire," in *Handbook of South American Archaeology*, edited by Helaine Silverman and William Isbell, 809–30 (New York: Springer, 2008); Terrence D'Altroy, *The Incas* (New York: John Wiley and Sons, 2014); Gordon F. McEwan, *The Incas: New Perspectives* (Santa Barbara, CA: ABC-Clio, 2006); Craig Morris and Adriana von Hagen, *The Incas* (New York: Thames and Hudson, 2011); Michael Moseley, *The Incas and Their Ancestors: The Archaeology of Peru* (New York: Thames and Hudson, 1997); John Rowe, "Inca Culture at the Time of the Spanish Conquest," in *Handbook of South American Indians*, edited by Julian Steward, 2:183–330 (Washington, DC: Smithsonian Institution, 1948). For an overview of Inca roads, see John Hyslop, *The Inka Road System* (New York: Academic, 1984). For examples of some of the constructions associated with the road network, see Brian S. Bauer, "Suspension Bridges of the Inca Empire," in *Andean Archaeology III*, edited by William Isbell and Helaine Silverman, 468–93 (New York: Springer, 2006); Donald E. Thompson and John V. Murra, "The Inca Bridges in the Huánuco Region," *American Antiquity* 31, no. 5 (1996): 632–39. For recent writings and travels on the Inca roads, see

Ricardo Manuel Espinosa, "The Great Inca Route: A Living Experience," *Museum International* 56, no. 3 (2004): 102–10.

6. See William L. Fox, "On the Road Home," *Places Journal* (July 2012), accessed July 29, 2015, https://placesjournal.org/article/on-the-road-home/.

7. Marc Augé, *Non-Places: Introduction to an Anthropology of Supermodernity*, translated by John Howe (London: Verso, 1995), 79.

8. See UNESCO, "Qhapaq Ñan, Andean Road System" (2014), accessed December 23, 2014, http://whc.unesco.org/en/list/1459.

9. Richard Holmes, *Footsteps: Adventures of a Romantic Biographer* (New York: Vintage, 1996), 69.

10. James Lockhart, *The Men of Cajamarca: A Social and Biographical Study of the First Conquerors of Peru* (Austin: University of Texas Press, 1972), 135.

11. Gonzalez Fernández de Oviedo, "Oviedo on Pizarro, Almagro and Luque," in *New Iberian World: A Documentary History of the Discovery and Settlement of Latin America to the Early 17th Century*, vol 4:, *The Andes*, edited by John Parry and Robert Keith, 7 (New York: Times Books, 1984).

12. For an overview, see John H. Elliott, *Imperial Spain, 1469–1716* (London: Penguin, 2002).

13. Cited in Lockhart, *Men of Cajamarca*, 5. It was common for Spaniards to apply to the Americas the language used during the reconquista when the Islamic Moors were expelled from the Iberian Peninsula, referring to Andean temples as "mosques" or—in this case—referring to South America as "the Levant" and indigenous kingdoms as "the Grand Turk."

14. Pedro Pizarro, *Relation of the Discovery and Conquest of the Kingdoms of Peru*, edited and translated by Philip Means (New York: Cortes Society, 1921 [1571]), 1:134–35.

15. Jared Diamond, *Guns, Germs, and Steel: The Fates of Human Societies* (New York: W. W. Norton, 1997), 80.

16. Augustín de Zárate, *The Discovery and Conquest of Peru*, translated by John M. Cohen (London: Folio Society, 1981 [1555]), 30.

17. "La Relación Samano-Xerez," in *Las relaciones primitivas de la conquista del Perú*, edited by Raúl Porras Barrenechea, 66–68 (Paris: Les Presses Modernes, 1937 [1528]).

18. Pedro Cieza de Leon, *The Discovery and Conquest of Peru: Chronicles of the New World Encounter*, edited and translated by Alexandra Parma Cook and Noble David Cook (Durham, NC: Duke University Press, 1998 [1553]), 97.

19. Ibid., 103.

20. Alonso Enriquez de Guzman, *The Life and Acts of Don Alonso Enriquez de Guzman: A Knight of Seville, of the Order of Santiago, AD 1518 to 1543*, translated and edited by Clement Markham (London: Hakylut Society, 1862 [1550]), 95.

21. Pedro Cieza de Leon, *La crónica del Perú* (Lima: PEISA, 1984 [1553]), 142–43, my translation.

22. See Carolina Vílchez and Fernando Mackie, *Cabeza de Vaca: Investigaciones Arqueologicas* (Tumbes, Peru: Minsterio de Cultura, 2013). For a brief summary in English, see Jerry Moore and Carolina Vílchez, "Spondylus and the Inka Empire on the Far North Coast of Peru: Recent Excavations at the Taller Conchales, Cabeza de Vaca, Tumbes," in *Making Value, Making Meaning: Techné in Pre-Columbian Mesoamerica and Andean South America*, edited by Cathy Costin (Washington, DC: Dumbarton Oaks, 2016), 221–51.

23. Cieza de Leon, *Discovery and Conquest of Peru*, 113.

24. Ibid., 112–13.

25. But the legend also contains elements of the conquerors' mythology: the power of the firearms, the stature of the conquistadors (apparently, Candia actually was one of the largest men among the Spaniards), and the natives' recognition of the conquerors' mystery and superiority. See John Staller, "Lightning (*Illapa*) and Its Manifestations: *Huacas* and *Ushnus*," in *Inca Sacred Space: Landscape, Site, and Symbol in the Andes*, edited by Frank Meddens, Katie Willis, Colin McEwan, and Nicholas Branch, 177–86 (London: Archetype, 2014).

26. On the conflicts between the conquistadors, see James Lockhart, *Spanish Peru, 1532–1560: A Social History* (Madison: University of Wisconsin Press, 1968). For a detailed analysis of the historiography surrounding a specific, pivotal battle, see Paul Stewart, "The Battle of Las Salinas, Peru, and Its Historians," *Sixteenth Century Journal* 19, no. 3 (1988): 407–34.

27. Joseph Conrad, *Nostromo: A Tale of the Seabord* (Oxford: Oxford University Press, 1984), 3.

28. Francisco de Jerez, *True Account of the Conquest of Peru*, translated by Clement Markham; edited by Ivan Reyna (New York: Peter Lang, 2013), 26.

29. Cieza de León, *La crónica del Perú*, 156, my translation: "deste valle de Tumbes se va en dos jornadas al valle de Solana (Guineal) que antiguamente fue muy poblado, y que había en él edificios y depósitos. El camino real de los Ingas pasa por estos valles entre arboledas y otras frescuras muy alegres."

30. Cristóbal Vaca de Castro, "Ordenanzas de Tambos—Distancias de Unos a ortos, modo de cargar los indios y obligaciones de las justicias respectivas hechas en la Ciudad del Cuzco en 31 de mayo de 1543," *Revista Histórica* 3: 427–94, 452.

31. Pizarro, *Relation of the Discovery and Conquest*, 167; Jorge Pável Elías Lequernaqué, "Don Sebastián de Colán y Pariña y sus ancestros: Caciques de dos pueblos de la costa del corregimiento de Piura (s. XVI–XVII)," *Bulletin de l'Institut Français d'Études Andines* 37, no. 1 (2007): 151–61; "Para la temprana conquista, Del Busto habla de una conspiración de los caciques que habitaban las orillas del río Chira y de los pescadores de las playas cercanas y que fue descubierta a tiempo por Pizarro, en julio de 1532, antes de la fundación de San Miguel de Tangarará. El marqués gobernador, para reprimenda de los indígenas y demás caciques, mandó que catorce de ellos fueran quemados vivos. Es probable que uno de estos jefes étnicos haya sido el del pueblo de Pariña," 156.

32. For discussions of Inca provincial ceramics, see Frances Hayashida, "Style, Technology, and State Production: Inka Pottery Manufacture in the Leche Valley, Peru," *Latin American Antiquity* 10, no. 4 (1999): 337–52; Tamara Bray, "Inka Pottery as Culinary Equipment: Food, Feasting, and Gender in Imperial State Design," *Latin American Antiquity* 14, no. 1 (2003): 3–28.

33. For an overview, see Noble David Cook, *Born to Die: Disease and New World Conquest, 1492–1650* (Cambridge: Cambridge University Press, 1998).

34. Victor Wolfgang von Hagen, *Highway of the Sun* (New York: Duell, Sloan, and Pearce, 1955), 276.

CHAPTER TEN

Epilogue

BACKWARD IN BOLIVIA

IN JULY 2000 I WAS ON THE EASTERN SHORE OF LAKE TITICACA IN highland Bolivia. It was midwinter in South America, clear and cold on the lakeshore, and to the northeast the peaks of the Cordillera Real were snow-capped and shimmering. I had flown into La Paz the day before, landing at El Alto airport, which at 4,062 m above sea level is the highest international airport in the Americas and the fifth-highest in the world. Oxygen tanks and masks were stationed in the gangway to revive light-headed lowlanders whose knees buckle in the high, thin air.

I was met in the airport terminal by the archaeologist Robin Beck Jr., who was working on doctoral research at a site called Alto Pukara, located near the Aymara community of Chiripa on the Taraco Peninsula on the east side of the lake.[1] Rob had invited me to visit his project because of my interest in and writings on cultural landscapes, Andean houses, and architecture. Flatteringly, Rob had said that his investigations had been influenced by my research, so he invited me to come to Chiripa and see his project in progress. We set a date for my arrival, scheduling it so he would be several weeks into the excavation when I arrived.

Unfortunately, things had not worked according to schedule. Rob's project had been beset by delays, which is not unusual in archaeology projects. Just as Charles Marie de La Condamine and his team had waited for months to begin their survey of the Avenue of the Volcanoes, it is not uncommon for archaeology projects to encounter setbacks for various reasons: essential scientific equipment is detained in customs, excavation permits submitted well in advance are not approved on schedule, or it takes time to rent a project house, buy gear, and get a project started. But the delays to Rob's project had a different cause.

Rob and his team were living in Chiripa, excavating on a farmer's land, and hiring local Aymara men to work on the excavation. These arrangements required extensive discussions and negotiations in meetings known as *reuniones*: Who would get to work on the project? How would the jobs be shared among different families? How would work on the excavation be balanced against other demands like farming and canal clearing? How much would workers get paid? And so on and so on. Rob, a thoughtful and generous guy, offered to provide a case of beer for each of the reuniones. This was a perfectly acceptable and expected Andean gesture: beer, *chicha* (maize beer), or *trago* (cane alcohol) usually accompanies meetings and rituals. The people of Chiripa appreciated Rob's largesse. However, the generous flow of beer had two effects: it eased the discussions, but there had been many, many reuniones. And thus the delays.

When I arrived at Chiripa, Rob was deeply frustrated as his time and grant money drained away in endless, well-lubricated reuniones. To make matters worse, he was having problems with the project vehicle, a twenty-year-old Toyota Land Cruiser. The vehicle was a venerable veteran of previous archaeological projects. The Land Cruiser had first seen duty in the late 1970s and 1980s in the highlands of central Peru, in the upper Mantaro Valley, during a large archaeological research project directed by Timothy Earle, then at UCLA, and his two doctoral students, Terrence D'Altroy and Christine Hastorf, both of whom became eminent Andean archaeologists. Their research in the Upper Mantaro was a major investigation into how the Inca Empire had transformed the region—co-opting local elites, creating state storehouses, and initiating other changes.[2] Unfortunately, the rise of the violent guerrilla movement Sendero Luminoso (Shining Path) in the mid-1980s made the region too dangerous for archaeological research, as the guerrillas' assassinations and bombings were met with violent military responses by Peru's armed forces. D'Altroy, Hastorf, and other doctoral students completed their dissertations and moved on to new projects. Hastorf began a long-term research project focused on the development of complex societies in the Lake Titicaca Basin, a project based at Chiripa.[3] As the Mantaro researchers dispersed, the project gear was divided up. Hastorf got the Land Cruiser.

The Land Cruiser presented its own problems. It was a sturdy but temperamental vehicle, with a sensitive carburetor and unreliable ignition. The Land Cruiser had the nasty habit of suddenly turning off, usually dying at a hairpin turn on a narrow dirt road at the edge of a gaping canyon. The Land Cruiser's unpredictable engine mystified the best mechanics in La Paz. In desperation, Christine made an expensive long-distance phone call from Bolivia to Tom and Ray Magliozzi, "Click and Clack, the Tappet Brothers," on WBUR in Boston's program *Car Talk* broadcast on National Public Radio. Tom and Ray said the Land Cruiser had a faulty fuel pump; they were wrong.

The Land Cruiser continued to provide lurching service for several more field seasons as Christine and her students worked on sites near Chiripa. When Rob Beck started his project in 2000, Christine loaned him the Land Cruiser. (Rob was studying with Tim Earle—Christine's former dissertation supervisor—so Rob was something like Christine's nephew in the fictive kinship we archaeologists often use among ourselves.)

During the first weeks of Rob's project, the Land Cruiser ran acceptably, but as the weeks of delay extended, the vehicle became more difficult as if it sensed the intensifying levels of frustration and wanted to add to them. The biggest problem was that the Land Cruiser became harder and harder to shift into gear. It had a manual transmission with a stick shift. The stick shift stuck. Whenever it was necessary to shift into a new gear—for example, from first into second—Rob would stomp the clutch pedal into the floorboard and grab the gear shift with both hands, pulling the stick backward and yanking it down as his face reddened with the effort. When he was on the dirt roads on the Taraco Peninsula, this was an annoyance but not a real risk; there were few other vehicles in the countryside, and it was possible to drive most places in first gear. But trips into La Paz to buy supplies or retrieve visitors (like me) were frustrating and dangerous.

When we arrived at the Chiripa project house, I met other folks working on the project or related studies. There were several Bolivian archaeologists and a handful of US graduate students. Most of the students studied with Hastorf—Bill Whitehead, Maria Bruno, and Andy Roddick—and were using the delays to Rob's excavations to analyze materials recovered during previous field seasons. It was a very congenial group, and it was pleasant to crowd into the small dining room and chat over bottles of Paceña Pilsner. Even indoors we wore down jackets and alpaca wool sweaters because it was midwinter and very, very cold. The only running water in the village was a public spigot out near the plaza, which would freeze solid until midmorning when it finally thawed in the Andean sunlight. At night, the temperature dropped into the teens. It was so cold in the house that a back room served as a refrigerated pantry, where cold pierced the concrete walls and raw chicken could be safely stored on an open shelf.

As we chatted around the dining room table, one of the Bolivian archaeologists joined us. He told Rob that he had spoken to the village headman who said Rob could begin working the day after tomorrow. After weeks of delay, this was a great relief to everyone—especially Rob. But, the Bolivian student reported, tomorrow the headman, all the villagers, and Rob would need to have one last reunion. Several cases of beer were required.

We were silent as Rob processed this information. Finally, I said to Rob: "Look, since there won't be any archaeology done tomorrow and you will be busy, why don't you give me some money and directions to your mechanic in La Paz, and I will take your vehicle and get the transmission fixed?"

"You would do that?" Rob asked. "That would be great!"

"Of course. No problem."

"I can go with Jerry," Bill volunteered. "I know where the mechanic is."

We all agreed to leave early the next morning. I was shown to the outbuilding where I would be sleeping. I unpacked my down sleeping bag, made a pad of empty grain sacks, and was soon snoring in the cold altiplano night.

Most of highland Bolivia is occupied by the Aymara, whose ancestors created the Formative mounds at Chiripa, the fabulous city and culture of Tiwanaku (AD 400–1000), and other sites and cultural landscapes in the southern Andes. Across the breadth of the Titicaca Basin, indigenous farmers constructed extensive swathes of raised-bed agricultural fields; about 190 km² of raised beds were built near the site of Tiwanaku alone.[4] Some of these fields were built at the command of the Tiwanaku state, but most were probably constructed by small groups of farmers working in cooperative groups. These raised beds had several advantages: they were very productive, they could be used to reclaim seasonally flooded lands from the lakeshore, and cold air floated from the tops of the beds down into the furrows, channeling freezing temperatures away from the plants. Raised fields are found on both sides of Lake Titicaca, in the Aymara region in Bolivia, and in the Quechua regions in Peru. Although modern agronomists may consider the altiplano an unproductive environment, suitable only for pastures for llamas, alpacas, and sheep, the archaeologist Clark Erickson has written that the prehistoric Titicaca Basin was "a totally human-created landscape, the result of thousands of years of both intentional management, and at times unintentional mismanagement, by its inhabitants."[5]

But the cultural landscape of the Titicaca Bain was more than the physically re-sculpted terrain; it also included the natural landscape that was culturally transformed and incorporated in language, ritual, myth, and memory. Consider an interesting spatial/temporal aspect of Aymara language: like many languages, Aymara references past/present/future in terms of the speaker's body. We do this in English, saying "the future is ahead of us" or "let's leave the past behind." But interestingly, Aymara speakers take an opposite approach: reasoning that since we have *seen* the past, it must be in *front* of us, whereas the *unseen* future must be *behind* us.[6]

From such basic concepts, the Aymara and other inhabitants of the Titicaca Basin developed a cultural landscape distinctly different from an average "Western" point of view about terrain. Erickson writes, for "the native inhabitants (the Quechua and the Aymara), the altiplano is a cosmic landscape, an ordered cultural space filled with sacred features (*huacas*), and the home of Pachamama ('earth mother'). As part of a complex belief system of reciprocity, the earth gives crops to the native farmers; in return, the farmers give elaborate *pagos* (offerings, 'payments') to the earth. To the archaeologist, historian, and geographer, this landscape is a palimpsest of past and present cultures, as each one has left significant traces of human modification on the local landscape."[7]

This is true throughout the Andes. The anthropologist Lynn Sikkink has written, "In the Andes the landscape is animated in specific ways. As the Andean geography is monumental, so are the beings that breathe life into mountains, plains, rivers, and rocky outcrops. For instance, a mountain is not just a place where a god walked, it is itself a god. A blocky rock the size of a small house is the missile flung from a sling in a fight between two peaks."[8]

Such complex conversations between people and landscapes are not limited to the Andes or South America; in fact, such ways of thinking about and interacting with terrain are global. As Keith Basso wrote about Cibecue Apache's conceptions of knowledge and wisdom in the lands in Arizona, "Knowledge of places and their cultural significance is crucial in this regard because it illustrates with numerous examples the mental conditions needed for wisdom as well as the practical advantages that wisdom confers on persons who possess it."[9] As is well-known, aboriginal peoples of Australia approach landscape as a geological record of history, kinship, and legend.[10]

Further, these discursive relationships between people and environment are not limited to non-Western societies: Robert Pogue Harrison has discussed Western ideas about forests from antiquity to modern times; Robert Macfarlane has documented the rich vocabulary applied to land, water, and sky in the British Isles; John Stillgoe explored the detailed language of landscape in Western Europe; and Barry Lopez and colleagues produced a remarkable dictionary in their book *Home Ground*.[11] So if we consider these relationships between people and terrain in the prehispanic Andes and South America to be somehow "strange," it is simply because we are not paying attention to our own connections to landscape. In every one of these instances—and many more left unmentioned—we see that "landscapes are topographies of the social and the cultural as much as they are physical contours."[12]

The cultural landscapes explored throughout this book exemplify these recursive relationships between humans and the terrains through which we journey and that we inhabit. These relationships can be surprisingly complex. Earthen mounds may seem to be simple piles of dirt, but they are made for specific cultural reasons in given historical moments, and this is equally true of the funerary barrows Thomas Jefferson studied in Virginia, the earthworks created by Michael Heizer and other twentieth-century artists, and the kuel created and revered by the Mapuche. Once constructed, such mounds are enmeshed in landscape, becoming both waypoints and actors in the complex interactions between people and place.

Although humans often modify natural landforms, material transformation is not absolutely necessary. Environmental features are culturally transformed through human actions—bestowing names on places that connote specific values or cultural connections, conducting processions and pilgrimages across the landscape that weave peaks and lakes into textures of meaning, or enacting specific rituals en route that honor and acknowledge the relationships among humans, mountains, water, and stars.

There is a common—if not universal—human desire to mark our presence on the Earth. Even in an environment like the wind-swept pampas of Argentina that seemingly selects for transience, we see the counterpuntal gesture of human presence, such as the stenciled hand motifs in the River of Paintings. Conversely, humans create permanent inscriptions and erasures that are material evidence of transient acts, such as the great geoglyphs on the pampas of Nasca, which record dynamic movements where pilgrims walked the land in proscribed routes of rites.

Andean landscapes were animate and unstable. In the Avenue of the Volcanoes, the prehistoric eruptions and consequent devastations were not simply the random circumstances of geological phenomena but also the cataclysmic responses of mountain deities offended by human misdeeds. But with this understanding of the way landscape responded to human transgressions came the inverse possibilities of human actions: the animate forces of the Andes could be honored, placated, and satisfied if proper respect was given. Thus, these were not inherently dangerous places to be avoided permanently. Rather, they were living landscapes where humans could settle and thrive as long as suitable respect was exhibited.

The contrast between Andean and Western ways of seeing the universe is evident in their different approaches to measuring the cosmos. As Charles Marie de La Condamine and his colleagues struggled to impose a geodesic grid in the Avenue of the Volcanoes, they never questioned the basic assumption that landscape was stable (even when they observed the explosive consequences of volcanic eruptions). Conversely, when Andean cosmographers established vista points and constructed benchmarks and solar pillars, it was to calibrate the movements and fluctuations of a cosmos that was inherently dynamic, its oscillations carefully observed and their outcomes influenced by proper ceremony and respect.

Finally, all of the cultural landscapes discussed in the book are intersected by human journeys sparked by different motives. South America was the last continent occupied by ancient peoples—Antarctica was only occupied by small outposts representing nations in the mid-twentieth century—and South America's inhabitants continued that great, millennia-long human journey out of Africa. This initial entry was followed by thousands of years of exploration, discovery, migration, and settlement. As people moved across and settled the continent, they adapted to South America's incredible environmental diversity: the sere pampas, the breathless mountains, verdant valleys, river deltas, vibrant jungles, starched deserts, tropical floodplains, coastal valleys, rugged drainages, and tangled mangrove swamps. Once settled in these new lands, ancient South Americans responded to changes in those environments—whether long-term shifts in temperature and rainfall or abrupt and cataclysmic disruptions of drought, flood, earthquakes, or volcanic eruptions.

Various material traces suggest these ancient journeys and far-flung interactions. Valued plants—potatoes, coca, tobacco, manioc, and quinoa, among others—were domesticated in different regions and then transported over vast distances.[13] Similarly, technologies and artifacts point to the movements of peoples, products, and ideas. Pottery may have been independently invented in several places at vastly different times, but then the technologies spread across much of the continent. Much later, it is possible to track the spread of artistic styles, religious ideas, and the expansion of empires by dating the occurrence of certain artifacts or motifs. Studies of mitochondrial DNA extracted from ancient bones indicate the complex movements of people across South America, while historical linguistics suggests that people moved across vast reaches of the continent. All of these lines of evidence point to the importance of travel in ancient South America.

My first solo trip in South America was in April 1981, from the Peruvian coastal town of Casma east to the highland center of Huaráz, where I went to see the celebration of Semana Santa, the Easter Holy Week. Casma and Huaráz are only about 80 km apart as the condor flies, but my all-night bus zigzagged along the drainage of the Río Casma, rising to about 3,353 m and cresting the Cordillera Negra before dropping into the valley of the upper Santa River that runs at the base of Cordillera Blanca, the tallest mountain range in Peru. The poor road and numerous stops en route combined to convert the 80 km trip into an 8-hour journey, and I arrived in Huaráz at 5:40 a.m. on a frigid morning just before dawn.

The bus let us out near the marketplace. I put on warmer clothes and hoisted my pack. The streets were still empty. I headed toward the *plaza de armas* to look for an open café and wait for dawn. As I walked up a silent street, a well-dressed woman approached me, asked if I was here for Semana Santa, and said it was very difficult to find rooms in Huaráz. She asked if I would like to stay in her sister's house, where I could sleep on a mattress on the floor.

I asked to see the place, and we walked a few blocks to a multi-floor apartment building, where we were buzzed into her sister's flat. Her sister's name was Nellie. The apartment was a small two-bedroom unit shared by five people, and although the bedrooms were occupied, there was a very comfortable space for a mattress under the kitchen table. I would get Nescafe and bread in the morning, and I could use the bathroom and hot shower. Although there wasn't much privacy under the kitchen table, it would be hard to find another place to sleep in Huaráz for 800 *soles*—then about $2—a night. I paid Nellie, rolled out my sleeping bag on the mattress, pulled off my boots, and took a little nap.

At around 9 a.m. I roused myself and went out to see the processions. Although not as impressive as the *pasos* in Seville or Antigua Guatemala, the processions involved people carrying a large wooden platform with life-sized images of Christ and other figures depicting the crucifixion and resurrection of Jesus. I fell in with two young boys named Darwin and Bonpland for the two great European naturalists (I am not making this up), who explained that Huaráz had eight barrios, each with its own paso. The devoted took turns marching with the pasos through the streets of the city, accompanied by plaintive brass bands and throngs of the faithful. The display was impressive, but in April 1981 my Spanish was not sufficient to pursue matters at any depth. I did notice that all the statues depicting evil Roman legions had blue glass eyes. Christ's eyes were brown, like the hundreds of eyes in the crowd that looked on his image in devotion.

At mid-afternoon I tucked into a café for a beer and a plate of *aji de gallina* and went back to my bed under the kitchen table. I said hello to everyone and slid under the table onto my bed. In my absence, the small apartment had become a densely occupied, multi-faith religious center. Nellie, wearing a headscarf and carrying her rosary beads, was just leaving to join a women's *cofradia* that would be carrying a paso of the Virgin Mary. In the living room, the other woman living in the house was meeting with two young Mormon missionaries—one Peruvian, the other North American—each dressed in a white shirt, black tie, gray slacks, and brilliantly polished black oxfords. A discreet nameplate pinned to their left-hand shirt pockets identified each of these young men as "Elder_____/Church of Jesus Christ of Latter Day Saints." After an opening prayer, the three of them discussed strategies for proselytizing the neighborhood.

While this was going on, the television played a Spanish-dubbed version of the 1965 Hollywood epic *The Greatest Story Ever Told*. Directed by George Stevens, the movie told the story of the life of Christ, from Bethlehem to Calvary to the Resurrection. The movie starred Max von Sydow, famous from Bergman's *Seventh Seal* but in his first English-speaking role as Jesus Christ. It was a bit disarming to watch the angular Scandinavian von Sydow walk down into the River Jordan—actually Kane Creek Canyon just outside Moab, Utah—where John the Baptist—played by a very hirsute Charleston Heston—called the faithful forward to be baptized, including the Messiah. "*Bautízame, Juan,*" von Sydow said with a piercing stare.

If this were not enough, I added my own religious—or at least philosophical—ideas into the mix. Very much influenced by the poet and sage Gary Snyder, I was in a Taoist phase and had brought a paperback version of Burton Watson's translations of the *Basic Writings* of Chuang Tzu, in which I read: "Great understanding is broad and unhurried; little understanding is cramped and busy. Great words are clear and limpid; little words are shrill and quarrelsome."[14]

And then I fell asleep.

Since that first journey, I eventually realized that my researches as an archaeologist were informed and molded by my journeys and their intersections with cultural landscapes, the incidence of travel. At first I traveled to look at archaeological sites, quickly realizing that I could learn more in a couple of hours walking over a site than I could in days of reading about it (which I also did). As my Spanish improved and my knowledge of Andean ethnography and history deepened, my travels allowed me to come somewhat closer to the experiences of the people who built and dwelt in these sites.

I do not mean to overstate this: I have never thought that I *actually* gained an insider's point of view or "really" understood what it was to live in these places centuries before. Rather, these journeys helped me extend my intellectual empathy and analytical reach. In a parallel manner, the domains of my archaeological research began to expand: my initial work on ancient commoners' houses on the coast of Peru remained a common theme but expanded in new directions as I studied elite households, the development of house societies, and the dynamics of construction and reconstruction in modern traditional houses. My interest in how architecture was designed as monuments of power in the ancient Andes led me to inquire into how unmodified but "culturally constructed" elements of landscape were imbued with meaning. Simultaneously, I became convinced that as an archaeologist I needed to write for multiple audiences—my colleagues working in South America, undergraduate and graduate students studying archaeology,

and a broader reading audience who deserves to understand archaeology's fundamental accomplishments: to retrieve those aspects of the
human experience that were unwritten, unnoticed, or forgotten and
to incorporate those experiences into the consultable record of what it
means to be human.

And thus this book.

Ironically, the contingencies of travel and discovery contrast with the deceptive solidity of an archaeological site. When a tourist visits any archaeological site, the first impression is of unoccupied timelessness. Consider the classic vista of Machu Picchu. The view is north across the site, visually anchored by the terraced peak of Huaynu Picchu separated from more distant mountains by the curving canyon of the Urubamba River. The emerald greenswards of the plazas form an angle in the midground, bisecting the two extensive blocks of a roofless stone room and leading to the staircase of terraces tumbling down the distant ridge. Except for the small bands of tourists led by guides, the ruins of Machu Picchu are still, silent, empty, what Pablo Neruda called "the glacial outposts on this Andean reef."[15]

But, of course, this was neither the reality at Machu Picchu nor that of any other archaeological site on the continent from Cueva de las Manos to Ciudad Perdida. Rather than stable and determined places, these were animated and contingent nodes of human action.

In a parallel sense, the journeys described in this book are marked by contingency. Pizarro's ultimate conquest of the Incas was fronted by decades of disaster. The expedition led by La Condamine constantly traversed failures. The scientific explorations of Gerardo Reichel-Dolmatoff in the Sierra Nevada de Santa Marta would never have occurred if the younger Reichel had continued on the murderous route of his youth. Of all the events in Pedro Korschenewski life—surviving the Holdomor and the Nazis' invasion of Ukraine, escaping to Argentina, reuniting with his family—none would have predicted that this quiet and private man would wander the pampas and coasts of Patagonia, studying archaeological sites and penguins. And who could have predicted that a poet like Raúl Zurita, once imprisoned by the dark forces of Pinochet, would survive to create the longest poem in the world?

Many of the archaeological insights described in this book were the products of accidental journeys. The discoveries of the Nasca lines—by Torribo Xesspe in 1927 and their "rediscovery" in 1939 by Paul Kosok—were the by-products of chance, as was Alceu Ranzi's spotting in the late 1990s of the massive geometric earthworks in recently deforested regions of western Amazonia. In a much more modest way, my own archaeological investigations and personal journeys were predicated upon chance: as a graduate student studying with an Andean scholar, Ulana Klymyshyn, and being invited to join the excavations at the Chimu site of Manchan, which Ulana co-directed with Carol Mackey. This unplanned opportunity led to more than thirty-five years of archaeological fieldwork and an undiminished passion for understanding ancient South America.

Every archaeologist I know would admit to the role of chance, contingency, and luck in his or her own investigations—but usually we do so over beers in bars at professional meetings. In our more formal reports and scientific presentations, the contingencies of archaeological research remain largely unmentioned. The archaeologist Joan Gero wrote about archaeologists' "lust for certitude," noting "how we insistently and silently dismiss the high degree of uncertainty that surrounds every phase and feature of our archaeological research. The archaeological literature is filled with pronouncements, declarations and assertions of knowledge wrested from archaeological sites without any discussion of the confusion and ambiguity that adheres to so many of the facts we recover. Even where we qualify archaeological conclusions by degrees of probability and temper them with calls for more data, it is certainty that characterizes how archaeological results are reported in our scholarly work and in the popular press."[16]

Gero was not suggesting that all our archaeological writings and reports be reduced to endless wailings of uncertainty; not every statement about method, evidence, or inference need be couched in the self-doubt of a Shakespearean soliloquy. Rather, Gero argued that archaeologists—or anyone else who claims knowledge of the past—should acknowledge the uneven sources and imperfect vistas of our views.

When we do not acknowledge the contingencies of our knowledge, it as if we archaeologists have adopted the Aymara perspective, in which the past—laid out in front of us—is perfectly visible and discerned. It is only the future that lies behind.

The next morning at Chiripa, I got up early and went into the field house to join the others for instant coffee and bread. Rob was already up. He looked across the kitchen table and asked, "Are you still up for taking the Land Cruiser into La Paz?"

"Sure. It's no problem. Just give me some money and the directions to your mechanic."

Rob said, "Bill knows the place, and it would be good to have someone else along."

"That sounds great," I said. I finished my coffee, went to the outhouse, washed my face at the cold outdoor spigot that trickled ice water, and was ready to go. Bill and I got in. I jammed the transmission into first gear, turned the key, and with a grind and a lurch we were on our way.

The road from Chiripa was a dirt track that cut south across the Taraco Peninsula toward the village and archaeological site of Tiwanaku. The fields were russet and fallow, fringed with fieldstone walls and rows of eucalyptus trees and spiky clumps of maguey. Since it was midwinter and between crops, Aymara farmers worked their plots with shovels and foot plows (*chaquitallaca*), levering large chunks of clay and turning dried wheat stubble into the soils. To the west, Lake Titicaca was azure and achingly beautiful.

The Land Cruiser grunted on in first gear as we followed the dirt road as it looped around the Taraco Peninsula before finally curving southeast toward the town of Tiwanaku. Despite being near the major archaeological site and one of the top tourist destinations in Bolivia, Tiwanaku is a small community of 10,000 residents in and immediately around the settlement. In those pre–cell phone days, the village of Tiwanaku was served by a single *gabinete telefónica* on the main plaza, where there was a *farmacia* and a few small stores that sold dry goods, farming implements, and other items.

But I was looking for a mechanic.

In my years as an archaeologist, I have driven across much of Latin America, literally from Baja California to Central America and from

Ecuador to Argentina. On many of those journeys, I have had car problems. Sometimes I could fix the problems myself. I once made a fan belt from a loop of rope encased in duct tape. I tried to seal small pinprick holes in a radiator with chewed wads of Chiclet gum: it didn't work very well, but it was enough to get me to a small town where a welder soldered the radiator using a homemade blowtorch improvised from a foot pump, a mason jar filled with gasoline, a rubber hose, and a nozzle made from bent and battered brass pipe. Once in southern Mexico, the brake fluid drained out my old Chevy Blazer as my friend Andrew Stewart and I were driving down a potholed cobbled road. I down-shifted into Low 1 as we lurched and bumped, and just when the vehicle slowed, Andrew jumped out of the truck, ran down the road, and shoved a boulder in front of me that I intentionally slammed into and finally stopped the vehicle. After Andrew and I regained our composure, we found the disconnected brake fluid line, stuck it back on the wheel drum, and added brake fluid to the reservoir, pumping the pedal until we had some brake pressure. We both got in, I pulled the Blazer around the boulder, and we lurched down the road until we came to the main highway, where I found a mechanic working at a roadside stand who bled the brake lines, fixing them properly.

Based on such experiences, I was *certain* I would find a mechanic in Tiwanaku. There *had* to be someone, I thought, who could help us with the transmission. When we pulled into the plaza, I thought we were in luck: from the corner of my eye, I spotted a small shop with cans of Penzoil motor oil for sale. I backed up the Land Cruiser and went inside.

"Good day," I said to the woman behind the counter.

"Good day, *señor*."

"I see you sell motor oil. Do you know where there is a mechanic here in Tiwanaku?"

"No, no, there isn't one."

"Really? There isn't a single mechanic in this town?"

"None."

"But you sell motor oil," I said pointing to the cans.

She shrugged, "Very little."

(Only later would I learn that, in fact, there were only about thirty motor vehicles among Tiwanaku's 10,000 inhabitants.)

She paused and thought for a moment. "But I do know someone who *has* a truck here. He lives around the corner and two doors down."

I stepped out of the shop, asked Bill to wait, and went around the corner where a well-used Nissan pickup was parked in front of a house. I knocked on the door, which eventually opened on creaking hinges. A barrel-chested man said, "Yes?"

"Good morning. I am with the gringo archaeologists working out at Chiripa. We are having problems with our vehicle. Is there a mechanic here in Tiwanaku?"

The man looked at the ground and shook his head. "No. No one. The closest mechanic shops are on the outskirts of La Paz."

I couldn't believe it. "Really? There is no one closer?"

The man thought for a moment and raised his eyes to the south. "Well, you know that they are working on the highway, Ruta Nacional 1. They have a big camp and work yard out on the highway. They have all sorts of equipment and trucks. There should be a mechanic there, probably many. The closest mechanic will be out there at the construction camp on Ruta 1. It's not close, but it's not too far."

So that was the only option: we had to get the Land Cruiser to the road construction camp.

I walked back to the vehicle, explained the situation to Bill, pushed in the clutch, turned on the engine, and tried to move the gear out of reverse. It was stuck. Using both hands and stomping the clutch to the floorboard, I tried to move the gear shift from reverse to first or second or any forward gear I could use to jump the Land Cruiser forward. Bill leaned over and we both tried to move the gear stick, grunting and swearing at the frozen spindle. We fell back exhausted from the effort.

After I caught my breath, I looked at Bill and said, "Okay. Let's do this."

I started the engine, looked backward over my right shoulder, let my foot off the clutch, and we rolled out of the plaza and toward Ruta 1, traveling in reverse.

The first 2 km weren't too bad, since there wasn't much traffic on the two-lane blacktop between Tiwanaku and the highway. Ruta Nacional 1 was a different matter. This is the principal highway linking La Paz to the border crossing at Desaguadero, and there is constant commerce between Bolivia and Peru. Huge semi-trucks, some hauling double trailers, hurtled past us as I waited for a pause to back onto the highway. A gap emerged, and I was able to back onto the highway. Lumbering trucks pulled deep on their horns as they swung past us, not believing their eyes.

And there on Ruta Nacional 1, as I drove in reverse toward La Paz, the past was there in front of me, but the future of this particular journey was invisible and behind me—as it always, actually is.

NOTES

1. Robin Beck Jr. completed his PhD in 2004 and is now associate professor of anthropology and associate curator at the Museum of Anthropology at the University of Michigan in Ann Arbor; for more information, see https://www.lsa.umich.edu/anthro/people/faculty/ci.beckrobin_ci.detail, accessed February 11, 2015.

2. For overviews of this research, see Timothy Earle, *Archaeological Field Research in the Upper Mantaro, Peru, 1982–1983: Investigations of Inka Expansion and Exchange* (Los Angeles: Institute of Archaeology, University of California, 1987); Terence D'Altroy and Timothy Earle, "Staple Finance, Wealth Finance, and Storage in the Inka Political Economy," *Current Anthropology* 26, no. 2 (1985): 187–206; Christine Hastorf, *Agriculture and the Onset of Political Inequality before the Inka* (Cambridge: Cambridge University Press, 1993).

3. For an early overview of this research, see Christine Hastorf, ed., *Early Settlement at Chiripa, Bolivia: Research of the Taraco Archaeological Project*, Contributions of the University of California Archaeological Research Facility 57 (Berkeley: University of California, 1999), accessed February 11, 2016, http://digitalassets.lib.berkeley.edu/anthpubs/ucb/text/arf057-001.pdf.

4. For introductions to the literature on the Titicaca Basin as an anthropogenic environment, see Clark Erickson, "The Lake Titicaca Basin: A Pre-Columbian Built Landscape," in *Imperfect Balance: Landscape Transformations in the Precolumbian Americas*, edited by David L. Lentz, 311–56 (New York: Columbia University Press, 2000); John Wayne Janusek and Alan L. Kolata, "Top-Down or Bottom-Up: Rural Settlement and Raised Field Agriculture in the Lake Titicaca Basin, Bolivia," *Journal of Anthropological Archaeology* 23 (2004): 404–30; Alan L. Kolata, "The Agricultural Foundations of the Tiwanaku State: A View from the Heartland," *American Antiquity* 51, no. 4 (1986): 748–62.

5. Clark Erickson, "Prehistoric Landscape Management in the Andean Highlands: Raised Field Agriculture and Its Environmental Impact," *Population and Environment* 13, no. 4 (1992): 285–300, 287.

6. For a discussion of this concept, see Rafael E. Núñez and Eve Sweetser, "With the Future behind Them: Convergent Evidence from Aymara Language and Gesture in the Crosslinguistic Comparison of Spatial Construals of Time," *Cognitive Science* 30 (2006): 401–45.

7. Erickson, "Prehistoric Landscape Management," 287.

8. Lynn Sikkink and Braulio Choque M., "Landscape, Gender, and Community: Andean Mountain Stories," *Anthropological Quarterly* 72, no. 4 (1999): 167–82, 167.

9. Keith Basso, "Wisdom Sits in Places: Notes on Western Apache Landscape," in *Senses of Place*, edited by Steven Feld and Keith Basso, 53–90 (Santa Fe: School of American Research Press, 1996), 73. For another distinct example from the American Southwest, see María Nieves Zedeño, "Landscapes, Land Use, and the History of Territory Formation: An Example from the Puebloan Southwest," *Journal of Archaeological Method and Theory* 4 (1997): 67–103.

10. See, among many other sources, classic articles by Howard Morphy, "Landscape and the Reproduction of the Ancestral Past," and Robert Layton, "Relating to the Country in the Western Desert," both in *The Anthropology of Landscapes: Perspectives on Space and Place*, edited by Eric Hirsch and Michael O'Hanlon, 210–31 (Oxford: Clarendon, 1995).

11. Robert Pogue Harrison, *Forests: The Shadow of Civilization* (Chicago: University of Chicago Press, 1992); Robert Macfarlane, *Landmarks* (London: Penguin Books, 2015); John Stillgoe, *What Is Landscape?* (Cambridge, MA: MIT Press, 2015); Barry Lopez, ed., *Home Ground: Language for an American Landscape* (San Antonio: Trinity University Press, 2006).

12. Bruno David and Julian Thomas, "Landscape Archaeology: An Introduction," in *Handbook of Landscape Archaeology*, edited by Bruno David and Julian Thomas, 27–43 (Walnut Creek, CA: Left Coast, 2008), 35.

13. Dolores Piperno, "The Origins of Plant Cultivation and Domestication in the New World Tropics: Patterns, Process, and New Developments," in *The Beginnings of Agriculture: New Data, New Ideas*, edited by T. Douglas Price and Ofer Bar-Yosef, special issue of *Current Anthropology* 52, no. S4 (2011): 453–70.

14. Chuang Tzu, *Basic Writings*, translated by Burton Watson (New York: Columbia University Press, 1964), 32.

15. Pablo Neruda, "Heights of Machu Picchu," in *Translating Neruda: The Way to Machu Picchu*, trans. John Felstiner, 202–39 (Stanford, CA: Stanford University Press, 1980), 219.

16. Joan Gero, *Yutopian: Archaeology, Ambiguity, and the Production of Knowledge in Northwest Argentina* (Austin: University of Texas Press, 2015), 12.

Acknowledgments

The journeys and encounters described in this book were made possible by the participation and support of numerous people over the three decades I have traveled in South America. First, I want to thank my compañeros del camino, the fellow travelers whose companionship informed and deeply enriched these travels: Angel Callañaupa Alvarez, Robin Beck Jr., Doug Bryant, Bill Fox, Paul Garcia, Jan Gasco, Patrick Kehoe, Bernardino Olaya, Andrew Stewart, Carolina Vílchez, Bill Whitehead, and Yorman. I also want to thank Jan Gasco and Nathan Moore for their support while I traveled and as I wrote this book.

I am fortunate to have a group of friends who read and critiqued earlier versions of this book, providing invaluable assessments, corrections, and suggestions: Bill Fox, Jan Gasco, Andrew Stewart, and Peg Videtta. I deeply appreciate the generosity of scholars who gave me permission to reproduce images of archaeological sites and other aspects of cultural landscapes: Doug Bryant, Tom Dillehay, Ivan Ghezzi, Clive

Ruggles, Sanna Saunaluoma, and David Wilson. A full list of illustration credits is found beginning on page 275.

The journeys and investigations described in this book were supported by numerous foundations and agencies over my three decades of research in South America. The research and travel discussed in this book were supported by the National Science Foundation/Archaeology Program (1981–82, Manchan; 2006–2007, Tumbes); the H. John Heinz Foundation (1996, Tumbes); the Curtis and Mary T. Brennan Foundation (2003, 2014, Tumbes); the California State University Dominguez Hills (CSUDH) Research and Scholarly and Creative Activities Program (1996, 2000, 2003, Tumbes); and the College of Natural and Behavioral Sciences Norris Summer Grant (2015, Cusco, Nasca, and Ecuador). I also want to thank Dr. Stephanie Brassley, Dean of the CSUDH Library, and Ms. Faye Phinsee-Clack, Inter-Library Loans, at CSUDH for their assistance and support of my research and writing projects.

An earlier version of chapter 6, "To The Lost City," appeared in three installments in the online journal *Berfrois* (see http://www.berfrois .com/2014/02/jerry-moore-to-the-lost-city/); I want to thank Russell Bennetts, editor-in-chief and founder of *Berfrois* for his interest and support.

It has been a great pleasure to work again with the outstanding staff of the University Press of Colorado. I deeply appreciate Jessica d'Arbonne's sustained interest and support in this project, as she shepherded the manuscript through the acquisition and review process. Laura Furney managed this project from manuscript to published book, and I so grateful for her prompt attention to my queries. I am indebted to Cheryl Carnahan, copyeditor extraordinaire, who wrestled with the orthographic inconsistencies of Quechua words as well as with my own self-induced erratic spellings. It was a delight to work with Daniel Pratt, whose thoughtful eye and hard work resulted in this book's excellent design. I thank Bill Nelson for preparing the maps in this volume. I am grateful to Beth Svinarich for overseeing the sales and marketing of *Incidence of Travel: Recent Journeys in Ancient South America*. I thank Darrin Pratt, director of the University Press of Colorado, for supporting this book and for his commitment to scholarly publishing. Finally, I want to thank my archaeological colleagues who anonymously reviewed the manuscript, made pointed and valuable suggestions about changes, and supported its publication. I deeply appreciate the contributions all these individuals have made to this project.

Illustration Credits

CHAPTER 6

CHAPTER 7

CHAPTER 10

Index